Practical Ansible 2

MW00845844

Automate infrastructure, manage configuration, and deploy applications with Ansible 2.9

Daniel Oh
James Freeman
Fabio Alessandro Locati

BIRMINGHAM - MUMBAI

Practical Ansible 2

Commissioning Editor: Vijin Boricha
Acquisition Editor: Meeta Rajani
Content Development Editor: Ronn Kurien
Senior Editor: Rahul Dsouza
Technical Editor: Sarvesh Jaywant
Copy Editor: Safis Editing
Project Coordinator: Neil Dmello
Proofreader: Safis Editing
Indexer: Rekha Nair
Production Designer: Jyoti Chauhan

First published: June 2020

Production reference: 1050620

Published by Packt Publishing Ltd.
Livery Place
35 Livery Street
Birmingham
B3 2PB, UK.

ISBN 978-1-78980-746-2

www.packt.com

About the authors

Daniel Oh is a principal technical marketing manager at Red Hat. He provides runtimes, frameworks, fast data access, and high-performance messaging in flexible, easy-to-use, cost-effective, open, and collaborative ways. He's also a CNCF ambassador and DevOps Institute ambassador who evangelizes how to design and develop cloud-native serverless microservices and deploy them to multi/hybrid cloud-native platforms based on CNCF projects. Daniel loves to share his developer experiences with DevOps folks in terms of how to evolve traditional microservices to cloud-native, event-driven, and serverless applications via technical workshops, brown bag sessions, hackathons, and hands-on labs across regions at many international conferences.

> *I would like to first and foremost thank my loving and patient wife and kids for their continued support, patience, and encouragement throughout the long process of writing this book. Thanks also to the SMEs (subject-matter experts) in the Ansible community project for their continuous contribution with their practical code – obviously critical references for this book.*

James Freeman is an accomplished IT consultant with over 20 years' experience in the technology industry. He has more than 5 years of first-hand experience of solving real-world enterprise problems in production environments using Ansible, frequently introducing Ansible as a new technology to businesses and CTOs for the first time. In addition, he has authored and facilitated bespoke Ansible workshops and training sessions, and has presented at both international conferences and meetups on Ansible.

> *I would like to thank Roland Whitehead and Terry Warren for providing me with the supportive workplace environment in which learning the skills to write this book were gained, and also for their continued support of my writing endeavors. I would also like to thank my son, Sam, who doesn't really understand why daddy hides at the computer all day, but is infinitely patient with me anyway.*

Fabio Alessandro Locati – commonly known as Fale – is an EMEA senior solution architect at Red Hat, a public speaker, an author, and an open source contributor. His primary areas of expertise are Linux, automation, security, and cloud technologies. Fale has more than 15 years of working experience in IT, with many of them spent consulting for many companies, including dozens of Fortune 500 companies. Fale has written *Learning Ansible 2.7*, *Learning Ansible 2*, and *OpenStack Cloud Security*, and has been part of the review process of multiple books.

> *I would like to thank the many people that, during my life, have motivated me to learn more, and that helped me in the process of writing this book.*

About the reviewers

Sam Doran is a Senior Software Engineer working on Red Hat Ansible Engine. He served in the US Air Force as an aircraft mechanic and is a proud alumnus of the Virginia Tech Corps of Cadets. He worked for the US Government as well as private industry in jobs ranging from professional photography and graphic design to Site Reliability Engineering, Network Engineering, and Information Security. He has used Ansible since 2013 to automate security monitoring infrastructure, cloud provisioning, application installation and configuration as well as helped Fortune 500 companies implement large scale deployments of Red Hat Ansible Tower. Sam loves automating anything and everything using Ansible.

Madhu Akula is a cloud native security researcher with extensive experience in cloud, containers, Kubernetes, and automation security. He frequently speaks and trains at security conferences around the world, including DEFCON, BlackHat, USENIX, GitHub, OWASP Appsec, AllDayDevOps, DevSecCon, Nullcon, and c0c0n. His research has identified vulnerabilities in 200+ companies and products like Google, Microsoft, AT&T, Wordpress, Ntop, and Adobe. He is a co-author of *Security Automation with Ansible 2*, a book that is listed as a technical resource by Red Hat. Madhu is an active member of international security, DevOps, and CloudNative communities and holds industry certifications like OSCP and CKA.

Packt is searching for authors like you

If you're interested in becoming an author for Packt, please visit `authors.packtpub.com` and apply today. We have worked with thousands of developers and tech professionals, just like you, to help them share their insight with the global tech community. You can make a general application, apply for a specific hot topic that we are recruiting an author for, or submit your own idea.

Table of Contents

Preface

Welcome to *Practical Ansible 2*, your guide to going from beginner to proficient Ansible automation engineer in a matter of a few chapters. This book will provide you with the knowledge and skills required to perform your very first installation and automation tasks with Ansible, and take you on a journey from simple one-line automation commands that perform single tasks, all the way through to writing your own complex custom code to extend the functionality of Ansible, and even automate cloud and container infrastructures. Throughout the book, practical examples will be given for you to not just read about Ansible automation, but actually try it out for yourself and understand how the code works. You will then be well placed to automate your infrastructure with Ansible in a manner that is scalable, repeatable, and reliable.

Who this book is for

This book is for anyone who has IT tasks they want to automate, from mundane day-to-day housekeeping tasks to complex infrastructure-as-code-based deployments. It is intended to appeal to anyone with prior experience of Linux-based environments who wants to get up to speed quickly with Ansible automation, and to appeal to a wide range of individuals, from system administrators to DevOps engineers to architects looking at overall automation strategy. It will even serve hobbyists well. Basic proficiency in Linux system administration and maintenance tasks is assumed; however, no previous Ansible or automation experience is required.

What this book covers

Chapter 1, *Getting Started with Ansible*, provides the steps you need for your very first installation of Ansible, and explains how to get up and running with this powerful automation.

Chapter 2, *Understanding the Fundamentals of Ansible*, explores the Ansible framework, gives you a sound understanding of the fundamentals of the Ansible language, and explains how to work with the various command-line tools that it comprises.

Chapter 3, *Defining Your Inventory*, gives you details about the Ansible inventory, its purpose, and how to create your own inventories and work with them. It also explores the differences between static and dynamic inventories, and when to leverage each type.

Chapter 4, *Playbooks and Roles*, provides you with an in-depth look at creating your own automation code in Ansible in the form of playbooks, and how to enable effective reuse of that code through roles.

Chapter 5, *Consuming and Creating Modules*, teaches you about Ansible modules and their purpose, and then provides you with the steps required to write your own module, and even to submit it to the Ansible project for inclusion.

Chapter 6, *Consuming and Creating Plugins*, explains the purpose of Ansible plugins, and covers the various types of plugin that Ansible uses. It then explains how to write your own plugins, and explains how to submit your code to the Ansible project.

Chapter 7, *Coding Best Practices*, provides an in-depth look at the best practices that you should adhere to while writing Ansible automation code to ensure that your solutions are manageable, easy to maintain, and easy to scale.

Chapter 8, *Advanced Ansible Topics*, explores some of the more advanced Ansible options and language directives, which are valuable in scenarios such as performing a roll-out to a highly available cluster. It also explains how to work with jump hosts to automate tasks on secure networks, and how to encrypt your variable data at rest.

Chapter 9, *Network Automation with Ansible*, provides a detailed look at the importance of network automation, explains why Ansible is especially well suited to this task, and takes you through practical examples of how to connect to a variety of network devices with Ansible.

Chapter 10, *Container and Cloud Management*, explores the manner in which Ansible supports working with both cloud and container platforms, and teaches you how to build containers with Ansible, along with methods to deploy infrastructure as code in a cloud environment using Ansible.

Chapter 11, *Troubleshooting and Testing Strategies*, teaches you how to test and debug your Ansible code, and gives you robust strategies to handle errors and unexpected failures both with playbooks and the agentless connections on which Ansible relies.

Chapter 12, *Getting Started with Ansible Tower*, provides an introduction to Ansible Tower and its upstream open source counterpart, AWX, demonstrating how this powerful tool provides a valuable complement to Ansible, especially in large, multi-user environments such as enterprises.

To get the most out of this book

All the chapters of this book assume you have access to at least one Linux machine running a relatively recent Linux distribution. All examples in this book were tested on CentOS 7 and Ubuntu Server 18.04, but should work on just about any other mainstream distribution. You will require Ansible 2.9 installed on at least one test machine too – installation steps will be covered in the very first chapter. Later versions of Ansible should also work, though there may be some subtle differences, and you should refer to the release notes and porting guide for newer Ansible versions. The final chapter also takes you through the installation of AWX, but this assumes a Linux server with Ansible installed. Most examples demonstrate automation across more than one host, and if you have more Linux hosts available you will be able to get more out of the examples; however, they can be scaled up or down as you require. Having more hosts is not mandatory, but enables you to get more out of the book.

Software/hardware covered in the book	OS requirements
At least one Linux server (virtual machine or physical)	CentOS 7 or Ubuntu Server 18.04, though other mainstream distributions (including newer versions of these operating systems) should work.
Ansible 2.9	As above
AWX release 10.0.0 or later	As above

If you are using the digital version of this book, we advise you to type the code yourself or access the code via the GitHub repository (link available in the next section). Doing so will help you avoid any potential errors related to the copying and pasting of code.

Download the example code files

You can download the example code files for this book from your account at www.packt.com. If you purchased this book elsewhere, you can visit www.packtpub.com/support and register to have the files emailed directly to you.

You can download the code files by following these steps:

1. Log in or register at www.packt.com.
2. Select the **Support** tab.
3. Click on **Code Downloads**.
4. Enter the name of the book in the **Search** box and follow the onscreen instructions.

Once the file is downloaded, please make sure that you unzip or extract the folder using the latest version of:

- WinRAR/7-Zip for Windows
- Zipeg/iZip/UnRarX for Mac
- 7-Zip/PeaZip for Linux

The code bundle for the book is also hosted on GitHub at `https://github.com/PacktPublishing/Practical-Ansible-2`. In case there's an update to the code, it will be updated on the existing GitHub repository.

We also have other code bundles from our rich catalog of books and videos available at `https://github.com/PacktPublishing/`. Check them out!

Download the color images

We also provide a PDF file that has color images of the screenshots/diagrams used in this book. You can download it here: `http://www.packtpub.com/sites/default/files/downloads/9781789807462_ColorImages.pdf`.

Conventions used

There are a number of text conventions used throughout this book.

`CodeInText`: Indicates code words in text, database table names, folder names, filenames, file extensions, pathnames, dummy URLs, user input, and Twitter handles. Here is an example: "Mount the downloaded `WebStorm-10*.dmg` disk image file as another disk in your system."

A block of code is set as follows:

```
html, body, #map {
 height: 100%;
 margin: 0;
 padding: 0
 }
```

When we wish to draw your attention to a particular part of a code block, the relevant lines or items are set in bold:

```
[default]
exten => s,1,Dial(Zap/1|30)
exten => s,2,Voicemail(u100)
exten => s,102,Voicemail(b100)
exten => i,1,Voicemail(s0)
```

Any command-line input or output is written as follows:

```
$ mkdir css
$ cd css
```

Bold: Indicates a new term, an important word, or words that you see onscreen. For example, words in menus or dialog boxes appear in the text like this. Here is an example: "Select **System info** from the **Administration** panel."

Warnings or important notes appear like this.

Tips and tricks appear like this.

Get in touch

Feedback from our readers is always welcome.

General feedback: If you have questions about any aspect of this book, mention the book title in the subject of your message and email us at customercare@packtpub.com.

Errata: Although we have taken every care to ensure the accuracy of our content, mistakes do happen. If you have found a mistake in this book, we would be grateful if you would report this to us. Please visit www.packtpub.com/support/errata, selecting your book, clicking on the Errata Submission Form link, and entering the details.

Piracy: If you come across any illegal copies of our works in any form on the Internet, we would be grateful if you would provide us with the location address or website name. Please contact us at copyright@packt.com with a link to the material.

If you are interested in becoming an author: If there is a topic that you have expertise in and you are interested in either writing or contributing to a book, please visit authors.packtpub.com.

Reviews

Please leave a review. Once you have read and used this book, why not leave a review on the site that you purchased it from? Potential readers can then see and use your unbiased opinion to make purchase decisions, we at Packt can understand what you think about our products, and our authors can see your feedback on their book. Thank you!

For more information about Packt, please visit packt.com.

Section 1: Learning the Fundamentals of Ansible

In this section, we will take a look at the very fundamentals of Ansible. We will start with the process of installing Ansible and then we will get to grips with the fundamentals, including the basics of the language and ad hoc commands. We will then explore Ansible inventories, before looking at writing our very first playbooks and roles to complete multi-stage automation tasks.

This section contains the following chapters:

- Chapter 1, *Getting Started with Ansible*
- Chapter 2, *Understanding the Fundamentals of Ansible*
- Chapter 3, *Defining Your Inventory*
- Chapter 4, *Playbooks and Roles*

Getting Started with Ansible 1

Ansible enables you to easily deploy applications and systems consistently and repeatably using native communication protocols such as SSH and WinRM. Perhaps most importantly, Ansible is agentless and so requires nothing to be installed on the managed systems (except for Python, which, these days, is present on most systems). As a result, it enables you to build a simple yet robust automation platform for your environment.

Ansible is simple and straightforward to install and comes packaged for most modern systems. Its architecture is serverless as well as agentless, and so it has a minimal footprint. You can choose to run it from a central server or your own laptop—the choice is entirely yours. You can manage anything from a single host to hundreds of thousands of remote hosts from one Ansible control machine. All remote machines can be (with sufficient playbooks being written) managed by Ansible, and with everything created correctly, you may never have to log in to any of these machines individually again.

In this chapter, we will begin to teach you the practical skills to cover the very fundamentals of Ansible, starting with how to install Ansible on a wide variety of operating systems. We will then look at how to configure Windows hosts to enable them to be managed with Ansible automation, before delving into greater depth on the topic of how Ansible connects to its target hosts. We'll then look at node requirements and how to validate your Ansible installation, before finally looking at how to obtain and run the very latest Ansible source code if you wish to either contribute to its development or gain access to the very latest of features.

In this chapter, we will cover the following topics:

- Installing and configuring Ansible
- Understanding your Ansible installation
- Running from source versus pre-built RPMs

Technical requirements

Ansible has a fairly minimal set of system requirements—as such, you should find that if you have a machine (either a laptop, a server, or a virtual machine) that is capable of running Python, then you will be able to run Ansible on it. Later in this chapter, we will demonstrate the installation methods for Ansible on a variety of operating systems—it is hence left to you to decide which operating systems are right for you.

The one exception to the preceding statement is Microsoft Windows—although there are Python environments available for Windows, there is as yet no native build of Ansible for Windows. Readers running more recent versions of Windows will be able to install Ansible using Windows Subsystem for Linux (henceforth, WSL) and by following the procedures outlined later for their chosen WSL environment (for example, if you install Ubuntu on WSL, you should simply follow the instructions given in this chapter for installing Ansible on Ubuntu).

Installing and configuring Ansible

Ansible is written in Python and, as such, can be run on a wide range of systems. This includes most popular flavors of Linux, FreeBSD, and macOS. The one exception to this is Windows, where though native Python distributions exist, there is as yet no native Ansible build. As a result, your best option at the time of writing is to install Ansible under WSL proceeding as if you were running on a native Linux host.

Once you have established the system on which you wish to run Ansible, the installation process is normally simple and straightforward. In the following sections, we will discuss how to install Ansible on a wide range of different systems, so that most readers should be able to get up and running with Ansible in a matter of minutes.

Installing Ansible on Linux and FreeBSD

The release cycle for Ansible is usually about four months, and during this short release cycle, there are normally many changes, from minor bug fixes to major ones, to new features and even sometimes fundamental changes to the language. The simplest way to not only get up and running with Ansible but to keep yourself up to date is to use the native packages built for your operating system where they are available.

For example, if you wish to run the latest version of Ansible on top of Linux distribution such as CentOS, Fedora, **Red Hat Enterprise Linux (RHEL)**, Debian, and Ubuntu, I strongly recommend that you use an operating system package manager such as yum on Red Hat-based distributions or apt on Debian-based ones. In this manner, whenever you update your operating system, you will update Ansible simultaneously.

Of course, it might be that you need to retain a specific version of Ansible for certain purposes—perhaps because your playbooks have been tested with this. In this instance, you would almost certainly choose an alternative installation method, but this is beyond the scope of this book. Also, it is recommended that, where possible, you create and maintain your playbooks in line with documented best practices, which should mean that they survive most Ansible upgrades.

The following are some examples showing how you might install Ansible on several Linux distributions:

- **Installing Ansible on Ubuntu**: To install the latest version of the Ansible control machine on Ubuntu, the apt packaging tool makes it easy using the following commands:

  ```
  $ sudo apt-get update
  $ sudo apt-get install software-properties-common
  $ sudo apt-add-repository --yes --update ppa:ansible/ansible
  $ sudo apt-get install ansible
  ```

  If you are running an older version of Ubuntu, you might need to replace software-properties-common with python-software-properties instead.

- **Installing Ansible on Debian:** You should add the following line into your /etc/apt/sources.list file:

  ```
  deb http://ppa.launchpad.net/ansible/ansible/ubuntu trusty main
  ```

  You will note that the word ubuntu appears in the preceding line of configuration along with trusty, which is an Ubuntu version. Debian builds of Ansible are, at the time of writing, taken from the Ansible repositories for Ubuntu and work without issue. You might need to change the version string in the preceding configuration according to your Debian build, but for most common use cases, the line quoted here will suffice.

Once this is done, you can install Ansible on Debian as follows:

```
$ sudo apt-key adv --keyserver keyserver.ubuntu.com --recv-keys
93C4A3FD7BB9C367
$ sudo apt-get update
$ sudo apt-get install ansible
```

- **Installing Ansible on Gentoo**: To install the latest version of the Ansible control machine on Gentoo, the `portage` package manager makes it easy with the following commands:

```
$ echo 'app-admin/ansible' >> /etc/portage/package.accept_keywords
$ emerge -av app-admin/ansible
```

- **Installing Ansible on FreeBSD**: To install the latest version of the Ansible control machine on FreeBSD, the PKG manager makes it easy with the following commands:

```
$ sudo pkg install py36-ansible
$ sudo make -C /usr/ports/sysutils/ansible install
```

- **Installing Ansible on Fedora**: To install the latest version of the Ansible control machine on Fedora, the `dnf` package manager makes it easy with the following commands:

```
$ sudo dnf -y install ansible
```

- **Installing Ansible on CentOS**: To install the latest version of the Ansible control machine on CentOS or RHEL, the `yum` package manager makes it easy with the following commands:

```
$ sudo yum install epel-release
$ sudo yum -y install ansible
```

If you execute the preceding commands on RHEL, you have to make sure that the Ansible repository is enabled. If it's not, you need to enable the relevant repository with the following commands:

```
$ sudo subscription-manager repos --enable rhel-7-server-
ansible-2.9-rpms
```

- **Installing Ansible on Arch Linux**: To install the latest version of the Ansible control machine on Arch Linux, the `pacman` package manager makes it easy with the following commands:

```
$ pacman -S ansible
```

Once you have installed Ansible on the specific Linux distribution that you use, you can begin to explore. Let's start with a simple example—when you run the `ansible` command, you will see output similar to the following:

```
$ ansible --version
ansible 2.9.6
 config file = /etc/ansible/ansible.cfg
 configured module search path =
[u'/home/jamesf_local/.ansible/plugins/modules',
u'/usr/share/ansible/plugins/modules']
 ansible python module location = /usr/lib/python2.7/dist-packages/ansible
 executable location = /usr/bin/ansible
 python version = 2.7.17 (default, Nov 7 2019, 10:07:09) [GCC 9.2.1
20191008]
```

Those who wish to test the very latest versions of Ansible, fresh from GitHub itself, might be interested in building an RPM package for installing to control machines. This method is, of course, only suitable for Red Hat-based distributions such as Fedora, CentOS, and RHEL. To do this, you will need to clone source code from the GitHub repository and build the RPM package as follows:

```
$ git clone https://github.com/ansible/ansible.git
$ cd ./ansible
$ make rpm
$ sudo rpm -Uvh ./rpm-build/ansible-*.noarch.rpm
```

Now that you have seen how to install Ansible on Linux, we'll take a brief look at how to install Ansible on macOS.

Installing Ansible on macOS

In this section, you will learn how to install Ansible on macOS. The easiest installation method is to use Homebrew, but you could also use the Python package manager. Let's get started by installing Homebrew, which is a fast and convenient package management solution for macOS.

If you don't already have Homebrew installed on macOS, you can easily install it as detailed here:

- **Installing Homebrew**: Normally the two commands shown here are all that is required to install Homebrew on macOS:

```
$ xcode-select --install
$ ruby -e "$(curl -fsSL
https://raw.githubusercontent.com/Homebrew/install/master/install)"
```

  If you have already installed the Xcode command-line tools for another purpose, you might see the following error message:

```
xcode-select: error: command line tools are already installed, use
"Software Update" to update
```

  You may want to open the App Store on macOS and check whether updates to Xcode are required, but as long as the command-line tools are installed, your Homebrew installation should proceed smoothly.

  If you wish to confirm that your installation of Homebrew was successful, you can run the following command, which will warn you about any potential issues with your install—for example, the following output is warning us that, although Homebrew is installed successfully, it is not in our PATH and so we may not be able to run any executables without specifying their absolute path:

```
$ brew doctor
Please note that these warnings are just used to help the Homebrew
maintainers
with debugging if you file an issue. If everything you use Homebrew
for is
working fine: please don't worry or file an issue; just ignore
this. Thanks!

Warning: Homebrew's sbin was not found in your PATH but you have
installed
formulae that put executables in /usr/local/sbin.
Consider setting the PATH for example like so
  echo 'export PATH="/usr/local/sbin:$PATH"' >> ~/.bash_profile
```

- **Installing the Python package manager (pip)**: If you don't wish to use Homebrew to install Ansible, you can instead install pip using with the following simple commands:

```
$ sudo easy_install pip
```

Also check that your Python version is at least 2.7, as Ansible won't run on anything older (this should be the case with almost all modern installations of macOS):

```
$ python --version
Python 2.7.16
```

You can use either Homebrew or the Python package manager to install the latest version of Ansible on macOS as follows:

- **Installing Ansible via Homebrew**: To install Ansible via Homebrew, run the following command:

```
$ brew install ansible
```

- **Installing Ansible via the Python package manager (pip)**: To install Ansible via `pip`, use the following command:

```
$ sudo pip install ansible
```

You might be interested in running the latest development version of Ansible direct from GitHub, and if so, you can achieve this by running the following command:

```
$ pip install git+https://github.com/ansible/ansible.git@devel
```

Now that you have installed Ansible using your preferred method, you can run the `ansible` command as before, and if all has gone according to plan, you will see output similar to the following:

```
$ ansible --version
ansible 2.9.6
  config file = None
  configured module search path = ['/Users/james/.ansible/plugins/modules',
'/usr/share/ansible/plugins/modules']
  ansible python module location =
/usr/local/Cellar/ansible/2.9.4_1/libexec/lib/python3.8/site-
packages/ansible
  executable location = /usr/local/bin/ansible
  python version = 3.8.1 (default, Dec 27 2019, 18:05:45) [Clang 11.0.0
(clang-1100.0.33.16)]
```

If you are running macOS 10.9, you may experience issues when installing Ansible using `pip`. The following is a workaround that should resolve the issue:

```
$ sudo CFLAGS=-Qunused-arguments CPPFLAGS=-Qunused-arguments pip install
ansible
```

If you want to update your Ansible version, `pip` makes it easy via the following command:

```
$ sudo pip install ansible --upgrade
```

Similarly, you can upgrade it using the `brew` command if that was your install method:

```
$ brew upgrade ansible
```

Now that you have learned the steps to install Ansible on macOS, let's see how to configure a Windows host for automation with Ansible.

Configuring Windows hosts for Ansible

As discussed earlier, there is no direct installation method for Ansible on Windows—simply, it is recommended that, where available, you install WSL and install Ansible as if you were running Linux natively, using the processes outlined earlier in this chapter.

Despite this limitation, however, Ansible is not limited to managing just Linux- and BSD-based systems—it is capable of the agentless management of Windows hosts using the native WinRM protocol, with modules and raw commands making use of PowerShell, which is available in every modern Windows installation. In this section, you will learn how to configure Windows to enable task automation with Ansible.

Let's look at what Ansible is capable of when automating Windows hosts:

- Gather facts about remote hosts.
- Install and uninstall Windows features.
- Manage and query Windows services.
- Manage user accounts and a list of users.
- Manage packages using Chocolatey (a software repository and accompanying management tool for Windows).
- Perform Windows updates.
- Fetch multiple files from a remote machine to the Windows host.
- Execute raw PowerShell commands and scripts on target hosts.

Ansible allows you to automate tasks on Windows machines by connecting with either a local user or a domain user. You can run actions as an administrator using the Windows `runas` support, just as with the `sudo` command on Linux distributions.

Also, as Ansible is open source software, it is easy to extend its functionality by creating your own modules in PowerShell or even sending raw PowerShell commands. For example, an InfoSec team could manage filesystem ACLs, configure Windows Firewall, and manage hostnames and domain membership with ease, using a mix of native Ansible modules and, where necessary, raw commands.

The Windows host must meet the following requirements for the Ansible control machine to communicate with it:

- Ansible attempts to support all Windows versions that are under either current or extended support from Microsoft, including desktop platforms such as Windows 7, 8.1, and 10, along with server operating systems including Windows Server 2008 (and R2), 2012 (and R2), 2016, and 2019.
- You will also need to install PowerShell 3.0 or later and at least .NET 4.0 on your Windows host.
- You will need to create and activate a WinRM listener, which is described in detail later. For security reasons, this is not enabled by default.

Let's look in more detail at how to prepare a Windows host to be automated by Ansible:

1. With regard to prerequisites, you have to make sure PowerShell 3.0 and .NET Framework 4.0 are installed on Windows machines. If you're still using the older version of PowerShell or .NET Framework, you need to upgrade them. You are free to perform this manually, or the following PowerShell script can handle it automatically for you:

```
$url =
"https://raw.githubusercontent.com/jborean93/ansible-windows/master
/scripts/Upgrade-PowerShell.ps1"
$file = "$env:temp\Upgrade-PowerShell.ps1" (New-Object -TypeName
System.Net.WebClient).DownloadFile($url, $file)

Set-ExecutionPolicy -ExecutionPolicy Unrestricted -Force &$file -
Verbose Set-ExecutionPolicy -ExecutionPolicy Restricted -Force
```

This script works by examining the programs that need to be installed (such as .NET Framework 4.5.2) and the required PowerShell version, rebooting if required, and setting the username and password parameters. The script will automatically restart and log on at reboot so that no more action is required and the script will continue until the PowerShell version matches the target version.

If the username and password parameters aren't set, the script will ask the user to reboot and log in manually if necessary, and the next time the user logs in, the script will continue at the point where it was interrupted. The process continues until the host meets the requirements for Ansible automation.

2. When PowerShell has been upgraded to at least version 3.0, the next step will be to configure the WinRM service so that Ansible can connect to it. WinRM service configuration defines how Ansible can interface with the Windows hosts, including the listener port and protocol.

If you have never set up a WinRM listener before, you have three options to do this:

- Firstly, you can use `winrm quickconfig` for HTTP and `winrm quickconfig -transport:https` for HTTPS. This is the simplest method to use when you need to run outside of the domain environment and just create a simple listener. This process has the advantage of opening the required port in the Windows firewall and automatically starting the WinRM service.
- If you are running in a domain environment, I strongly recommend using **Group Policy Objects (GPOs)** because if the host is the domain member, then the configuration is done automatically without user input. There are many documented procedures for doing this available, and as this is a very Windows domain-centric task, it is beyond the scope of this book.
- Finally, you can create a listener with a specific configuration by running the following PowerShell commands:

```
$selector_set = @{
    Address = "*"
    Transport = "HTTPS"
}
$value_set = @{
    CertificateThumbprint =
"E6CDAA82EEAF2ECE8546E05DB7F3E01AA47D76CE"
}

New-WSManInstance -ResourceURI "winrm/config/Listener" -SelectorSet
$selector_set -ValueSet $value_set
```

 The preceding `CertificateThumbprint` should match the thumbprint of a valid SSL certificate that you previously created or imported into the Windows Certificate Store.

If you are running in PowerShell v3.0, you might face an issue with the WinRM service that limits the amount of memory available. This is a known bug and a hotfix is available to resolve it. An example process (written in PowerShell) to apply this hotfix is given here:

```
$url =
"https://raw.githubusercontent.com/jborean93/ansible-windows/master/scripts
/Install-WMF3Hotfix.ps1"
$file = "$env:temp\Install-WMF3Hotfix.ps1"

(New-Object -TypeName System.Net.WebClient).DownloadFile($url, $file)
powershell.exe -ExecutionPolicy ByPass -File $file -Verbose
```

Configuring the WinRM listeners can be a complex task, so it is important to be able to check the results of your configuration process. The following command (which can be run from Command Prompt) will display the current WinRM listener configuration:

```
winrm enumerate winrm/config/Listener
```

If all goes well, you should have output similar to this:

```
Listener
    Address = *
    Transport = HTTP
    Port = 5985
    Hostname
    Enabled = true
    URLPrefix = wsman
    CertificateThumbprint
    ListeningOn = 10.0.2.15, 127.0.0.1, 192.168.56.155, ::1,
fe80::5efe:10.0.2.15%6, fe80::5efe:192.168.56.155%8, fe80::
ffff:ffff:fffe%2, fe80::203d:7d97:c2ed:ec78%3, fe80::e8ea:d765:2c69:7756%7

Listener
    Address = *
    Transport = HTTPS
    Port = 5986
    Hostname = SERVER2016
    Enabled = true
    URLPrefix = wsman
    CertificateThumbprint = E6CDAA82EEAF2ECE8546E05DB7F3E01AA47D76CE
    ListeningOn = 10.0.2.15, 127.0.0.1, 192.168.56.155, ::1,
fe80::5efe:10.0.2.15%6, fe80::5efe:192.168.56.155%8, fe80::
ffff:ffff:fffe%2, fe80::203d:7d97:c2ed:ec78%3, fe80::e8ea:d765:2c69:7756%7
```

According to the preceding output, two listeners are active—one to listen on port 5985 over HTTP and the other to listen on port 5986 over HTTPS providing greater security. By way of additional explanation, the following parameters are also displayed in the preceding output:

- `Transport`: This should be set to either HTTPS or HTTPS, though it is strongly recommended that you use the HTTPS listener to ensure your automation commands are not subject to snooping or manipulation.
- `Port`: This is the port on which the listener operates, by default 5985 for HTTP or 5986 for HTTPS.
- `URLPrefix`: This is the URL prefix to communicate with, by default, `wsman`. If you change it, you must set the `ansible_winrm_path` host on your Ansible control host to the same value.
- `CertificateThumbprint`: If running on an HTTPS listener, this is the certificate thumbprint of the Windows Certificate Store used by the connection.

If you need to debug any connection issues after setting up your WinRM listener, you may find the following commands valuable as they perform WinRM-based connections between Windows hosts without Ansible—hence, you can use them to distinguish whether an issue you might be experiencing is related to your Ansible host or whether there is an issue with the WinRM listener itself:

```
# test out HTTP
winrs -r:http://<server address>:5985/wsman -u:Username -p:Password
ipconfig

# test out HTTPS (will fail if the cert is not verifiable)
winrs -r:https://<server address>:5986/wsman -u:Username -p:Password -ssl
ipconfig

# test out HTTPS, ignoring certificate verification
$username = "Username"
$password = ConvertTo-SecureString -String "Password" -AsPlainText -Force
$cred = New-Object -TypeName System.Management.Automation.PSCredential -
ArgumentList $username, $password

$session_option = New-PSSessionOption -SkipCACheck -SkipCNCheck -
SkipRevocationCheck
Invoke-Command -ComputerName server -UseSSL -ScriptBlock { ipconfig } -
Credential $cred -SessionOption $session_option
```

If one of the preceding commands fails, you should investigate your WinRM listener setup before attempting to set up or configure your Ansible control host.

At this stage, Windows should be ready to receive communication from Ansible over WinRM. To complete this process, you will need to also perform some additional configuration on your Ansible control host. First of all, you will need to install the `winrm` Python module, which, depending on your control hosts' configuration, may or may not have been installed before. The installation method will vary from one operating system to another, but it can generally be installed on most platforms with `pip` as follows:

```
$ pip install winrm
```

Once this is complete, you will need to define some additional inventory variables for your Windows hosts—don't worry too much about inventories for now as we will cover these later in this book. The following example is just for reference:

```
[windows]
192.168.1.52

[windows:vars]
ansible_user=administrator
ansible_password=password
ansible_connection=winrm
ansible_winrm_server_cert_validation=ignore
```

Finally, you should be able to run the Ansible `ping` module to perform an end-to-end connectivity test with a command like the following (adjust for your inventory):

```
$ ansible -i inventory -m ping windows
192.168.1.52 | SUCCESS => {
    "changed": false,
    "ping": "pong"
}
```

Now that you have learned the necessary steps to configure Windows hosts for Ansible, let's see how to connect multiple hosts via Ansible in the next section.

Understanding your Ansible installation

By this stage in this chapter, regardless of your operating system choice for your Ansible control machine, you should have a working installation of Ansible with which to begin exploring the world of automation. In this section, we will carry out a practical exploration of the fundamentals of Ansible to help you to understand how to work with it. Once you have mastered these basic skills, you will then have the knowledge required to get the most out of the remainder of this book. Let's get started with an overview of how Ansible connects to non-Windows hosts.

Understanding how Ansible connects to hosts

With the exception of Windows hosts (as discussed at the end of the previous section), Ansible uses the SSH protocol to communicate with hosts. The reasons for this choice in the Ansible design are many, not least that just about every Linux/FreeBSD/macOS host has it built in, as do many network devices such as switches and routers. This SSH service is normally integrated with the operating system authentication stack, enabling you to take advantage of things such as Kerberos to improve authentication security. Also, features of OpenSSH such as `ControlPersist` are used to increase the performance of the automation tasks and SSH jump hosts for network isolation and security.

`ControlPersist` is enabled by default on most modern Linux distributions as part of the OpenSSH server installation. However, on some older operating systems such as Red Hat Enterprise Linux 6 (and CentOS 6), it is not supported, and so you will not be able to use it. Ansible automation is still perfectly possible, but longer playbooks might run slower.

Ansible makes use of the same authentication methods that you will already be familiar with, and SSH keys are normally the easiest way to proceed as they remove the need for users to input the authentication password every time a playbook is run. However, this is by no means mandatory, and Ansible supports password authentication through the use of the `--ask-pass` switch. If you are connecting to an unprivileged account on the hosts, and need to perform the Ansible equivalent of running commands under `sudo`, you can also add `--ask-become-pass` when you run your playbooks to allow this to be specified at runtime as well.

The goal of automation is to be able to run tasks securely but with the minimum of user intervention. As a result, it is highly recommended that you use SSH keys for authentication, and if you have several keys to manage, then be sure to make use of `ssh-agent`.

Every Ansible task, whether it is run singly or as part of a complex playbook, is run against an inventory. An inventory is, quite simply, a list of the hosts that you wish to run the automation commands against. Ansible supports a wide range of inventory formats, including the use of dynamic inventories, which can populate themselves automatically from an orchestration provider (for example, you can generate an Ansible inventory dynamically from your Amazon EC2 instances, meaning you don't have to keep up with all of the changes in your cloud infrastructure).

Dynamic inventory plugins have been written for most major cloud providers (for example, Amazon EC2, Google Cloud Platform, and Microsoft Azure), as well as on-premises systems such as OpenShift and OpenStack. There are even plugins for Docker. The beauty of open source software is that, for most of the major use cases you can dream of, someone has already contributed the code and so you don't need to figure it out or write it for yourself.

> Ansible's agentless architecture and the fact that it doesn't rely on SSL means that you don't need to worry about DNS not being set up or even time skew problems as a result of NTP not working—these can, in fact, be tasks performed by an Ansible playbook! Ansible really was designed to get your infrastructure running from a virtually bare operating system image.

For now, let's focus on the INI formatted inventory. An example is shown here with four servers, each split into two groups. Ansible commands and playbooks can be run against an entire inventory (that is, all four servers), one or more groups (for example, `webservers`), or even down to a single server:

```
[webservers]
web1.example.com
web2.example.com

[apservers]
ap1.example.com
ap2.example.com
```

Let's use this inventory file along with the Ansible `ping` module, which is used to test whether Ansible can successfully perform automation tasks on the inventory host in question. The following example assumes you have installed the inventory in the default location, which is normally `/etc/ansible/hosts`. When you run the following `ansible` command, you see a similar output to this:

```
$ ansible webservers -m ping
web1.example.com | SUCCESS => {
    "changed": false,
    "ping": "pong"
}
web2.example.com | SUCCESS => {
    "changed": false,
    "ping": "pong"
}
$
```

Notice that the `ping` module was only run on the two hosts in the `webservers` group and not the entire inventory—this was by virtue of us specifying this in the command-line parameters.

The `ping` module is one of many thousands of modules for Ansible, all of which perform a given set of tasks (from copying files between hosts, to text substitution, to complex network device configuration). Again, as Ansible is open source software, there is a veritable army of coders out there who are writing and contributing modules, which means if you can dream of a task, there's probably already an Ansible module for it. Even in the instance that no module exists, Ansible supports sending raw shell commands (or PowerShell commands for Windows hosts) and so even in this instance, you can complete your desired tasks without having to move away from Ansible.

As long as the Ansible control host can communicate with the hosts in your inventory, you can automate your tasks. However, it is worth giving some consideration to where you place your control host. For example, if you are working exclusively with a set of Amazon EC2 machines, it arguably would make more sense for your Ansible control machine to be an EC2 instance—in this way, you are not sending all of your automation commands over the internet. It also means that you don't need to expose the SSH port of your EC2 hosts to the internet, hence keeping them more secure.

We have so far covered a brief explanation of how Ansible communicates with its target hosts, including what inventories are and the importance of SSH communication to all except Windows hosts. In the next section, we will build on this by looking in greater detail at how to verify your Ansible installation.

Verifying the Ansible installation

In this section, you will learn how you can verify your Ansible installation with simple ad hoc commands.

As discussed previously, Ansible can authenticate with your target hosts several ways. In this section, we will assume you want to make use of SSH keys, and that you have already generated your public and private key pair and applied your public key to all of your target hosts that you will be automating tasks on.

The `ssh-copy-id` utility is incredibly useful for distributing your public SSH key to your target hosts before you proceed any further. An example command might be `ssh-copy-id -i ~/.ssh/id_rsa ansibleuser@web1.example.com`.

To ensure Ansible can authenticate with your private key, you could make use of `ssh-agent`—the commands show a simple example of how to start `ssh-agent` and add your private key to it. Naturally, you should replace the path with that to your own private key:

```
$ ssh-agent bash
$ ssh-add ~/.ssh/id_rsa
```

As we discussed in the previous section, we must also define an inventory for Ansible to run against. Another simple example is shown here:

```
[frontends]
frt01.example.com
frt02.example.com
```

The `ansible` command that we used in the previous section has two important switches that you will almost always use: `-m <MODULE_NAME>` to run a module on the hosts from your inventory that you specify and, optionally, the module arguments passed using the `-a OPT_ARGS` switch. Commands run using the `ansible` binary are known as ad hoc commands.

Following are three simple examples that demonstrate ad hoc commands—they are also valuable for verifying both the installation of Ansible on your control machine and the configuration of your target hosts, and they will return an error if there is an issue with any part of the configuration:

- **Ping hosts**: You can perform an Ansible "ping" on your inventory hosts using the following command:

  ```
  $ ansible frontends -i hosts -m ping
  ```

- **Display gathered facts**: You can display gathered facts about your inventory hosts using the following command:

  ```
  $ ansible frontends -i hosts -m setup | less
  ```

- **Filter gathered facts**: You can filter gathered facts using the following command:

  ```
  $ ansible frontends -i hosts -m setup -a
  "filter=ansible_distribution*"
  ```

For every ad hoc command you run, you will get a response in JSON format—the following example output results from running the `ping` module successfully:

```
$ ansible frontends -m ping
frontend01.example.com | SUCCESS => {
    "changed": false,
```

```
    "ping": "pong"
}
frontend02.example.com | SUCCESS => {
    "changed": false,
    "ping": "pong"
}
```

Ansible can also gather and return "facts" about your target hosts—facts are all manner of useful information about your hosts, from CPU and memory configuration to network parameters, to disk geometry. These facts are intended to enable you to write intelligent playbooks that perform conditional actions—for example, you might only want to install a given software package on hosts with more than 4 GB of RAM or perhaps perform a specific configuration only on macOS hosts. The following is an example of the filtered facts from a macOS-based host:

```
$ ansible frontend01.example.com -m setup -a "filter=ansible_distribution*"
frontend01.example.com | SUCCESS => {
 ansible_facts": {
 "ansible_distribution": "macOS",
 "ansible_distribution_major_version": "10",
 "ansible_distribution_release": "18.5.0",
 "ansible_distribution_version": "10.14.4"
 },
 "changed": false
```

Ad hoc commands are incredibly powerful, both for verifying your Ansible installation and for learning Ansible and how to work with modules as you don't need to write a whole playbook—you can just run a module with an ad hoc command and learn how it responds. Here are some more ad hoc examples for you to consider:

- Copy a file from the Ansible control host to all hosts in the frontends group with the following command:

    ```
    $ ansible frontends -m copy -a "src=/etc/yum.conf
    dest=/tmp/yum.conf"
    ```

- Create a new directory on all hosts in the frontends inventory group, and create it with specific ownership and permissions:

    ```
    $ ansible frontends -m file -a "dest=/path/user1/new mode=777
    owner=user1 group=user1 state=directory"
    ```

- Delete a specific directory from all hosts in the frontends group with the following command:

    ```
    $ ansible frontends -m file -a "dest=/path/user1/new state=absent"
    ```

- Install the `httpd` package with `yum` if it is not already present—if it is present, do not update it. Again, this applies to all hosts in the `frontends` inventory group:

  ```
  $ ansible frontends -m yum -a "name=httpd state=present"
  ```

- The following command is similar to the previous one, except that changing `state=present` to `state=latest` causes Ansible to install the (latest version of the) package if it is not present, and update it to the latest version if it is present:

  ```
  $ ansible frontends -m yum -a "name=demo-tomcat-1 state=latest"
  ```

- Display all facts about all the hosts in your inventory (warning—this will produce a lot of JSON!):

  ```
  $ ansible all -m setup
  ```

Now that you have learned more about verifying your Ansible installation and about how to run ad hoc commands, let's proceed to look in a bit more detail at the requirements of the nodes that are to be managed by Ansible.

Managed node requirements

So far, we have focused almost exclusively on the requirements for the Ansible control host and have assumed that (except for the distribution of the SSH keys) the target hosts will just work. This, of course, is not always the case, and for example, while a modern installation of Linux installed from an ISO will often just work, cloud operating system images are often stripped down to keep them small, and so might lack important packages such as Python, without which Ansible cannot operate.

If your target hosts are lacking Python, it is usually easy to install it through your operating system's package management system. Ansible requires you to install either Python version 2.7 or 3.5 (and above) on both the Ansible control machine (as we covered earlier in this chapter) and on every managed node. Again, the exception here is Windows, which relies on PowerShell instead.

If you are working with operating system images that lack Python, the following commands provide a quick guide to getting Python installed:

- To install Python using `yum` (on older releases of Fedora and CentOS/RHEL 7 and below), use the following:

  ```
  $ sudo yum -y install python
  ```

- On RHEL and CentOS version 8 and newer versions of Fedora, you would use the `dnf` package manager instead:

  ```
  $ sudo dnf install python
  ```

  You might also elect to install a specific version to suit your needs, as in this example:

  ```
  $ sudo dnf install python37
  ```

- On Debian and Ubuntu systems, you would use the `apt` package manager to install Python, again specifying a version if required (the example given here is to install Python 3.6 and would work on Ubuntu 18.04):

  ```
  $ sudo apt-get update
  $ sudo apt-get install python3.6
  ```

The `ping` module we discussed earlier in this chapter for Ansible not only checks connectivity and authentication with your managed hosts, but it uses the managed hosts' Python environment to perform some basic host checks. As a result, it is a fantastic end-to-end test to give you confidence that your managed hosts are configured correctly as hosts, with the connectivity and authentication set up perfectly, but where Python is missing, it would return a `failed` result.

Of course, a perfect question at this stage would be: how can Ansible help if you roll out 100 cloud servers using a stripped-down base image without Python? Does that mean you have to manually go through all 100 nodes and install Python by hand before you can start automating?

Thankfully, Ansible has you covered even in this case, thanks to the `raw` module. This module is used to send raw shell commands to the managed nodes—and it works both with SSH-managed hosts and Windows PowerShell-managed hosts. As a result, you can use Ansible to install Python on a whole set of systems from which it is missing, or even run an entire shell script to bootstrap a managed node. Most importantly, the raw module is one of very few that does not require Python to be installed on the managed node, so it is perfect for our use case where we must roll out Python to enable further automation.

The following are some examples of tasks in an Ansible playbook that you might use to bootstrap a managed node and prepare it for Ansible management:

```
- name: Bootstrap a host without python2 installed
  raw: dnf install -y python2 python2-dnf libselinux-python

- name: Run a command that uses non-posix shell-isms (in this example
/bin/sh doesn't handle redirection and wildcards together but bash does)
  raw: cat < /tmp/*txt
  args:
    executable: /bin/bash

- name: safely use templated variables. Always use quote filter to avoid
injection issues.
  raw: "{{package_mgr|quote}} {{pkg_flags|quote}} install {{python|quote}}"
```

We have now covered the basics of setting up Ansible both on the control host and on the managed nodes, and we have given you a brief primer on configuring your first connections. Before we wrap up this chapter, we will look in more detail at how you might run the latest development version of Ansible, direct from GitHub.

Running from source versus pre-built RPMs

Ansible is always rapidly evolving, and there may be times, either for early access to a new feature (or module) or as part of your own development efforts, that you wish to run the latest, bleeding-edge version of Ansible from GitHub. In this section, we will look at how you can quickly get up and running with the source code. The method outlined in this chapter has the advantage that, unlike package-manager-based installs that must be performed as root, the end result is a working installation of Ansible without the need for any root privileges.

Let's get started by checking out the very latest version of the source code from GitHub:

1. You must clone the sources from the git repository first, and then change to the directory containing the checked-out code:

```
$ git clone https://github.com/ansible/ansible.git --recursive
$ cd ./ansible
```

2. Before you can proceed with any development work, or indeed to run Ansible from the source code, you must set up your shell environment. Several scripts are provided for just that purpose, each being suitable for different shell environments. For example, if you are running the venerable Bash shell, you would set up your environment with the following command:

```
$ source ./hacking/env-setup
```

Conversely, if you are running the Fish shell, you would set up your environment as follows:

```
$ source ./hacking/env-setup.fish
```

3. Once you have set up your environment, you must install the `pip` Python package manager, and then use this to install all of the required Python packages (note: you can skip the first command if you already have `pip` on your system):

```
$ sudo easy_install pip
$ sudo pip install -r ./requirements.txt
```

Note that, when you have run the `env-setup` script, you'll be running from your source code checkout, and the default inventory file will be /etc/ansible/hosts. You can optionally specify an inventory file other than /etc/ansible/hosts.

4. When you run the `env-setup` script, Ansible runs from the source code checkout, and the default inventory file is /etc/ansible/hosts; however, you can optionally specify an inventory file wherever you want on your machine (see *Working with Inventory*, https://docs.ansible.com/ansible/latest/user_guide/intro_inventory.html#inventory, for more details). The following command provides an example of how you might do this, but obviously, your filename and contents are almost certainly going to vary:

```
$ echo "ap1.example.com" > ~/my_ansible_inventory
$ export ANSIBLE_INVENTORY=~/my_ansible_inventory
```

 ANSIBLE_INVENTORY applies to Ansible version 1.9 and above and replaces the deprecated ANSIBLE_HOSTS environment variable.

Once you have completed these steps, you can run Ansible exactly as we have discussed throughout this chapter, with the exception that you must specify the absolute path to it. For example, if you set up your inventory as in the preceding code and clone the Ansible source into your home directory, you could run the ad hoc `ping` command that we are now familiar with, as follows:

```
$ ~/ansible/bin/ansible all -m ping
ap1.example.com | SUCCESS => {
    "changed": false,
    "ping": "pong"
}
```

Of course, the Ansible source tree is constantly changing and it is unlikely you would just want to stick with the copy you cloned. When the time comes to update it, you don't need to clone a new copy; you can simply update your existing working copy using the following commands (again, assuming that you initially cloned the source tree into your home directory):

```
$ git pull --rebase
$ git submodule update --init --recursive
```

That concludes our introduction to setting up both your Ansible control machine and managed nodes. It is hoped that the knowledge you have gained in this chapter will help you to get your own Ansible installation up and running and set the groundwork for the rest of this book.

Summary

Ansible is a powerful and versatile yet simple automation tool, of which the key benefits are its agentless architecture and its simple installation process. Ansible was designed to get you from zero to automation rapidly and with minimal effort, and we have demonstrated the simplicity with which you can get up and running with Ansible in this chapter.

In this chapter, you learned the basics of setting up Ansible—how to install it to control other hosts and the requirements for nodes being managed by Ansible. You learned about the fundamentals required to set up SSH and WinRM for Ansible automation, as well as how to bootstrap managed nodes to ensure they are suitable for Ansible automation. You also learned about ad hoc commands and their benefits. Finally, you learned how to run the latest version of the code directly from GitHub, which both enables you to contribute directly to the development of Ansible and gives you access to the very latest features should you wish to make use of them on your infrastructure.

In the next chapter, we will learn Ansible language fundamentals to enable you to write your first playbooks and to help you to create templated configurations and start to build up complex automation workflows.

Questions

1. On which operating systems can you install Ansible? (Multiple correct answers)

    A) Ubuntu

    B) Fedora

    C) Windows 2019 server

    D) HP-UX

    E) Mainframe

2. Which protocol does Ansible use to connect the remote machine for running tasks?

    A) HTTP

    B) HTTPS

    C) SSH

    D) TCP

    E) UDP

3. To execute a specific module in the Ansible ad hoc command line, you need to use the −m option.

    A) True

    B) False

Further reading

- For any questions about installation via Ansible Mailing Liston Google Groups, see the following:

      https://groups.google.com/forum/#!forum/ansible-project

- How to install the latest version of `pip` can be found here:

      https://pip.pypa.io/en/stable/installing/#installation

- Specific Windows modules using PowerShell can be found here:

      https://github.com/ansible/ansible-modules-core/tree/devel/windows

- If you have a GitHub account and want to follow the GitHub project, you can keep tracking issues, bugs, and ideas for Ansible:

      https://github.com/ansible/ansible

Understanding the Fundamentals of Ansible

Ansible is, at its heart, a simple framework that pushes a small program called an **Ansible module** to target nodes. Modules are at the heart of Ansible and are responsible for performing all of the automation's hard work. The Ansible framework goes beyond this, however, and also includes plugins and dynamic inventory management, as well as tying all of this together with playbooks to automate infrastructure provisioning, configuration management, application deployment, network automation, and much more, as shown:

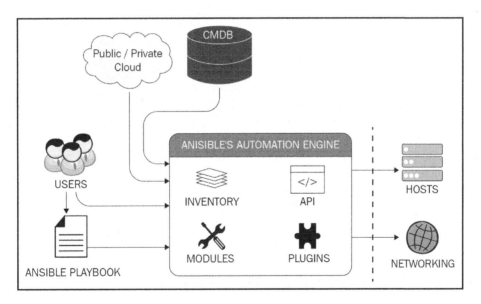

Ansible only needs to be installed on the management node; from there, it distributes the required modules over the network's transport layer (usually SSH or WinRM) to perform tasks and deletes them once the tasks are complete. In this way, Ansible retains its agentless architecture and does not clutter up your target nodes with code that might be required for a one-off automation task.

In this chapter, you will learn more about the composition of the Ansible framework and its various components, as well as how to use them together in playbooks written in YAML syntax. So, you will learn how to create automation code for your IT operations tasks and learn how to apply this using both ad hoc tasks and more complex playbooks. Finally, you will learn how Jinja2 templating allows you to repeatably build dynamic configuration files using variables and dynamic expressions.

In this chapter, we will cover the following topics:

- Getting familiar with the Ansible framework
- Exploring the configuration file
- Command-line arguments
- Defining variables
- Understanding Jinja2 filters

Technical requirements

This chapter assumes that you have successfully installed the latest version of Ansible (2.9, at the time of writing) onto a Linux node, as discussed in Chapter 1, *Getting Started with Ansible*. It also assumes that you have at least one other Linux host to test automation code on; the more hosts you have available, the more you will be able to develop the examples in this chapter and learn about Ansible. SSH communication between the Linux hosts is assumed, as is a working knowledge of them.

The code bundle for this chapter is available at https://github.com/PacktPublishing/Ansible-2-Cookbook/tree/master/Chapter%202.

Getting familiar with the Ansible framework

In this section, you will understand how the Ansible framework fits into IT operations automation. We will explain how to start Ansible for the first time. Once you understand this framework, you will be ready to start learning more advanced concepts, such as creating and running playbooks with your own inventory.

In order to run Ansible's ad hoc commands via an SSH connection from your Ansible control machine to multiple remote hosts, you need to ensure you have the latest Ansible version installed on the control host. Use the following command to confirm the latest Ansible version:

```
$ ansible --version
ansible 2.9.6
 config file = /etc/ansible/ansible.cfg
 configured module search path =
[u'/home/jamesf_local/.ansible/plugins/modules',
u'/usr/share/ansible/plugins/modules']
 ansible python module location = /usr/lib/python2.7/dist-packages/ansible
 executable location = /usr/bin/ansible
 python version = 2.7.17 (default, Nov 7 2019, 10:07:09) [GCC 9.2.1
20191008]
```

You also need to ensure SSH connectivity with each remote host that you will define in the inventory. You can use a simple, manual SSH connection on each of your remote hosts to test the connectivity, as Ansible will make use of SSH during all remote Linux-based automation tasks:

```
$ ssh <username>@frontend.example.com
The authenticity of host 'frontend.example.com (192.168.1.52)' can't be
established.
ED25519 key fingerprint is SHA256:hU+saFERGFDERW453tasdFPAkpVws.
Are you sure you want to continue connecting (yes/no)? yes
password:<Input_Your_Password>
```

In this section, we will walk you through how Ansible works, starting with some simple connectivity testing. You can learn how the Ansible framework accesses multiple host machines to execute your tasks by following this simple procedure:

1. Create or edit your default inventory file, /etc/ansible/hosts (you can also specify the path with your own inventory file by passing options such as --inventory=/path/inventory_file). Add some example hosts to your inventory—these must be the IP addresses or hostnames of real machines for Ansible to test against. The following are examples from my network, but you need to substitute these for your own devices. Add one hostname (or IP address) per line:

   ```
   frontend.example.com
   backend1.example.com
   backend2.example.com
   ```

All hosts should be specified with a resolvable address—that is, a **Fully Qualified Domain Name (FQDN)**—if your hosts have DNS entries (or are in /etc/hosts on your Ansible control node). This can be IP addresses if you do not have DNS or host entries set up. Whatever format you choose for your inventory addresses, you should be able to successfully ping each host. See the following output as an example:

```
$ ping frontend.example.com
PING frontend.example.com (192.168.1.52): 56 data bytes
64 bytes from 192.168.1.52: icmp_seq=0 ttl=64 time=0.040 ms
64 bytes from 192.168.1.52: icmp_seq=1 ttl=64 time=0.115 ms
64 bytes from 192.168.1.52: icmp_seq=2 ttl=64 time=0.097 ms
64 bytes from 192.168.1.52: icmp_seq=3 ttl=64 time=0.130 ms
```

2. To make the automation process seamless, we'll generate an SSH authentication key pair so that we don't have to type in a password every time we want to run a playbook. If you do not already have an SSH key pair, you can generate one using the following command:

```
$ ssh-keygen
```

When you run the ssh-keygen tool, you will see an output similar to the following. Note that you should leave the passphrase variable blank when prompted; otherwise, you will need to enter a passphrase every time you want to run an Ansible task, which removes the convenience of authenticating with SSH keys:

```
$ ssh-keygen
Generating public/private rsa key pair.
Enter file in which to save the key (/Users/doh/.ssh/id_rsa):
<Enter>
Enter passphrase (empty for no passphrase): <Press Enter>
Enter same passphrase again: <Press Enter>
Your identification has been saved in /Users/doh/.ssh/id_rsa.
Your public key has been saved in /Users/doh/.ssh/id_rsa.pub.
The key fingerprint is:
SHA256:1IF0KMMTVAMEQF62kTwcG59okGZLiMmi4Ae/BGBT+24 doh@danieloh.com
The key's randomart image is:
+---[RSA 2048]----+
|=*=*BB==+oo |
|B=*+*B=.o+ . |
|=+=o=.o+. . |
|...=. . |
| o .. S |
| .. |
```

```
| E |
| . |
| |
+----[SHA256]-----+
```

3. Although there are conditions that your SSH keys are automatically picked up with, it is recommended that you make use of `ssh-agent` as this allows you to load multiple keys to authenticate against a variety of targets. This will be very useful to you in the future, even if it isn't right now. Start `ssh-agent` and add your new authentication key, as follows (note that you will need to do this for every shell that you open):

```
$ ssh-agent bash
$ ssh-add ~/.ssh/id_rsa
```

4. Before you can perform key-based authentication with your target hosts, you need to apply the public key from the key pair you just generated to each host. You can copy the key to each host, in turn, using the following command:

```
$ ssh-copy-id -i ~/.ssh/id_rsa.pub frontend.example.com
/usr/bin/ssh-copy-id: INFO: Source of key(s) to be installed:
"~/.ssh/id_rsa.pub"
/usr/bin/ssh-copy-id: INFO: attempting to log in with the new
key(s), to filter out any that are already installed
/usr/bin/ssh-copy-id: INFO: 1 key(s) remain to be installed -- if
you are prompted now it is to install the new keys
doh@frontend.example.com's password:

Number of key(s) added: 1

Now try logging into the machine, with: "ssh
'frontend.example.com'"
and check to make sure that only the key(s) you wanted were added.
```

5. With this complete, you should now be able to perform an Ansible `ping` command on the hosts you put in your inventory file. You will find that you are not prompted for a password at any point as the SSH connections to all the hosts in your inventory are authenticated with your SSH key pair. So, you should see an output similar to the following:

```
$ ansible all -i hosts -m ping
frontend.example.com | SUCCESS => {
    "changed": false,
    "ping": "pong"
}
backend1.example.com | SUCCESS => {
```

```
        "changed": false,
        "ping": "pong"
}
backend2.example.com | SUCCESS => {
        "changed": false,
        "ping": "pong"
}
```

This example output is generated with Ansible's default level of verbosity. If you run into problems during this process, you can increase Ansible's level of verbosity by passing one or more -v switches to the ansible command when you run it. For most issues, it is recommended that you use -vvvv, which gives you ample debugging information, including the raw SSH commands and the output from them. For example, assume that a certain host (such as backend2.example.com) can't be connected to and you receive an error similar to the following:

```
backend2.example.com | FAILED => SSH encountered an unknown error during
the connection. We recommend you re-run the command using -vvvv, which will
enable SSH debugging output to help diagnose the issue
```

Note that even Ansible recommends the use of the -vvvv switch for debugging. This could potentially produce pages of output but will include many useful details, such as the raw SSH command that was used to generate the connection to the target host in the inventory, along with any error messages that may have resulted from that call. This can be incredibly useful when debugging connectivity or code issues, although the output might be a little overwhelming at first. However, with some practice, you will quickly learn to interpret it.

By now, you should have a good idea of how Ansible communicates with its clients over SSH. Let's proceed to the next section, where we will look in more detail at the various components that make up Ansible, as this will help us understand how to work with it better.

Breaking down the Ansible components

Ansible allows you to define policies, configurations, task sequences, and orchestration steps in playbooks—the limit is really only your imagination. A playbook can be executed to manage your tasks either synchronously or asynchronously on a remote machine, although you will find that most examples are synchronous. In this section, you will learn about the main components of Ansible and understand how Ansible employs those components to communicate with remote hosts.

In order to understand the various components, we first need an inventory to work from. Let's create an example one, ideally with multiple hosts in it—this could be the same as the one you created in the previous section. As discussed in that section, you should populate the inventory with the hostnames or IP addresses of the hosts that you can reach from the control host itself:

```
remote1.example.com
remote2.example.com
remote3.example.com
```

To really understand how Ansible—as well as its various components—works, we first need to create an Ansible playbook. While the ad hoc commands that we have experimented with so far are just single tasks, playbooks are organized groups of tasks that are (usually) run in sequence. Conditional logic can be applied and in any other programming language, they would be considered your code. At the head of the playbook, you should specify the name of your play—although this is not mandatory, it is good practice to name all your plays and tasks as without this, it would be quite hard for someone else to interpret what the playbook does, or even for you to if you come back to it after a period of time. Let's get started with building our first example playbook:

1. Specify the play name and inventory hosts to run your tasks against at the very top of your playbook. Also, note the use of `---`, which denotes the beginning of a YAML file (Ansible playbooks that are written in YAML):

```
---
- name: My first Ansible playbook
  hosts: all
```

2. After this, we will tell Ansible that we want to perform all the tasks in this playbook as a superuser (usually `root`). We do this with the following statement (to aid your memory, think of `become` as shorthand for `become superuser`):

```
become: yes
```

3. After this header, we will specify a task block that will contain one or more tasks to be run in sequence. For now, we will simply create one task to update the version of Apache using the `yum` module (because of this, this playbook is only suitable for running against RHEL-, CentOS-, or Fedora-based hosts). We will also specify a special element of the play called a handler. Handlers will be covered in greater detail in `Chapter 4`, *Playbooks and Roles*, so don't worry too much about them for now. Simply put, a handler is a special type of task that is called only if something changes. So, in this example, it restarts the web server, but only if it changes, preventing unnecessary restarts if the playbook is run several times and there are no updates for Apache. The following code performs these functions exactly and should form the basis of your first playbook:

```
tasks:
- name: Update the latest of an Apache Web Server
  yum:
    name: httpd
    state: latest
  notify:
    - Restart an Apache Web Server

handlers:
- name: Restart an Apache Web Server
  service:
    name: httpd
    state: restarted
```

Congratulations, you now have your very first Ansible playbook! If you run this now, you should see it iterate through all the hosts in your inventory, as well as on each update in the Apache package, and then restart the service where the package was updated. Your output should look something as follows:

```
$ PLAY [My first Ansible playbook]
************************************************

TASK [Gathering Facts]
******************************************************
ok: [remote2.example.com]
ok: [remote1.example.com]
ok: [remote3.example.com]

TASK [Update the latest of an Apache Web Server]
*******************************
changed: [remote2.example.com]
changed: [remote3.example.com]
changed: [remote1.example.com]
```

```
RUNNING HANDLER [Restart an Apache Web Server]
*********************************
changed: [remote3.example.com]
changed: [remote1.example.com]
changed: [remote2.example.com]

PLAY RECAP
*******************************************************************
remote1.example.com : ok=3 changed=2 unreachable=0 failed=0 skipped=0
rescued=0 ignored=0
remote2.example.com : ok=3 changed=2 unreachable=0 failed=0 skipped=0
rescued=0 ignored=0
remote3.example.com : ok=3 changed=2 unreachable=0 failed=0 skipped=0
rescued=0 ignored=0
```

If you examine the output from the playbook, you can see the value in naming not only the play but also each task that is executed, as it makes interpreting the output of the run a very simple task. You will also see that there are multiple possible results from running a task; in the preceding example, we can see two of these results—ok and changed. Most of these results are fairly self-explanatory, with ok meaning the task ran successfully and that nothing changed as a result of the run. An example of this in the preceding playbook is the Gathering Facts stage, which is a read-only task that gathers information about the target hosts. As a result, it can only ever return ok or a failed status, such as unreachable, if the host is down. It should never return changed.

However, you can see in the preceding output that all three hosts need to upgrade their Apache package and, as a result of this, the results from the Update the latest of an Apache Web Server task is changed for all the hosts. This changed result means that our handler variable is notified and the web server service is restarted.

If we run the playbook a second time, we know that it is very unlikely that the Apache package will need upgrading again. Notice how the playbook output differs this time:

```
PLAY [My first Ansible playbook]
***********************************************
TASK [Gathering Facts]
***********************************************************
ok: [remote1.example.com]
ok: [remote2.example.com]
ok: [remote3.example.com]

TASK [Update the latest of an Apache Web Server]
*******************************
ok: [remote2.example.com]
ok: [remote3.example.com]
```

```
ok: [remote1.example.com]

PLAY RECAP
*****************************************************************
remote1.example.com : ok=2 changed=0 unreachable=0 failed=0 skipped=0
rescued=0 ignored=0
remote2.example.com : ok=2 changed=0 unreachable=0 failed=0 skipped=0
rescued=0 ignored=0
remote3.example.com : ok=2 changed=0 unreachable=0 failed=0 skipped=0
rescued=0 ignored=0
```

You can see that this time, the output from the `Update the latest of an Apache Web Server` task is `ok` for all three hosts, meaning no changes were applied (the package was not updated). As a result of this, our handler is not notified and does not run—you can see that it does not even feature in the preceding playbook output. This distinction is important—the goal of an Ansible playbook (and the modules that underpin Ansible) should be to only make changes when they need to be made. If everything is all up to date, then the target host should not be altered. Unnecessary restarts to services should be avoided, as should unnecessary alterations to files. In short, Ansible playbooks are (and should be) designed to be efficient and to achieve a target machine state.

This has very much been a crash course on writing your first playbook, but hopefully, it gives you a taste of what Ansible can do when you move from single ad hoc commands through to more complex playbooks. Before we explore the Ansible language and components any further, let's take a more in-depth look at the YAML language that playbooks are written in.

Learning the YAML syntax

In this section, you will learn how to write a YAML file with the correct syntax and best practices and tips for running a playbook on multiple remote machines. Ansible uses YAML because it is easier for humans to read and write than other common data formats, such as XML or JSON. There are no commas, curly braces, or tags to worry about, and the enforced indentation in the code ensures that it is tidy and easy on the eye. In addition, there are libraries available in most programming languages for working with YAML.

This reflects one of the core goals of Ansible—to produce easy-to-read (and write) code that described the target state of a given host. Ansible playbooks are (ideally) supposed to be self-documenting, as documentation is often an afterthought in busy technology environments—so, what better way to document than through the automation system responsible for deploying code?

Before we dive into YAML structure, a word on the files themselves. Files written in YAML can optionally begin with --- (as seen in the example playbook in the previous section) and end with . . . . This applies to all files in YAML, regardless of whether it is employed by Ansible or another system, and indicates that the file is in the YAML language. You will find that most examples of Ansible playbooks (as well as roles and other associated YAML files) start with --- but do not end with . . .—the header is sufficient to clearly denote that the file uses the YAML format.

Let's explore the YAML language through the example playbook we created in the preceding section:

1. Lists are an important construct in the YAML language—in fact, although it might not be obvious, the `tasks:` block of the playbook is actually a YAML list. A list in YAML lists all of its items at the same indentation level, with each line starting with -. For example, we updated the `httpd` package from the preceding playbook using the following code:

```
- name: Update the latest of an Apache Web Server
  yum:
    name: httpd
    state: latest
```

However, we could have specified a list of packages to be upgraded as follows:

```
- name: Update the latest of an Apache Web Server
  yum:
    name:
      - httpd
      - mod_ssl
    state: latest
```

Now, rather than passing a single value to the `name:` key, we pass a YAML-formatted list containing the names of two packages to be updated.

2. Dictionaries are another important concept in YAML—they are represented by a `key: value` format, as we have already extensively seen, but all of the items in the dictionary are indented by one more level. This is easiest explained by an example, so consider the following code from our example playbook:

```
service:
  name: httpd
  state: restarted
```

In this example (from `handler`), the `service` definition is actually a dictionary and both the `name` and `state` keys are indented with two more spaces than the `service` key. This higher level of indentation means that the `name` and `state` keys are associated with the `service` key, therefore, in this case, telling the `service` module which service to operate on (`httpd`) and what to do with it (restart it).

Already, we have observed in these two examples that you can produce quite complicated data structures by mixing lists and dictionaries.

3. As you become more advanced at playbook design (we will see examples of this later on in this book), you may very well start to produce quite complicated variable structures that you will put into their own separate files to keep your playbook code readable. The following is an example of a `variables` file that provides the details of two employees of a company:

```
---
employees:
  - name: daniel
    fullname: Daniel Oh
    role: DevOps Evangelist
    level: Expert
    skills:
      - Kubernetes
      - Microservices
      - Ansible
      - Linux Container
  - name: michael
    fullname: Michael Smiths
    role: Enterprise Architect
    level: Advanced
    skills:
      - Cloud
      - Middleware
      - Windows
      - Storage
```

In this example, you can see that we have a dictionary containing the details of each employee. The employees themselves are list items (you can spot this because the lines start with –) and equally, the employee skills are denoted as list items. You will notice the `fullname`, `role`, `level`, and `skills` keys are at the same indentation level as `name` but do not feature – before them. This tells you that they are in the dictionary with the list item itself, and so they represent the details of the employee.

4. YAML is very literal when it comes to parsing the language and a new line always represents a new line of code. What if you actually need to add a block of text (for example, to a variable)? In this case, you can use a literal block scalar, |, to write multiple lines and YAML will faithfully preserve the new lines, carriage returns, and all the whitespace that follows each line (note, however, that the indentation at the beginning of each line is part of the YAML syntax):

```
Specialty: |
  Agile methodology
  Cloud-native app development practices
  Advanced enterprise DevOps practices
```

So, if we were to get Ansible to print the preceding contents to the screen, it would display as follows (note that the preceding two spaces have gone—they were interpreted correctly as part of the YAML language and not printed):

```
Agile methodology
Cloud-native app development practices
Advanced enterprise DevOps practices
```

Similar to the preceding is the folded block scalar, >, which does the same as the literal block scalar but does not preserve line endings. This is useful for very long strings that you want to print on a single line, but also want to wrap across multiple lines in your code for the purpose of readability. Take the following variation on our example:

```
Specialty: >
  Agile methodology
  Cloud-native app development practices
  Advanced enterprise DevOps practices
```

Now, if we were to print this, we would see the following:

```
Agile methodologyCloud-native app development practicesAdvanced enterprise
DevOps practices
```

We could add trailing spaces to the preceding example to stop the words from running into each other, but I have not done this here as I wanted to provide you with an easy-to-interpret example.

As you review playbooks, variable files, and so on, you will see these structures used over and over again. Although simple in definition, they are very important—a missed level of indentation or a missing – instance at the start of a list item can cause your entire playbook to fail to run. As we discovered, you can put all of these various constructs together. One additional example is provided in the following code block of a `variables` file for you to consider, which shows the various examples we have covered all in one place:

```
---
servers:
  - frontend
  - backend
  - database
  - cache
employees:
  - name: daniel
    fullname: Daniel Oh
    role: DevOps Evangelist
    level: Expert
    skills:
      - Kubernetes
      - Microservices
      - Ansible
      - Linux Container
  - name: michael
    fullname: Michael Smiths
    role: Enterprise Architect
    level: Advanced
    skills:
      - Cloud
      - Middleware
      - Windows
      - Storage
    Speciality: |
      Agile methodology
      Cloud-native app development practices
      Advanced enterprise DevOps practices
```

You can also express both dictionaries and lists in an abbreviated form, known as **flow collections**. The following example shows exactly the same data structure as our original `employees` variable file:

```
---
employees: [{"fullname": "Daniel Oh","level": "Expert","name":
"daniel","role": "DevOps Evangelist","skills":
["Kubernetes","Microservices","Ansible","Linux Container"]},{"fullname":
"Michael Smiths","level": "Advanced","name": "michael","role": "Enterprise
Architect","skills":["Cloud","Middleware","Windows","Storage"]}]
```

Although this displays exactly the same data structure, you can see how difficult it is to read with the naked eye. Flow collections are not used extensively in YAML and I would not recommend you to make use of them yourself, but it is important to understand them in case you come across them. You will also notice that although we've started talking about variables in YAML, we haven't expressed any variable types. YAML tries to make assumptions about variable types based on the data they contain, so if you want assign `1.0` to a variable, YAML will assume it is a floating-point number. If you need to express it as a string (perhaps because it is a version number), you need to put quotation marks around it, which causes the YAML parser to interpret it as a string instead, such as in the following example:

```
version: "2.0"
```

This completes our look at the YAML language syntax. Now that's complete, in the next section, let's take a look at ways that you can organize your automation code to keep it manageable and tidy.

Organizing your automation code

As you can imagine, if you were to write all of your required Ansible tasks in one massive playbook, it would quickly become unmanageable—that is to say, it would be difficult to read, difficult for someone else to pick up and understand, and—most of all—difficult to debug when things go wrong. Ansible provides a number of ways for you to divide your code into manageable chunks; perhaps the most important of these is the use of roles. Roles (for the sake of a simple analogy) behave like a library in a conventional high-level programming language. We will go into more detail about roles in Chapter 4, *Playbooks and Roles*.

There are, however, other ways that Ansible supports splitting your code into manageable chunks, which we will explore briefly in this section as a precursor to the more in-depth exploration of roles later in this book.

Let's build up a practical example. To start, we know that we need to create an inventory for Ansible to run against. In this instance, we'll create four notional groups of servers, with each group containing two servers. Our hypothetical example will contain a frontend server and application servers for a fictional application, located in two different geographic locations. Our inventory file will be called `production-inventory` and the example contents are as follows:

```
[frontends_na_zone]
frontend1-na.example.com
frontend2-na.example.com
```

```
[frontends_emea_zone]
frontend1-emea.example.com
frontend2-emea.example.com

[appservers_na_zone]
appserver1-na.example.com
appserver2-na.example.com

[appservers_emea_zone]
appserver1-emea.example.com
appserver2-emea.example.com
```

Now, obviously, we could just write one massive playbook to address the required tasks on these different hosts, but as we have already discussed, this would be cumbersome and inefficient. Let's instead break the task of automating these different hosts down into smaller playbooks:

1. Create a playbook to run a connection test on a specific host group, such as `frontends_na_zone`. Put the following contents into the playbook:

   ```
   ---
   - hosts: frontends_na_zone
     remote_user: danieloh
     tasks:
       - name: simple connection test
         ping:
   ```

2. Now, try running this playbook against the hosts (note that we have configured it to connect to a remote user on the inventory system, called `danieloh`, so you will either need to create this user and set up the appropriate SSH keys or change the user in the `remote_user` line of your playbook). When you run the playbook after setting up the authentication, you should see an output similar to the following:

   ```
   $ ansible-playbook -i production-inventory frontends-na.yml

   PLAY [frontends_na_zone]
   ********************************************************

   TASK [Gathering Facts]
   *********************************************************
   ok: [frontend1-na.example.com]
   ok: [frontend2-na.example.com]

   TASK [simple connection test]
   ****************************************************
   ok: [frontend1-na.example.com]
   ```

```
ok: [frontend2-na.example.com]

PLAY RECAP
*****************************************************************
**
frontend1-na.example.com : ok=2 changed=0 unreachable=0 failed=0
skipped=0 rescued=0 ignored=0
frontend2-na.example.com : ok=2 changed=0 unreachable=0 failed=0
skipped=0 rescued=0 ignored=0
```

3. Now, let's extend our simple example by creating a playbook that will only run on the application servers. Again, we will use the Ansible `ping` module to perform a connection test, but in a real-world situation, you would perform more complex tasks, such as installing packages or modifying files. Specify that this playbook is run against this host group from the `appservers_emea_zone` inventory. Add the following contents to the playbook:

```
   ---
   - hosts: appservers_emea_zone
     remote_user: danieloh
     tasks:
       - name: simple connection test
         ping:
```

As before, you need to ensure you can access these servers, so either create the `danieloh` user and set up authentication to that account or change the `remote_user` line in the example playbook. Once you have done this, you should be able to run the playbook and you will see an output similar to the following:

```
$ ansible-playbook -i production-inventory appservers-emea.yml

PLAY [appservers_emea_zone]
**************************************************

TASK [Gathering Facts]
**************************************************
ok: [appserver2-emea.example.com]
ok: [appserver1-emea.example.com]

TASK [simple connection test]
**************************************************
ok: [appserver2-emea.example.com]
ok: [appserver1-emea.example.com]

PLAY RECAP
*****************************************************************
```

```
**
appserver1-emea.example.com : ok=2 changed=0 unreachable=0 failed=0
skipped=0 rescued=0 ignored=0
appserver2-emea.example.com : ok=2 changed=0 unreachable=0 failed=0
skipped=0 rescued=0 ignored=0
```

4. So far, so good. However, we now have two playbooks that we need to run manually, which only addresses two of our inventory host groups. If we want to address all four groups, we need to create a total of four playbooks, all of which need to be run manually. This is hardly reflective of best automation practices. What if there was a way to take these individual playbooks and run them together from one top-level playbook? This would enable us to divide our code to keep it manageable, but also prevents a lot of manual effort when it comes to running the playbooks. Fortunately, we can do exactly that by taking advantage of the import_playbook directive in a top-level playbook that we will call site.yml:

```
---

- import_playbook: frontend-na.yml
- import_playbook: appserver-emea.yml
```

Now, when you run this single playbook using the (by now, familiar) ansible-playbook command, you will see that the effect is the same as if we had actually run both playbooks back to back. In this way, even before we explore the concept of roles, you can see that Ansible supports splitting up your code into manageable chunks without needing to run each chunk manually:

```
$ ansible-playbook -i production-inventory site.yml

PLAY [frontends_na_zone]
********************************************************

TASK [Gathering Facts]
*********************************************************
ok: [frontend2-na.example.com]
ok: [frontend1-na.example.com]

TASK [simple connection test]
**************************************************
ok: [frontend1-na.example.com]
ok: [frontend2-na.example.com]

PLAY [appservers_emea_zone]
****************************************************

TASK [Gathering Facts]
```

```
**********************************************************
ok: [appserver2-emea.example.com]
ok: [appserver1-emea.example.com]

TASK [simple connection test]
***************************************************
ok: [appserver2-emea.example.com]
ok: [appserver1-emea.example.com]

PLAY RECAP
**************************************************************
**
appserver1-emea.example.com : ok=2 changed=0 unreachable=0 failed=0
skipped=0 rescued=0 ignored=0
appserver2-emea.example.com : ok=2 changed=0 unreachable=0 failed=0
skipped=0 rescued=0 ignored=0
frontend1-na.example.com : ok=2 changed=0 unreachable=0 failed=0
skipped=0 rescued=0 ignored=0
frontend2-na.example.com : ok=2 changed=0 unreachable=0 failed=0
skipped=0 rescued=0 ignored=0
```

There's much more that you can do with geographically diverse environments, such as our simple example here, as we have not even touched on things such as placing variables in your inventory (which, for example, associates different parameters with different environments). We will explore this in more detail in `Chapter 3`, *Defining Your Inventory*.

However, hopefully that has armed with enough knowledge so that you can start making informed choices about how to organize the code for your playbooks. As you complete further chapters of this book, you will be able to establish whether you wish to make use of roles or the `import_playbook` directive (or perhaps even both) as part of your playbook organization.

Let's carry on with our crash course on Ansible, in the next section, with a look at the configuration file and some of the key directives that you might find valuable.

Exploring the configuration file

Ansible's behavior is, in part, defined by its configuration file. The central configuration file (which impacts the behavior of Ansible for all users on the system) can be found at `/etc/ansible/ansible.cfg`. However, this is not the only place Ansible will look for its configuration; in fact, it will look in the following locations, from the top to the bottom.

The first instance of the file is the configuration it will use; all of the others are ignored, even if they are present:

1. ANSIBLE_CONFIG: The file location specified by the value of this environment variable, if set
2. ansible.cfg: In the current working directory
3. ~/.ansible.cfg: In the home directory of the user
4. /etc/ansible/ansible.cfg: The central configuration that we previously mentioned

If you installed Ansible through a package manager, such as yum or apt, you will almost always find a default configuration file called ansible.cfg in /etc/ansible. However, if you built Ansible from the source or installed it via pip, the central configuration file will not exist and you will need to create it yourself. A good starting point is to reference the example Ansible configuration file that is included with the source code, a copy of which can be found on GitHub at https://raw.githubusercontent.com/ansible/ansible/devel/examples/ansible.cfg.

In this section, we will detail how to locate Ansible's running configuration and how to manipulate it. Most people who install Ansible through a package find that they can get a long way with Ansible before they have to modify the default configuration, as it has been carefully designed to work in a great many scenarios. However, it is important to know a little about configuring Ansible in case you come across an issue in your environment that can only be changed by modifying the configuration.

Obviously, if you don't have Ansible installed, there's little point in exploring its configuration, so let's just check whether you have Ansible installed and working by issuing a command such as the following (the output shown is from the latest version of Ansible at the time of writing, installed on macOS with Homebrew):

```
$ ansible 2.9.6
  config file = None
  configured module search path = ['/Users/james/.ansible/plugins/modules',
'/usr/share/ansible/plugins/modules']
  ansible python module location =
/usr/local/Cellar/ansible/2.9.6_1/libexec/lib/python3.8/site-
packages/ansible
  executable location = /usr/local/bin/ansible
  python version = 3.8.2 (default, Mar 11 2020, 00:28:52) [Clang 11.0.0
(clang-1100.0.33.17)]
```

Let's get started by exploring the default configuration that is provided with Ansible:

1. The command in the following code block lists the current configuration parameters supported by Ansible. It is incredibly useful because it tells you both the environment variable that can be used to change the setting (see the env field) as well as the configuration file parameter and section that can be used (see the ini field). Other valuable information, including the default configuration values and a description of the configuration, is given (see the default and description fields, respectively). All of the information is sourced from lib/constants.py. Run the following command to explore the output:

```
$ ansible-config list
```

The following is an example of the kind of output you will see. There are, of course, many pages to it, but a snippet is shown here as an example:

```
$ ansible-config list
ACTION_WARNINGS:
  default: true
  description:
  - By default Ansible will issue a warning when received from a
task action (module
    or action plugin)
  - These warnings can be silenced by adjusting this setting to
False.
  env:
  - name: ANSIBLE_ACTION_WARNINGS
  ini:
  - key: action_warnings
    section: defaults
  name: Toggle action warnings
  type: boolean
  version_added: '2.5'
AGNOSTIC_BECOME_PROMPT:
  default: true
  description: Display an agnostic become prompt instead of
displaying a prompt containing
    the command line supplied become method
  env:
  - name: ANSIBLE_AGNOSTIC_BECOME_PROMPT
  ini:
  - key: agnostic_become_prompt
    section: privilege_escalation
  name: Display an agnostic become prompt
  type: boolean
  version_added: '2.5'
```

```
yaml:
  key: privilege_escalation.agnostic_become_prompt
.....
```

2. If you want to see a straightforward display of all the possible configuration parameters, along with their current values (regardless of whether they are configured from environment variables or a configuration file in one of the previously listed locations), you can run the following command:

```
$ ansible-config dump
```

The output shows all the configuration parameters (in an environment variable format), along with the current settings. If the parameter is configured with its default value, you are told so (see the (default) element after each parameter name):

```
$ ansible-config dump
ACTION_WARNINGS(default) = True
AGNOSTIC_BECOME_PROMPT(default) = True
ALLOW_WORLD_READABLE_TMPFILES(default) = False
ANSIBLE_CONNECTION_PATH(default) = None
ANSIBLE_COW_PATH(default) = None
ANSIBLE_COW_SELECTION(default) = default
ANSIBLE_COW_WHITELIST(default) = ['bud-frogs', 'bunny', 'cheese',
'daemon', 'default', 'dragon', 'elephant-in-snake', 'elephant',
'eyes', 'hellokitty', 'kitty', 'luke-koala', 'meow', 'milk',
'moofasa', 'moose', 'ren', 'sheep', 'small', 'stegosaurus',
'stimpy', 'supermilker', 'three-eyes', 'turkey', 'turtle', 'tux',
'udder', 'vader-koala', 'vader', 'www']
ANSIBLE_FORCE_COLOR(default) = False
ANSIBLE_NOCOLOR(default) = False
ANSIBLE_NOCOWS(default) = False
ANSIBLE_PIPELINING(default) = False
ANSIBLE_SSH_ARGS(default) = -C -o ControlMaster=auto -o
ControlPersist=60s
ANSIBLE_SSH_CONTROL_PATH(default) = None
ANSIBLE_SSH_CONTROL_PATH_DIR(default) = ~/.ansible/cp
....
```

3. Let's see the effect on this output by editing one of the configuration parameters. Let's do this by setting an environment variable, as follows (this command has been tested in the bash shell, but may differ for other shells):

```
$ export ANSIBLE_FORCE_COLOR=True
```

Now, let's re-run the `ansible-config` command, but this time get it to tell us only the parameters that have been changed from their default values:

```
$ ansible-config dump --only-change
ANSIBLE_FORCE_COLOR(env: ANSIBLE_FORCE_COLOR) = True
```

Here, you can see that `ansible-config` tells us that we have only changed `ANSIBLE_FORCE_COLOR` from the default value, that it is set to `True`, and that we set it through an `env` variable. This is incredibly valuable, especially if you have to debug configuration issues.

When working with the Ansible configuration file itself, you will note that it is in INI format, meaning it has sections such as `[defaults]`, parameters in the format `key = value`, and comments beginning with either `#` or `;`. You only need to place the parameters you wish to change from their defaults in your configuration file, so if you wanted to create a simple configuration to change the location of your default inventory file, it might look as follows:

```
# Set my configuration variables
[defaults]
inventory = /Users/danieloh/ansible/hosts ; Here is the path of the
inventory file
```

As discussed earlier, one of the possible valid locations for the `ansible.cfg` configuration file is in your current working directory. It is likely that this is within your home directory, so on a multi-user system, we strongly recommend you restrict access to the Ansible configuration file to your user account alone. You should take all the usual precautions when it comes to securing important configuration files on a multi-user system, especially as Ansible is normally used to configure multiple remote systems and so, a lot of damage could be done if a configuration file is inadvertently compromised!

Of course, Ansible's behavior is not just controlled by the configuration files and switches—the command-line arguments that you pass to the various Ansible executables are also of vital importance. In fact, we have already worked with one already—in the preceding example, we showed you how to change where Ansible looks for its inventory file using the `inventory` parameter in `ansible.cfg`. However, in many of the examples that we previously covered in this book, we overrode this with the `-i` switch when running Ansible. So, let's proceed to the next section to look at the use of command-line arguments when running Ansible.

Command-line arguments

In this section, you will learn about the use of command-line arguments for playbook execution and how to employ some of the more commonly used ones to your advantage. We are already very familiar with one of these arguments, the --version switch, which we use to confirm that Ansible is installed (and which version is installed):

```
$ ansible 2.9.6
  config file = None
  configured module search path = ['/Users/james/.ansible/plugins/modules',
'/usr/share/ansible/plugins/modules']
  ansible python module location =
/usr/local/Cellar/ansible/2.9.6_1/libexec/lib/python3.8/site-
packages/ansible
  executable location = /usr/local/bin/ansible
  python version = 3.8.2 (default, Mar 11 2020, 00:28:52) [Clang 11.0.0
(clang-1100.0.33.17)]
```

Just as we were able to learn about the various configuration parameters directly through Ansible, we can also learn about the command-line arguments. Almost all of the Ansible executables have a --help option that you can run to display the valid command-line parameters. Let's try this out now:

1. You can view all the options and arguments when you execute the ansible command line. Use the following command:

   ```
   $ ansible --help
   ```

   You will see a great deal of helpful output when you run the preceding command; an example of this is shown in the following code block (you might want to pipe this into a pager, such as less, so that you can read it all easily):

   ```
   $ ansible --help
   usage: ansible [-h] [--version] [-v] [-b] [--become-method
   BECOME_METHOD] [--become-user BECOME_USER] [-K] [-i INVENTORY] [--
   list-hosts] [-l SUBSET] [-P POLL_INTERVAL] [-B SECONDS] [-o] [-t
   TREE] [-k]
                     [--private-key PRIVATE_KEY_FILE] [-u REMOTE_USER] [-
   c CONNECTION] [-T TIMEOUT] [--ssh-common-args SSH_COMMON_ARGS] [--
   sftp-extra-args SFTP_EXTRA_ARGS] [--scp-extra-args SCP_EXTRA_ARGS]
                     [--ssh-extra-args SSH_EXTRA_ARGS] [-C] [--syntax-
   check] [-D] [-e EXTRA_VARS] [--vault-id VAULT_IDS] [--ask-vault-
   pass | --vault-password-file VAULT_PASSWORD_FILES] [-f FORKS]
                     [-M MODULE_PATH] [--playbook-dir BASEDIR] [-a
   MODULE_ARGS] [-m MODULE_NAME]
                     pattern
   ```

Define and run a single task 'playbook' against a set of hosts

positional arguments:
  pattern host pattern

optional arguments:
  --ask-vault-pass ask for vault password
  --list-hosts outputs a list of matching hosts; does not execute
anything else
  --playbook-dir BASEDIR
                        Since this tool does not use playbooks, use
this as a substitute playbook directory.This sets the relative path
for many features including roles/ group_vars/ etc.
  --syntax-check perform a syntax check on the playbook, but do not
execute it
  --vault-id VAULT_IDS the vault identity to use
  --vault-password-file VAULT_PASSWORD_FILES
                        vault password file
  --version show program's version number, config file location,
configured module search path, module location, executable location
and exit
  -B SECONDS, --background SECONDS
                        run asynchronously, failing after X seconds
(default=N/A)
  -C, --check don't make any changes; instead, try to predict some
of the changes that may occur
  -D, --diff when changing (small) files and templates, show the
differences in those files; works great with --check
  -M MODULE_PATH, --module-path MODULE_PATH
                        prepend colon-separated path(s) to module
library
(default=~/.ansible/plugins/modules:/usr/share/ansible/plugins/modu
les)
  -P POLL_INTERVAL, --poll POLL_INTERVAL
                        set the poll interval if using -B
(default=15)
  -a MODULE_ARGS, --args MODULE_ARGS
                        module arguments
  -e EXTRA_VARS, --extra-vars EXTRA_VARS
                        set additional variables as key=value or
YAML/JSON, if filename prepend with @

2. We could take one example from the preceding code to build on our previous use of `ansible`; so far, we have almost exclusively used it to run ad hoc tasks with the `-m` and `-a` parameters. However, `ansible` can also perform useful tasks such as telling us about the hosts in a group within our inventory. We could explore this using the `production-inventory` file we used earlier in this chapter:

```
$ ansible -i production-inventory --list-host appservers_emea_zone
```

When you run this, you should see the members of the `appservers_emea_zone` inventory group listed. Although perhaps a little contrived, this example is incredibly valuable when you start working with dynamic inventory files and you can no longer just `cat` your inventory file to the terminal to view the contents:

```
$ ansible -i production-inventory --list-host appservers_emea_zone
  hosts (2):
    appserver1-emea.example.com
    appserver2-emea.example.com
```

The same is true for the `ansible-playbook` executable file, too. We have already seen a few of these in the previous examples of this book and there's more that we can do. For example, earlier, we discussed the use of `ssh-agent` to manage multiple SSH authentication keys. While this makes running playbooks simple (as you don't have to pass any authentication parameters to Ansible), it is not the only way of doing this. You can use one of the command-line arguments for `ansible-playbook` to specify the private SSH key file, instead, as follows:

```
$ ansible-playbook -i production-inventory site.yml --private-key
~/keys/id_rsa
```

Similarly, in the preceding section, we specified the `remote_user` variable for Ansible to connect with in the playbook. However, command-line arguments can also set this parameter for the playbook; so, rather than editing the `remote_user` line in the playbook, we could remove it altogether and instead have run it using the following command-line string:

```
$ ansible-playbook -i production-inventory site.yml --user danieloh
```

The ultimate aim of Ansible is to make your life simpler and to remove mundane day-to-day tasks from your list. As a result, there is no right or wrong way to do this—you can specify your private SSH key using a command-line argument or make it available using `ssh-agent`. Similarly, you can put the `remote_user` line in your playbook or user the `--user` parameter on the command line. Ultimately, the choice is yours, but it is important to consider that if you are distributing a playbook to multiple users and they all have to remember to specify the remote user on the command line, will they actually remember to do it? What will the consequences be if they don't? If the `remote_user` line is present in the playbook, will that make their lives easier and be less prone to error because the user account has been set in the playbook itself?

As with the configuration of Ansible, you will use a small handful of the command-line arguments frequently and there will be many that you may never touch. The important thing is that you know they are there and how to find out about them, and you can make informed decisions about when to use them. Let's proceed to the next section, where we will look in a bit more detail at ad hoc commands with Ansible.

Understanding ad hoc commands

We have already seen a handful of ad hoc commands so far in this book, but to recap, they are single commands you can run with Ansible, making use of Ansible modules without the need to create or save playbooks. They are very useful for performing quick, one-off tasks on a number of remote machines or for testing and understanding the behavior of the Ansible modules that you intend to use in your playbooks. They are both a great learning tool and a quick and dirty (because you never document your work with a playbook!) automation solution.

As with every Ansible example, we need an inventory to run against. Let's reuse our `production-inventory` file from before:

```
[frontends_na_zone]
frontend1-na.example.com
frontend2-na.example.com

[frontends_emea_zone]
frontend1-emea.example.com
frontend2-emea.example.com

[appservers_na_zone]
appserver1-na.example.com
appserver2-na.example.com
```

```
[appservers_emea_zone]
appserver1-emea.example.com
appserver2-emea.example.com
```

Now, let's start with perhaps the quickest and dirtiest of ad hoc commands—running a raw shell command on a group of remote machines. Suppose that you want to check that the date and time of all the frontend servers in EMEA are in sync—you could do this by using a monitoring tool or by manually logging into each server in turn and checking the date and time. However, you can also use an Ansible ad hoc command:

1. Run the following ad hoc command to retrieve the current date and time from all of the `frontends_emea_zone` servers:

   ```
   $ ansible -i production-inventory frontends_emea_zone -a
   /usr/bin/date
   ```

   You will see that Ansible faithfully logs in to each machine in turn and runs the `date` command, returning the current date and time. Your output will look something as follows:

   ```
   $ ansible -i production-inventory frontends_emea_zone -a
   /usr/bin/date
   frontend1-emea.example.com | CHANGED | rc=0 >>
   Sun 5 Apr 18:55:30 BST 2020
   frontend2-emea.example.com | CHANGED | rc=0 >>
   Sun 5 Apr 18:55:30 BST 2020
   ```

2. This command is run with the user account you are logged in to when the command is run. You can use a command-line argument (discussed in the previous section) to run as a different user:

   ```
   $ ansible -i production-inventory frontends_emea_zone -a
   /usr/sbin/pvs -u danieloh

   frontend2-emea.example.com | FAILED | rc=5 >>
     WARNING: Running as a non-root user. Functionality may be
   unavailable.
     /run/lvm/lvmetad.socket: access failed: Permission denied
     WARNING: Failed to connect to lvmetad. Falling back to device
   scanning.
     /run/lock/lvm/P_global:aux: open failed: Permission denied
     Unable to obtain global lock.non-zero return code
   frontend1-emea.example.com | FAILED | rc=5 >>
     WARNING: Running as a non-root user. Functionality may be
   unavailable.
     /run/lvm/lvmetad.socket: access failed: Permission denied
     WARNING: Failed to connect to lvmetad. Falling back to device
   ```

```
scanning.
  /run/lock/lvm/P_global:aux: open failed: Permission denied
  Unable to obtain global lock.non-zero return code
```

3. Here, we can see that the `danieloh` user account does not have the privileges
    required to successfully run the `pvs` command. However, we can fix this by
    adding the `--become` command-line argument, which tells Ansible to become
    `root` on the remote systems:

    ```
    $ ansible -i production-inventory frontends_emea_zone -a
    /usr/sbin/pvs -u danieloh --become

    frontend2-emea.example.com | FAILED | rc=-1 >>
    Missing sudo password
    frontend1-emea.example.com | FAILED | rc=-1 >>
    Missing sudo password
    ```

4. We can see that the command still fails because although `danieloh` is in
    `/etc/sudoers`, it is not allowed to run commands as `root` without entering a
    `sudo` password. Luckily, there's a switch to get Ansible to prompt us for this at
    run time, meaning we don't need to edit our `/etc/sudoers` file:

    ```
    $ ansible -i production-inventory frontends_emea_zone -a
    /usr/sbin/pvs -u danieloh --become --ask-become-pass
    BECOME password:

    frontend1-emea.example.com | CHANGED | rc=0 >>
      PV VG Fmt Attr PSize PFree
      /dev/sda2 centos lvm2 a-- <19.00g 0
    frontend2-emea.example.com | CHANGED | rc=0 >>
      PV VG Fmt Attr PSize PFree
      /dev/sda2 centos lvm2 a-- <19.00g 0
    ```

5. By default, if you don't specify a module using the `-m` command-line argument,
    Ansible assumes you want to use the `command` module (see `https://docs.`
    `ansible.com/ansible/latest/modules/command_module.html`). If you wish to
    use a specific module, you can add the `-m` switch to the command-line arguments
    and then specify the module arguments under the `-a` switch, as in the following
    example:

    ```
    $ ansible -i production-inventory frontends_emea_zone -m copy -a
    "src=/etc/yum.conf dest=/tmp/yum.conf"
    frontend1-emea.example.com | CHANGED => {
        "ansible_facts": {
            "discovered_interpreter_python": "/usr/bin/python"
        },
    ```

```
    "changed": true,
    "checksum": "e0637e631f4ab0aaebef1a6b8822a36f031f332e",
    "dest": "/tmp/yum.conf",
    "gid": 0,
    "group": "root",
    "md5sum": "a7dc0d7b8902e9c8c096c93eb431d19e",
    "mode": "0644",
    "owner": "root",
    "size": 970,
    "src": "/root/.ansible/tmp/ansible-
tmp-1586110004.75-208447517347027/source",
    "state": "file",
    "uid": 0
}
frontend2-emea.example.com | CHANGED => {
    "ansible_facts": {
        "discovered_interpreter_python": "/usr/bin/python"
    },
    "changed": true,
    "checksum": "e0637e631f4ab0aaebef1a6b8822a36f031f332e",
    "dest": "/tmp/yum.conf",
    "gid": 0,
    "group": "root",
    "md5sum": "a7dc0d7b8902e9c8c096c93eb431d19e",
    "mode": "0644",
    "owner": "root",
    "size": 970,
    "src": "/root/.ansible/tmp/ansible-
tmp-1586110004.75-208447517347027/source",
    "state": "file",
    "uid": 0
}
```

The preceding output not only shows that the copy was performed successfully to both hosts but also all the output values from the copy module. This, again, can be very helpful later when you are developing playbooks as it enables you to understand exactly how the module works and what output it produces in cases where you need to perform further work with that output. This is a more advanced topic, however, that is beyond the scope of this introductory chapter.

You will also note that all arguments passed to the module must be enclosed in quotation marks ("). All arguments are specified as key=value pairs and no spaces should be added between key and value (for example, key = value is not acceptable). If you need to place quotation marks around one of your argument values, you can escape them using the backslash character (for example, -a "src=/etc/yum.conf dest=\"/tmp/yum file.conf\"")

All examples we have performed so far are very quick to execute and run, but this is not always the case with computing tasks. When you have to run an operation for a long time, say more than two hours, you should consider running it as a background process. In this instance, you can run the command asynchronously and confirm the result of that execution later.

For example, to execute `sleep 2h` asynchronously in the background with a timeout of 7,200 seconds (-B) and without polling (-P), use this command:

```
$ ansible -i production-inventory frontends_emea_zone -B 7200 -P 0 -a
"sleep 2h"
frontend1-emea.example.com | CHANGED => {
    "ansible_facts": {
        "discovered_interpreter_python": "/usr/bin/python"
    },
    "ansible_job_id": "537978889103.8857",
    "changed": true,
    "finished": 0,
    "results_file": "/root/.ansible_async/537978889103.8857",
    "started": 1
}
frontend2-emea.example.com | CHANGED => {
    "ansible_facts": {
        "discovered_interpreter_python": "/usr/bin/python"
    },
    "ansible_job_id": "651461662130.8858",
    "changed": true,
    "finished": 0,
    "results_file": "/root/.ansible_async/651461662130.8858",
    "started": 1
}
```

Note that the output from this command gives a unique job ID for each task on each host. Let's now say that we want to see how this task proceeds on the second frontend server. Simply issue the following command from your Ansible control machine:

```
$ ansible -i production-inventory frontend2-emea.example.com -m
async_status -a "jid=651461662130.8858"
frontend2-emea.example.com | SUCCESS => {
    "ansible_facts": {
        "discovered_interpreter_python": "/usr/bin/python"
    },
    "ansible_job_id": "651461662130.8858",
    "changed": false,
    "finished": 0,
    "started": 1
}
```

Here, we can see that the job has started but not finished. If we now kill the `sleep` command that we issued and check on the status again, we can see the following:

```
$ ansible -i production-inventory frontend2-emea.example.com -m
async_status -a "jid=651461662130.8858"
frontend2-emea.example.com | FAILED! => {
    "ansible_facts": {
        "discovered_interpreter_python": "/usr/bin/python"
    },
    "ansible_job_id": "651461662130.8858",
    "changed": true,
    "cmd": [
        "sleep",
        "2h"
    ],
    "delta": "0:03:16.534212",
    "end": "2020-04-05 19:18:08.431258",
    "finished": 1,
    "msg": "non-zero return code",
    "rc": -15,
    "start": "2020-04-05 19:14:51.897046",
    "stderr": "",
    "stderr_lines": [],
    "stdout": "",
    "stdout_lines": []
}
```

Here, we see a `FAILED` status result because the `sleep` command was killed; it did not exit cleanly and returned a `-15` code (see the `rc` parameter). When it was killed, no output was sent to either `stdout` or `stderr`, but if it had been, Ansible would have captured it and displayed it in the preceding code, which would aid you in debugging the failure. Lots of other useful information is included, including how long the task actually ran for, the end time, and so on. Similarly, the useful output is returned when the task exits cleanly.

That concludes our look at ad hoc commands in Ansible. By now, you should have a fairly solid grasp of the fundamentals of Ansible, but there's one important thing we haven't looked at yet, even though we briefly touched on it—variables and how to define them. We'll proceed to look at this in the next section.

Defining variables

In this section, we will cover the topic of variables and how they can be defined in Ansible. You will learn how variables should be defined step by step and understand how to work with them in Ansible.

Although automation removes much of the repetition from previously manual tasks, not every single system is identical. If two systems differ in some minor way, you could write two unique playbooks—one for each system. However, this would be inefficient and wasteful, as well as difficult to manage as time goes on (for example, if the code in one playbook is changed, how can you ensure that it is updated in the second variant?).

Equally, you might need to use a value from one system in another—perhaps you need to obtain the hostname of a database server and make it available to another. All of these issues can be addressed with variables as they allow the same automation code to run with parameter variations, as well as values to pass from one system to another (although this must be handled with some care).

Let's get started with a practical look at defining variables in Ansible.

Variables in Ansible should have well-formatted names that adhere to the following rules:

- The name of the variable must only include letters, underscores, and numbers—spaces are not allowed.
- The name of the variable can only begin with a letter—they can contain numbers, but cannot start with one.

For example, the following are good variable names:

- `external_svc_port`
- `internal_hostname_ap1`

The following examples are all invalid, however, and cannot be used:

- `appserver-zone-na`
- `cache server ip`
- `dbms.server.port`
- `01appserver`

As discussed in the *Learning the YAML syntax* section, variables can be defined in a dictionary structure, such as the following. All values are declared in key-value pairs:

```
region:
  east: app
  west: frontend
  central: cache
```

In order to retrieve a specific field from the preceding dictionary structure, you can use either one of the following notations:

```
# bracket notation
region['east']

# dot notation
region.east
```

There are some exceptions to this; for example, you should use bracket notation if the variable name starts and ends with two underscores (for example, __variable__) or contains known public attributes, such as the following:

- as_integer_ratio
- symmetric_difference

You can find more information on this at https://docs.ansible.com/ansible/latest/user_guide/playbooks_variables.html#creating-valid-variable-names.

This dictionary structure is valuable when defining host variables; although earlier in this chapter we worked with a fictional set of employee records defined as an Ansible variables file, you could use this to specify something, such as some redis server parameters:

```
---
redis:
  - server: cacheserver01.example.com
    port: 6379
    slaveof: cacheserver02.example.com
```

These could then be applied through your playbook and one common playbook could be used for all redis servers, regardless of their configuration, as changeable parameters such as the port and master servers are all contained in the variables.

You can also pass set variables directly in a playbook, and even pass them to roles that you call. For example, the following playbook code calls four hypothetical roles and each assigns a different value to the username variable for each one. These roles could be used to set up various administration roles on a server (or multiple servers), with each passing a changing list of usernames as people come and go from the company:

```
roles:
  - role: dbms_admin
    vars:
      username: James
  - role: system_admin
```

```
      vars:
        username: John
  - role: security_amdin
      vars:
        username: Rock
  - role: app_admin
      vars:
        username: Daniel
```

To access variables from within a playbook, you simply place the variable name inside quoted pairs of curly braces. Consider the following example playbook (based loosely on our previous `redis` example):

```
---
- name: Display redis variables
  hosts: all

  vars:
    redis:
      server: cacheserver01.example.com
      port: 6379
      slaveof: cacheserver02.example.com

  tasks:
    - name: Display the redis port
      debug:
        msg: "The redis port for {{ redis.server }} is {{ redis.port }}"
```

Here, we define a variable in the playbook itself called `redis`. This variable is a dictionary, containing a number of parameters that might be important for our server. To access the contents of these variables, we use pairs of curly braces around them (as described previously) and the entire string is encased in quotation marks, which means we don't have to individually quote the variables. If you run the playbook on a local machine, you should see an output that looks as follows:

```
$ ansible-playbook -i localhost, redis-playbook.yml

PLAY [Display redis variables]
************************************************

TASK [Gathering Facts]
*****************************************************
ok: [localhost]

TASK [Display the redis port]
************************************************
ok: [localhost] => {
```

```
        "msg": "The redis port for cacheserver01.example.com is 6379"
    }

    PLAY RECAP
    **********************************************************************
    localhost : ok=2 changed=0 unreachable=0 failed=0 skipped=0 rescued=0
    ignored=0
```

Although we are accessing these variables here to print them in a debug message, you could use the same curly brace notation to assign them to module parameters, or for any other purpose that your playbook requires them for.

Ansible, just like many languages, has specially reserved variables that take on particular meaning in playbooks. In Ansible, these are known as magic variables and you can find a full list of them at https://docs.ansible.com/ansible/latest/reference_appendices/special_variables.html. Needless to say, you should not attempt to use any magic variable names for your own variables. Some common magic variables you might come across are as follows:

- inventory_hostname: The hostname for the current host that is iterated over in the play
- groups: A dictionary of the host groups in the inventory, along with the host membership of each group
- group_names: A list of the groups the current host (specified by inventory_hostname) is part of
- hostvars: A dictionary of all the hosts in the inventory and the variables assigned to each of them

For example, the host variables for all the hosts can be accessed at any point in the playbook using hostvars, even if you are only operating on one particular host. Magic variables are surprisingly useful in playbooks and you will rapidly start to find yourself using them, so it is important to be aware of their existence.

You should also note that you can specify Ansible variables in multiple locations. Ansible has a strict order of variable precedence and you can take advantage of this by setting default values for variables in a place that has low precedence and then overriding them later in the play. This is useful for a variety of reasons, especially where an undefined variable could cause havoc when a playbook is run (or even when the playbook would fail as a result of this). We have not yet discussed all of the places that variables can be stored, so the full list of variable precedence order is not given here.

In addition, it can change between Ansible releases, so it is important that you refer to the documentation when working with and understanding variable precedence—go to `https:/ /docs.ansible.com/ansible/latest/user_guide/playbooks_variables.html#variable- precedence-where-should-i-put-a-variable` for more information.

That concludes our brief overview of variables in Ansible, although we will see them used again in later examples in this book. Let's now round off this chapter with a look at Jinja2 filters, which add a whole world of power to your variable definitions.

Understanding Jinja2 filters

As Ansible is written in Python, it inherits an incredibly useful and powerful templating engine called Jinja2. We will look at the concept of templating later in this book, so for now, we will focus on one particular aspect of Jinja2 known as filtering. Jinja2 filters provide an incredibly powerful framework that you can use to manipulate and transform your data. Perhaps you have a string that you need to convert to lowercase, for example—you could apply a Jinja2 filter to achieve this. You can also use it to perform pattern matching, search and replace operations, and much more. There are many hundreds of filters for you to work with and in this section, we hope to empower you with a basic understanding of Jinja2 filters and some practical knowledge about how to apply them, as well as show you where to get more information about them if you wish to explore the subject further.

It is worth noting that Jinja2 operations are performed on the Ansible control host and only the results of the filter operation are sent to the remote hosts. This is done by design, both for consistency and to reduce the workload on the individual nodes as much as possible.

Let's explore this through a practical example. Suppose we have a YAML file containing some data that we want to parse. We can quite easily read a file from the machine filesystem and capture the result using the `register` keyword (`register` captures the result of the task and stores it in a variable—in the case of running the `shell` module, it captures all the output from the command that was run).

Our YAML data file might look as follows:

```
tags:
  - key: job
    value: developer
  - key: language
    value: java
```

Now, we could create a playbook to read this file and register the result, but how can we actually turn it into a variable structure that Ansible can understand and work with? Let's consider the following playbook:

```
---
- name: Jinja2 filtering demo 1
  hosts: localhost

  tasks:
    - copy:
        src: multiple-document-strings.yaml
        dest: /tmp/multiple-document-strings.yaml
    - shell: cat /tmp/multiple-document-strings.yaml
      register: result
    - debug:
        msg: '{{ item }}'
        loop: '{{ result.stdout | from_yaml_all | list }}'
```

The `shell` module does not necessarily run from the directory that the playbook is stored in, so we cannot guarantee that it will find our `multiple-document-strings.yaml` file. The `copy` module does, however, source the file from the current directory, so it is useful to use it to copy it to a known location (such as `/tmp`) for the `shell` module to read the file from. The `debug` module is then run in a `loop` module. The `loop` module is used to iterate over all of the lines of `stdout` from the `shell` command, as we are using two Jinja2 filters—`from_yaml_all` and `list`.

The `from_yaml_all` filter parses the source document lines as YAML and then the `list` filter converts the parsed data into a valid Ansible list. If we run the playbook, we should see Ansible's representation of the data structure from within our original file:

```
$ ansible-playbook -i localhost, jinja-filtering1.yml

PLAY [Jinja2 filtering demo 1]
**************************************************

TASK [Gathering Facts]
*******************************************************
ok: [localhost]

TASK [copy]
*****************************************************************
ok: [localhost]

TASK [shell]
*****************************************************************
changed: [localhost]
```

```
TASK [debug]
*******************************************************************
ok: [localhost] => (item={'tags': [{'value': u'developer', 'key': u'job'},
{'value': u'java', 'key': u'language'}]}) => {
    "msg": {
        "tags": [
            {
                "key": "job",
                "value": "developer"
            },
            {
                "key": "language",
                "value": "java"
            }
        ]
    }
}

PLAY RECAP
*******************************************************************
localhost : ok=4 changed=1 unreachable=0 failed=0 skipped=0 rescued=0
ignored=0
```

As you can see, we have generated a list of dictionaries that in themselves contain the key-value pairs.

If this data structure was already stored in our playbook, we could take this one step further and use the items2dict filter to turn the list into true key: value pairs, removing the key and value items from the data structure. For example, consider this second playbook:

```
---
- name: Jinja2 filtering demo 2
  hosts: localhost
  vars:
    tags:
      - key: job
        value: developer
      - key: language
        value: java

  tasks:
    - debug:
        msg: '{{ tags | items2dict }}'
```

Now, if we run this, we can see that our data is converted into a nice neat set of `key:` `value` pairs:

```
$ ansible-playbook -i localhost, jinja2-filtering2.yml
[WARNING]: Found variable using reserved name: tags

PLAY [Jinja2 filtering demo 2]
**************************************************

TASK [Gathering Facts]
*****************************************************
ok: [localhost]

TASK [debug]
*********************************************************************
ok: [localhost] => {
    "msg": {
        "job": "developer",
---
        "language": "java"
    }
}

PLAY RECAP
*********************************************************************
localhost : ok=2 changed=0 unreachable=0 failed=0 skipped=0 rescued=0
ignored=0
```

Observe the warning at the top of the playbook. Ansible displays a warning if you attempt to use a reserved name for a variable, as we did here. Normally, you should not create a variable with a reserved name, but the example here demonstrates both how the filter works and how Ansible will attempt to warn you if you do something that might cause problems.

Earlier in this section, we used the `shell` module to read a file and used `register` to store the result in a variable. This is perfectly fine, if a little inelegant. Jinja2 contains a series of `lookup` filters that, among other things, can read the contents of a given file. Let's examine the behavior of this following playbook::

```
---
- name: Jinja2 filtering demo 3
  hosts: localhost
  vars:
    ping_value: "{{ lookup('file', '/etc/hosts') }}"
```

```
    tasks:
      - debug:
          msg: "ping value is {{ ping_value }}"
```

When we run this, we can see that Ansible has captured the contents of the /etc/hosts file for us, without us needing to resort to the copy and shell modules as we did earlier:

```
$ ansible-playbook -i localhost, jinja2-filtering3.yml

PLAY [Jinja2 filtering demo 3]
**************************************************

TASK [Gathering Facts]
*****************************************************
ok: [localhost]

TASK [debug]
***************************************************************
ok: [localhost] => {
    "msg": "ping value is 127.0.0.1 localhost localhost.localdomain
localhost4 localhost4.localdomain4\n::1 localhost localhost.localdomain
localhost6 localhost6.localdomain6\n\n"
}

PLAY RECAP
***************************************************************
localhost : ok=2 changed=0 unreachable=0 failed=0 skipped=0 rescued=0
ignored=0
```

There are many other filters that you might be interested in exploring and a full list can be found in the official Jinja2 documentation (https://jinja.palletsprojects.com/en/2.11.x/). The following are a handful of other examples that will give you an idea of the kinds of things that Jinja2 filters can achieve for you, from quoting strings to concatenating lists to obtaining useful path information for a file:

```
# Add some quotation in the shell
- shell: echo {{ string_value | quote }}

# Concatenate a list into a specific string
{{ list | join("$") }}

# Have the last name of a specific file path
{{ path | basename }}

# Have the directory from a specific path
{{ path | dirname }}
```

```
# Have the directory from a specific windows path
{{ path | win_dirname }}
```

That concludes our look at Jinja2 filtering. It is a massive topic that deserves a book all to itself, but, as ever, I hope that this practical guide has given you some pointers on how to get started and where to find information.

Summary

Ansible is a very powerful and versatile automation engine that can be used for a wide variety of tasks. Understanding the basics of how to work it is of paramount importance, before addressing the more complex challenges of playbook creation and large-scale automation. Ansible relies on a language called YAML, a simple-to-read (and write) syntax that supports the rapid development of easy-to-read and easy-to-maintain code and inherits a number of valuable features from the Python language that it is written in, including Jinja2 filtering.

In this chapter, you learned the fundamentals of working with various Ansible programs. You then learned about the YAML syntax and the ways that you can break down your code into manageable chunks to make it easier to read and maintain. We explored the use of ad hoc commands in Ansible, variable definition and structure, and how to make use of Jinja2 filters to manipulate the data in your playbooks.

In the next chapter, we will take a more in-depth look at Ansible inventories and explore some of the more advanced concepts of working with them that you may find useful.

Questions

1. Which component of Ansible allows you to define a block to execute task groups as a play?

   A) `handler`

   B) `service`

   C) `hosts`

   D) `tasks`

   E) `name`

2. Which basic syntax from the YAML format do you use to start a file?

   A) `###`

   B) `---`

   C) `%%%`

   D) `===`

   E) `***`

3. True or false – in order to interpret and transform output data in Ansible, you need to use Jinja2 templates.

   A) True

   B) False

Further reading

- To find out about more configuration variables, go to `https://docs.ansible.com/ansible/latest/reference_appendices/config.html#ansible-configuration-settings`.

Defining Your Inventory 3

As we have already discussed in the first two chapters, Ansible cannot do anything until you tell it what hosts it is responsible for. This is, of course, logical—you wouldn't want any automation tool, regardless of how easy it is to use and set up, to simply go out and take control of every single device on your network. Hence, at the bare minimum, you must tell Ansible what hosts it is going to automate tasks on, and this, in the most fundamental terms, is what an inventory is.

However, there is so much more to inventories than just a list of automation targets. Ansible inventories can be provided in several formats; they can be either static or dynamic, and they can contain important variables that define how Ansible interacts with each host (or groups of hosts). Hence, they deserve a chapter to themselves, and in this chapter, we shall perform a practical exploration of inventories and how to use them to your best advantage as you automate your infrastructure with Ansible.

In this chapter, we will cover the following topics:

- Creating an inventory file and adding hosts
- Generating a dynamic inventory file
- Special host management using patterns

Technical requirements

This chapter assumes that you have set up your control host with Ansible, as detailed in Chapter 1, *Getting Started with Ansible,* and you are using the most recent version available—the examples in this chapter were tested with Ansible 2.9. This chapter also assumes that you have at least one additional host to test against, and ideally this should be Linux-based. Although we will give specific examples of hostnames in this chapter, you are free to substitute them with your own hostname and/or IP addresses, and details of how to do this will be provided in the appropriate places.

The code bundle for this chapter is available here: https://github.com/PacktPublishing/Ansible-2-Cookbook/tree/master/Chapter%203.

Creating an inventory file and adding hosts

Whenever you see a reference to "creating an inventory" in Ansible, you are normally quite safe to assume that it is a static inventory. Ansible supports two types of inventory—static and dynamic, and we will cover the latter of these two later in this chapter. Static inventories are by their very nature static; they are unchanging unless a human being goes and manually edits them. This is great when you are starting out and testing Ansible, as it provides you with a very quick and easy way to get up and running quickly. Even in small, closed environments, static inventories are a great way to manage your environment, especially when changes to the infrastructure are infrequent.

Most Ansible installations will look for a default inventory file in /etc/ansible/hosts (though this path is configurable in the Ansible configuration file, as discussed in Chapter 2, *Understanding the Fundamentals of Ansible*). You are welcome to populate this file or to provide your own inventory for each playbook run, and it is commonplace to see inventories provided alongside playbooks. After all, there's rarely a "one size fits all" playbook, and although you can subdivide your inventory with groups (more on this later), it can often be just as easy to provide a smaller static inventory file alongside a given playbook. As you will have seen in the earlier chapters of this book, most Ansible commands use the -i flag to specify the location of the inventory file if not using the default. Hypothetically, this might look like the following example:

```
$ ansible -i /home/cloud-user/inventory all -m ping
```

Most static inventory files you will come across are created in INI format, though it is important to note that other formats are possible. The most common format you will find after INI-formatted files are YAML ones—more details of the types of inventory files you can work with may be found here: https://docs.ansible.com/ansible/latest/user_guide/intro_inventory.html.

In this chapter, we will provide some examples of both INI and YAML formatted inventory files for you to consider, as you must have an awareness of both. Personally, I have worked with Ansible for many years and worked with either INI-formatted files or dynamic inventories, but they say knowledge is power and so it will do no harm to learn a little about both formats.

Let's start by creating a static inventory file. This inventory file will be separate from the default inventory.

Create an inventory file in /etc/ansible/my_inventory using the following INI-formatted code:

```
target1.example.com ansible_host=192.168.81.142 ansible_port=3333

target2.example.com ansible_port=3333 ansible_user=danieloh

target3.example.com ansible_host=192.168.81.143 ansible_port=5555
```

The blank lines between inventory hosts are not required—they have been inserted simply to make the inventory more readable in this book. This inventory file is very simple and does not include any grouping; however, when referencing the inventory, you can still refer to all the hosts together using the special all group, which is implicitly defined regardless of how you format and divide your inventory file.

Each line in the preceding file contains one inventory host. The first column contains the inventory hostname that Ansible will use (and can be accessed through the inventory_hostname magic variable we discussed in Chapter 2, *Understanding the Fundamentals of Ansible*). All parameters on the same line after that are variables that are assigned to the host. These can be user-defined variables or special Ansible variables as we have set here.

There are many such variables, but the preceding examples specifically include the following:

- `ansible_host`: If the inventory hostname cannot be accessed directly—perhaps because it is not in DNS, for example, this variable contains the hostname or IP address that Ansible will connect to instead.
- `ansible_port`: By default, Ansible attempts all communication over port 22 for SSH—if you have an SSH daemon running on another port, you can tell Ansible about it using this variable.
- `ansible_user`: By default, Ansible will attempt to connect to the remote host using the current user account you are running the Ansible command from—you can override this in several ways, of which this is one.

Hence, the preceding three hosts can be summarized as follows:

- The `target1.example.com` host should be connected to using the `192.168.81.142` IP address, on port `3333`.
- The `target2.example.com` host should be connected to on port `3333` also, but this time using the `danieloh` user rather than the account running the Ansible command.
- The `target3.example.com` host should be connected to using the `192.168.81.143` IP address, on port `5555`.

In this way, even with no further constructs, you can begin to see the power of static INI-formatted inventories.

Now, if you wanted to create exactly the same inventory as the preceding, but this time, format it as YAML, you would specify it as follows:

```yaml
---
ungrouped:
  hosts:
    target1.example.com:
      ansible_host: 192.168.81.142
      ansible_port: 3333
    target2.example.com:
      ansible_port: 3333
      ansible_user: danieloh
    target3.example.com:
      ansible_host: 192.168.81.143
      ansible_port: 5555
```

You may come across inventory file examples containing parameters such as `ansible_ssh_port`, `ansible_ssh_host`, and `ansible_ssh_user`–these variable names (and others like them) were used in Ansible versions before 2.0. Backward compatibility has been maintained for many of these, but you should update them where possible as this compatibility may be removed at some point in the future.

Now if you were to run the preceding inventory within Ansible, using a simple `shell` command, the result would appear as follows:

```
$ ansible -i /etc/ansible/my_inventory.yaml all -m shell -a 'echo hello-
yaml' -f 5
target1.example.com | CHANGED | rc=0 >>
hello-yaml
target2.example.com | CHANGED | rc=0 >>
hello-yaml
target3.example.com | CHANGED | rc=0 >>
hello-yaml
```

That covers the basics of creating a simple static inventory file. Let's now expand upon this by adding host groups into the inventory in the next part of this chapter.

Using host groups

There is rarely one playbook that will suit an entire infrastructure, and although it is easy to tell Ansible to use an alternate inventory for a different playbook, this could get very messy, very quickly, with potentially hundreds of small inventory files dotted around your network. You can imagine how quickly this would get unmanageable, and Ansible is supposed to make things more manageable, not the opposite. One possible simple solution to this is to start adding groups into your inventories.

Let's assume you have a simple three-tier web architecture, with multiple hosts in each tier for high availability and/or load balancing. The three tiers in this architecture might be the following:

- Frontend servers
- Application servers
- Database servers

With this architecture set out, let's set about creating an inventory for it, again mixing up the YAML and INI formats to give you experience in both. To keep the examples clear and concise, we'll assume that you can access all servers using their **Fully Qualified Domain Names (FQDNs)**, and hence won't add any host variables into these inventory files. There is nothing to stop you from doing this of course, and every example is different.

Let's, first of all, create the inventory for the three-tier frontend using the INI format. We will call this file `hostsgroups-ini`, and the contents of this file should look something like this:

```
loadbalancer.example.com

[frontends]
frt01.example.com
frt02.example.com

[apps]
app01.example.com
app02.example.com

[databases]
dbms01.example.com
dbms02.example.com
```

In the preceding inventory, we have created three groups called `frontends`, `apps`, and `databases`. Note that, in INI-formatted inventories, group names go inside square braces. Under each group name goes the server names that belong in each group, so the preceding example shows two servers in each group. Notice the outlier at the top, `loadbalancer.example.com`—this host isn't in any group. All ungrouped hosts must go at the very top of an INI-formatted file.

Before we proceed any further, it's worth noting that inventories can also contain groups of groups, which is incredibly useful for processing certain tasks by a different division. The preceding inventory stands in its own right, but what if our frontend servers are built on Ubuntu, and the app and database servers are built on CentOS? There will be some fundamental differences in the ways we handle these hosts—for example, we might use the `apt` module to manage packages on Ubuntu and the `yum` module on CentOS.

We could, of course, handle this case using facts gathered from each host as these will contain the operating system details. We could also create a new version of the inventory, as follows:

```
loadbalancer.example.com

[frontends]
```

```
frt01.example.com
frt02.example.com

[apps]
app01.example.com
app02.example.com

[databases]
dbms01.example.com
dbms02.example.com

[centos:children]
apps
databases

[ubuntu:children]
frontends
```

With the use of the `children` keyword in the group definition (inside the square braces), we can create groups of groups; hence, we can perform clever groupings to help our playbook design without having to specify each host more than once.

This structure in INI format is quite readable but takes some getting used to when it is converted into YAML format. The code listed next shows the YAML version of the preceding inventory—the two are identical as far as Ansible is concerned, but it is left to you to decide which format you prefer working with:

```
all:
  hosts:
    loadbalancer.example.com:
  children:
    centos:
      children:
        apps:
          hosts:
            app01.example.com:
            app02.example.com:
        databases:
          hosts:
            dbms01.example.com:
            dbms02.example.com:
    ubuntu:
      children:
        frontends:
          hosts:
            frt01.example.com:
            frt02.example.com:
```

You can see that the `children` keyword is still used in the YAML-formatted inventory, but now the structure is more hierarchical than it was in the INI format. The indentation might be easier for you to follow, but note how the hosts are ultimately defined at quite a high level of indentation—this format could be more difficult to extend depending on your desired approach.

When you want to work with any of the groups from the preceding inventory, you would simply reference it either in your playbook or on the command line. For example, in the last section we ran, we can use the following:

```
$ ansible -i /etc/ansible/my_inventory.yaml all -m shell -a 'echo hello-yaml' -f 5
```

Note the `all` keyword in the middle of that line. That is the special `all` group that is implicit in all inventories and is explicitly mentioned in your previous YAML example. If we wanted to run the same command, but this time on just the `centos` group hosts from the previous YAML inventory, we would run this variation of the command:

```
$ ansible -i hostgroups-yml centos -m shell -a 'echo hello-yaml' -f 5
app01.example.com | CHANGED | rc=0 >>
hello-yaml
app02.example.com | CHANGED | rc=0 >>
hello-yaml
dbms01.example.com | CHANGED | rc=0 >>
hello-yaml
dbms02.example.com | CHANGED | rc=0 >>
hello-yaml
```

As you can see, this is a powerful way of managing your inventory and making it easy to run commands on just the hosts you want to. The possibility of creating multiple groups makes life simple and easy, especially when you want to run different tasks on different groups of servers.

As an aside to developing your inventories, it is worth noting that there is a quick shorthand notation that you can use to create multiple hosts. Let's assume you have 100 app servers, all named sequentially, as follows:

```
[apps]
app01.example.com
app02.example.com
...
app99.example.com
app100.example.com
```

This is entirely possible, but would be tedious and error-prone to create by hand and would produce some very hard to read and interpret inventories. Luckily, Ansible provides a quick shorthand notation to achieve this, and the following inventory snippet actually produces an inventory with the same 100 app servers that we could create manually:

```
[apps]
app[01:100].prod.com
```

It is also possible to use alphabetic ranges as well as numeric ones—extending our example to add some cache servers, you might have the following:

```
[caches]
cache-[a:e].prod.com
```

This is the same as manually creating the following:

```
[caches]
cache-a.prod.com
cache-b.prod.com
cache-c.prod.com
cache-d.prod.com
cache-e.prod.com
```

Now that we've completed our exploration of the various static inventory formats and how to create groups (and indeed, child groups), let's expand in the next section on our previously brief look at host variables.

Adding host and group variables to your inventory

We have already touched upon host variables—we saw them earlier in this chapter when we used them to override connection details such as the user account to connect with, the address to connect to, and the port to use. However, there is so much more you can do with Ansible and inventory variables, and it is important to note that they can be defined not only at the host level but also at the group level, which again provides you with some incredibly powerful ways in which to efficiently manage your infrastructure from one central inventory.

Let's build on our previous three-tier example and suppose that we need to set two variables for each of our two frontend servers. These are not special Ansible variables, but instead are variables entirely of our own choosing, which we will use later on in the playbooks that run against this server. Suppose that these variables are as follows:

- `https_port`, which defines the port that the frontend proxy should listen on
- `lb_vip`, which defines the FQDN of the load-balancer in front of the frontend servers

Let's see how this is done:

1. We could simply add these to each of the hosts in the `frontends` part of our inventory file, just as we did before with the Ansible connection variables. In this case, a portion of our INI-formatted inventory might look like this:

```
[frontends]
frt01.example.com https_port=8443 lb_vip=lb.example.com
frt02.example.com https_port=8443 lb_vip=lb.example.com
```

If we run an ad hoc command against this inventory, we can see the contents of both of these variables:

```
$ ansible -i hostvars1-hostgroups-ini frontends -m debug -a
"msg=\"Connecting to {{ lb_vip }}, listening on {{ https_port }}\""
frt01.example.com | SUCCESS => {
    "msg": "Connecting to lb.example.com, listening on 8443"
}
frt02.example.com | SUCCESS => {
    "msg": "Connecting to lb.example.com, listening on 8443"
}
```

This has worked just as we desired, but the approach is inefficient as you have to add the same variables to every single host.

2. Luckily, you can assign variables to a host group as well as to hosts individually. If we edited the preceding inventory to achieve this, the `frontends` section would now look like this:

```
[frontends]
frt01.example.com
frt02.example.com

[frontends:vars]
https_port=8443
lb_vip=lb.example.com
```

Notice how much more readable that is? Yet, if we run the same command as before against our newly organized inventory, we see that the result is the same:

```
$ ansible -i groupvars1-hostgroups-ini frontends -m debug -a
"msg=\"Connecting to {{ lb_vip }}, listening on {{ https_port }}\""
frt01.example.com | SUCCESS => {
    "msg": "Connecting to lb.example.com, listening on 8443"
}
frt02.example.com | SUCCESS => {
    "msg": "Connecting to lb.example.com, listening on 8443"
}
```

3. There will be times when you want to work with host variables for individual hosts, and times when group variables are more relevant. It is up to you to determine which is better for your scenario; however, remember that host variables can be used in combination. It is also worth noting that host variables override group variables, so if we need to change the connection port to 8444 on the frt01.example.com one, we could do this as follows:

```
[frontends]
frt01.example.com https_port=8444
frt02.example.com

[frontends:vars]
https_port=8443
lb_vip=lb.example.com
```

Now if we run our ad hoc command again with the new inventory, we can see that we have overridden the variable on one host:

```
$ ansible -i hostvars2-hostgroups-ini frontends -m debug -a
"msg=\"Connecting to {{ lb_vip }}, listening on {{ https_port }}\""
frt01.example.com | SUCCESS => {
    "msg": "Connecting to lb.example.com, listening on 8444"
}
frt02.example.com | SUCCESS => {
    "msg": "Connecting to lb.example.com, listening on 8443"
}
```

Of course, doing this for one host alone when there are only two might seem a little pointless, but when you have an inventory with hundreds of hosts in it, this method of overriding one host will suddenly become very valuable.

4. Just for completeness, if we were to add the host variables we defined previously to our YAML version of the inventory, the `frontends` section would appear as follows (the rest of the inventory has been removed to save space):

```
frontends:
  hosts:
    frt01.example.com:
      https_port: 8444
    frt02.example.com:
  vars:
    https_port: 8443
    lb_vip: lb.example.com
```

Running the same ad hoc command as before, you can see that the result is the same as for our INI-formatted inventory:

```
$ ansible -i hostvars2-hostgroups-yml frontends -m debug -a
"msg=\"Connecting to {{ lb_vip }}, listening on {{ https_port }}\""
frt01.example.com | SUCCESS => {
    "msg": "Connecting to lb.example.com, listening on 8444"
}
frt02.example.com | SUCCESS => {
    "msg": "Connecting to lb.example.com, listening on 8443"
}
```

5. So far, we have covered several ways of providing host variables and group variables to your inventory; however, there is another way that deserves special mention and will become valuable to you as your inventory becomes larger and more complex.

Right now, our examples are small and compact and only contain a handful of groups and variables; however, when you scale this up to a full infrastructure of servers, using a single flat inventory file could, once again, become unmanageable. Luckily, Ansible also provides a solution to this. Two specially-named directories, `host_vars` and `group_vars`, are automatically searched for appropriate variable content if they exist within the playbook directory. We can test this out by recreating the preceding frontend variables example using this special directory structure, rather than putting the variables into the inventory file.

Let's start by creating a new directory structure for this purpose:

```
$ mkdir vartree
$ cd vartree
```

6. Now, under this directory, we'll create two more directories for the variables:

```
$ mkdir host_vars group_vars
```

7. Now, under the host_vars directory, we'll create a file with the name of our host that needs the proxy setting, with .yml appended to it (that is, frt01.example.com.yml). This file should contain the following:

```
---
https_port: 8444
```

8. Similarly, under the group_vars directory, create a YAML file named after the group to which we want to assign variables (that is, frontends.yml) with the following contents:

```
---
https_port: 8443
lb_vip: lb.example.com
```

9. Finally, we will create our inventory file as before, except that it contains no variables:

```
loadbalancer.example.com

[frontends]
frt01.example.com
frt02.example.com

[apps]
app01.example.com
app02.example.com

[databases]
dbms01.example.com
dbms02.example.com
```

Just for clarity, your final directory structure should look like this:

```
$  tree
.
├──  group_vars
│    └──  frontends.yml
├──  host_vars
│    └──  frt01.example.com.yml
└──  inventory

2 directories, 3 files
```

10. Now, let's try running our familiar ad hoc command and see what happens:

```
$ ansible -i inventory frontends -m debug -a "msg=\"Connecting to
{{ lb_vip }}, listening on {{ https_port }}\""
frt02.example.com | SUCCESS => {
    "msg": "Connecting to lb.example.com, listening on 8443"
}
frt01.example.com | SUCCESS => {
    "msg": "Connecting to lb.example.com, listening on 8444"
}
```

As you can see, this works exactly as before, and without further instruction, Ansible has traversed the directory structure and ingested all of the variable files.

11. If you have many hundreds of variables (or need an even finer-grained approach), you can replace the YAML files with directories named after the hosts and groups. Let's recreate the directory structure but now with directories instead:

```
$ tree
.
├── group_vars
│   └── frontends
│       ├── https_port.yml
│       └── lb_vip.yml
├── host_vars
│   └── frt01.example.com
│       └── main.yml
└── inventory
```

Notice how we now have directories named after the `frontends` group and the `frt01.example.com` host? Inside the `frontends` directory, we have split the variables into two files, and this can be incredibly useful for logically organizing variables in groups, especially as your playbooks get bigger and more complex.

The files themselves are simply an adaptation of our previous ones:

```
$ cat host_vars/frt01.example.com/main.yml
---
https_port: 8444

$ cat group_vars/frontends/https_port.yml
---
https_port: 8443

$ cat group_vars/frontends/lb_vip.yml
---
lb_vip: lb.example.com
```

Even with this more finely divided directory structure, the result of running the ad hoc command is still the same:

```
$ ansible -i inventory frontends -m debug -a "msg=\"Connecting to
{{ lb_vip }}, listening on {{ https_port }}\""
frt01.example.com | SUCCESS => {
    "msg": "Connecting to lb.example.com, listening on 8444"
}
frt02.example.com | SUCCESS => {
    "msg": "Connecting to lb.example.com, listening on 8443"
}
```

12. One final thing of note before we conclude this chapter is if you define the same variable at both a group level and a child group level, the variable at the child group level takes precedence. This is not as obvious to figure out as it first sounds. Consider our earlier inventory where we used child groups to differentiate between CentOS and Ubuntu hosts—if we add a variable with the same name to both the ubuntu child group and the frontends group (which is a **child** of the ubuntu group) as follows, what will the outcome be? The inventory would look like this:

```
loadbalancer.example.com

[frontends]
frt01.example.com
frt02.example.com

[frontends:vars]
testvar=childgroup

[apps]
app01.example.com
app02.example.com
```

```
[databases]
dbms01.example.com
dbms02.example.com

[centos:children]
apps
databases

[ubuntu:children]
frontends

[ubuntu:vars]
testvar=group
```

Now, let's run an ad hoc command to see what value of testvar is actually set:

```
$ ansible -i hostgroups-children-vars-ini ubuntu -m debug -a
"var=testvar"
frt01.example.com | SUCCESS => {
    "testvar": "childgroup"
}
frt02.example.com | SUCCESS => {
    "testvar": "childgroup"
}
```

It's important to note that the frontends group is a child of the ubuntu group in this inventory (hence, the group definition is [ubuntu:children]), and so the variable value we set at the frontends group level wins as this is the child group in this scenario.

By now, you should have a pretty good idea of how to work with static inventory files. No look at Ansible's inventory capabilities is complete, however, without a look at dynamic inventories, and we shall do exactly this in the next section.

Generating a dynamic inventory file

In these days of cloud computing and infrastructure-as-code, the hosts you may wish to automate could change on a daily if not hourly basis! Keeping a static Ansible inventory up to date could become a full-time job, and hence, in many large-scale scenarios, it becomes unrealistic to attempt to use a static inventory on an ongoing basis.

This is where Ansible's dynamic inventory support comes in. In short, Ansible can gather its inventory data from just about any executable file (though you will find that most dynamic inventories are written in Python)—the only requirement is that the executable returns the inventory data in a specified JSON format. You are free to create your own inventory scripts if you wish, but thankfully, many have been created already for you to use that cover a multitude of potential inventory sources including Amazon EC2, Microsoft Azure, Red Hat Satellite, LDAP directories, and many more systems.

When writing a book, it is difficult to know for certain which dynamic inventory script to use as an example as it is not a given that everyone will have an Amazon EC2 account they can freely use to test against (for example). As a result, we will use the Cobbler provisioning system by way of example, as this is freely available and easy to roll out on a CentOS system. For those interested, Cobbler is a system for dynamically provisioning and building Linux systems, and it can handle all aspects of this including DNS, DHCP, PXE booting, and so on. Hence, if you were to use this to provision virtual or physical machines in your infrastructure, it would make sense to also use this as your inventory source as Cobbler was responsible for building the systems in the first place, and so knows all of the system names.

This example will demonstrate for you the fundamentals of working with a dynamic inventory, which you can then take forward to use the dynamic inventory scripts for other systems. Let's get started with this process by first of all installing Cobbler—the process outlined here was tested on CentOS 7.8:

1. Your first task is to install the relevant Cobbler packages using yum. Note that, at the time of writing, the SELinux policy provided with CentOS 7 did not support Cobbler's functionality and blocks some aspects from working. Although this is not something you should do in a production environment, your simplest path to getting this demo up and running is to simply disable SELinux:

   ```
   $ yum install -y cobbler cobbler-web
   $ setenforce 0
   ```

2. Next, ensure that the cobblerd service is configured to listen on the loopback address by checking the settings in /etc/cobbler/settings—the relevant snippet of the file is shown here and should appear as follows:

   ```
   # default, localhost
   server: 127.0.0.1
   ```

This is not a public listening address, so please *do not use* 0.0.0.0. You can also set it to the IP address of the Cobbler server.

3. With this step complete, you can start the `cobblerd` service using `systemctl`:

```
$ systemctl start cobblerd.service
$ systemctl enable cobblerd.service
$ systemctl status cobblerd.service
```

4. With the Cobbler service up and running, we'll now step through the process of adding a distribution to Cobbler to create some hosts off of. This process is fairly simple, but you do need to add a kernel file and an initial RAM disk file. The easiest source to obtain these from is your `/boot` directory, assuming you have installed Cobbler on CentOS 7. On the test system used for this demo, the following commands were used—however, you must replace the version number in the `vmlinuz` and `initramfs` filenames with the appropriate version numbers from your system's `/boot` directory:

```
$ cobbler distro add --name=CentOS --
kernel=/boot/vmlinuz-3.10.0-957.el7.x86_64 --
initrd=/boot/initramfs-3.10.0-957.el7.x86_64.img

$ cobbler profile add --name=webservers --distro=CentOS
```

This definition is quite rudimentary and would not necessarily be able to produce working server images; however, it will suffice for our simple demo as we can add some systems based on this notional CentOS-based image. Note that the profile name we are creating, `webservers`, will later become our inventory group name in our dynamic inventory.

5. Let's now add those systems to Cobbler. The following two commands will add two hosts called `frontend01` and `frontend02` to our Cobbler system, using the `webservers` profile we created previously:

```
$ cobbler system add --name=frontend01 --profile=webservers --dns-
name=frontend01.example.com --interface=eth0

$ cobbler system add --name=frontend02 --profile=webservers --dns-
name=frontend02.example.com --interface=eth0
```

Note that, for Ansible to work, it must be able to reach these FQDNs specified in the `--dns-name` parameter. To achieve this, I am also adding entries to `/etc/hosts` on the Cobbler system for these two machines to ensure we can reach them later. These entries can point to any two systems of your choosing as this is just a test.

At this point, you have successfully installed Cobbler, created a profile, and added two hypothetical systems to this profile. The next stage in our process is to download and configure the Ansible dynamic inventory scripts to work with these entries. To achieve this, let's get started on the process given here:

1. Download the Cobbler dynamic inventory file from the GitHub Ansible repository and the associated configuration file template. Note that most dynamic inventory scripts provided with Ansible also have a templated configuration file, which will contain parameters that you may need to set to get the dynamic inventory script working. For our simple example, we will download these files into our current working directory:

```
$ wget
https://raw.githubusercontent.com/ansible/ansible/devel/contrib/inv
entory/cobbler.py
$ wget
https://raw.githubusercontent.com/ansible/ansible/devel/contrib/inv
entory/cobbler.ini
$ chmod +x cobbler.py
```

It is important to remember to make whatever dynamic inventory script you download executable, as shown previously; if you don't do this, then Ansible won't be able to run the script even if everything else is set up perfectly.

2. Edit the `cobbler.ini` file and ensure that it points to the localhost as, for this example, we are going to run Ansible and Cobbler on the same system. In real life, you would point it at the remote URL of your Cobbler system. A snippet of the configuration file is shown here to give you an idea of what to configure:

```
[cobbler]

# Specify IP address or Hostname of the cobbler server. The default
variable is here:
host = http://127.0.0.1/cobbler_api

# (Optional) With caching, you will have responses of API call with
the cobbler server quicker
cache_path = /tmp
cache_max_age = 900
```

3. You can now run an Ansible ad hoc command in the manner you are used to—the only difference this time is that you will specify the filename of the dynamic inventory script rather than the name of the static inventory file. Assuming you have set up hosts at the two addresses we entered into Cobbler earlier, your output should look something like that shown here:

```
$  ansible -i cobbler.py webservers -m ping
frontend01.example.com | SUCCESS => {
    "ansible_facts": {
        "discovered_interpreter_python": "/usr/bin/python"
    },
    "changed": false,
    "ping": "pong"
}
frontend02.example.com | SUCCESS => {
    "ansible_facts": {
        "discovered_interpreter_python": "/usr/bin/python"
    },
    "changed": false,
    "ping": "pong"
}
```

That's it! You have just implemented your first dynamic inventory in Ansible. Of course, we know that many readers won't be using Cobbler, and some of the other dynamic inventory plugins are a little more complex to get going. For example, the Amazon EC2 dynamic inventory script requires your authentication details for Amazon Web Services (or a suitable IAM account) and the installation of the Python `boto` and `boto3` libraries. How would you know to do all of this? Luckily, it is all documented in the headers of either the dynamic inventory script or the configuration file, so the most fundamental piece of advice I can give is this: whenever you download a new dynamic inventory script, be sure to check out the files themselves in your favorite editor as their requirements have most likely been documented for you.

Before we end this section of this book, let's have a look at a few other handy hints for working with inventories, starting with the use of multiple inventory sources in the next section.

Using multiple inventory sources in the inventory directories

So far in this book, we have been specifying our inventory file (either static or dynamic) using the -i switch in our Ansible commands. What might not be apparent is that you can specify the -i switch more than once and so use multiple inventories at the same time. This enables you to perform tasks such as running a playbook (or ad hoc command) across hosts from both static and dynamic inventories at the same time. Ansible will work out what needs to be done—static inventories should not be marked as executable and so will not be processed as such, whereas dynamic inventories will be. This small but clever trick enables you to combine multiple inventory sources with ease. Let's move on in the next section to looking at the use of static inventory groups in combination with dynamic ones, an extension of this multiple-inventory functionality.

Using static groups with dynamic groups

Of course, the possibility of mixing inventories brings with it an interesting question—what happens to the groups from a dynamic inventory and a static inventory if you define both? The answer is that Ansible combines both, and this leads to an interesting possibility. As you will have observed, our Cobbler inventory script produced an Ansible group called webservers from a Cobbler profile that we called webservers. This is common for most dynamic inventory providers; most inventory sources (for example, Cobbler and Amazon EC2) are not Ansible-aware and so do not offer groups that Ansible can directly use. As a result, most dynamic inventory scripts will use some facet of information from the inventory source to produce groupings, the Cobbler machine profile being one such example.

Let's extend our Cobbler example from the preceding section by mixing a static inventory. Suppose that we want to make our webservers machines a child group of a group called centos so that we can, in the future, group all CentOS machines together. We know that we only have a Cobbler profile called webservers, and ideally, we don't want to start messing with the Cobbler setup to do something solely Ansible-related.

The answer to this is to create a static inventory file with two group definitions. The first must be the same name as the group you are expecting from the dynamic inventory, except that you should leave it blank. When Ansible combines the static and dynamic inventory contents, it will overlap the two groups and so add the hosts from Cobbler to these webservers groups.

The second group definition should state that `webservers` is a child group of the `centos` group. The resulting file should look something like this:

```
[webservers]

[centos:children]
webservers
```

Now let's run a simple ad hoc `ping` command in Ansible to see how it evaluates the two inventories together. Notice how we will specify the `centos` group to run `ping` against, instead of the `webservers` group. We know that Cobbler has no `centos` group because we never created one, and we know that any hosts in this group must come via the `webservers` group when you combine the two inventories, as our static inventory has no hosts in it. The results will look something like this:

```
$ ansible -i static-groups-mix-ini -i cobbler.py centos -m ping
frontend01.example.com | SUCCESS => {
    "ansible_facts": {
        "discovered_interpreter_python": "/usr/bin/python"
    },
    "changed": false,
    "ping": "pong"
}
frontend02.example.com | SUCCESS => {
    "ansible_facts": {
        "discovered_interpreter_python": "/usr/bin/python"
    },
    "changed": false,
    "ping": "pong"
}
```

As you can see from the preceding output, we have referenced two different inventories, one static and the other dynamic. We have combined groups, taking hosts that only exist in one inventory source, and combining them with a group that only exists in another. As you can see, this is an incredibly simple example, and it would be easy to extend this to combine lists of static and dynamic hosts or to add a custom variable to a host that comes from a dynamic inventory.

This is a trick of Ansible that is little known but can be very powerful as your inventories expand and grow. As we have worked through this chapter, you will have observed that we have been very precise about specifying our inventory hosts either individually or by group; for example, we explicitly told `ansible` to run the ad hoc command against all hosts in the `webservers` group. In the next section, we will build on this to look at how Ansible can manage a set of hosts specified using patterns.

Special host management using patterns

We have already established that you will often want to run either an ad hoc command or a playbook against only a subsection of your inventory. So far, we have been quite precise in doing that, but let's now expand upon this by looking at how Ansible can work with patterns to figure out which hosts a command (or playbook) should be run against.

As a starting point, let's consider again an inventory that we defined earlier in this chapter for the purposes of exploring host groups and child groups. For your convenience, the inventory contents are provided again here:

```
loadbalancer.example.com

[frontends]
frt01.example.com
frt02.example.com

[apps]
app01.example.com
app02.example.com

[databases]
dbms01.example.com
dbms02.example.com

[centos:children]
apps
databases

[ubuntu:children]
frontends
```

To demonstrate host/group selection by pattern, we shall use the `--list-hosts` switch with the `ansible` command to see which hosts Ansible would operate on. You are welcome to expand the example to use the `ping` module, but we'll use `--list-hosts` here in the interests of space and keeping the output concise and readable:

1. We have already mentioned the special `all` group to specify all hosts in the inventory:

```
$ ansible -i hostgroups-children-ini all --list-hosts
  hosts (7):
    loadbalancer.example.com
    frt01.example.com
    frt02.example.com
    app01.example.com
```

```
      app02.example.com
      dbms01.example.com
      dbms02.example.com
```

The asterisk character has the same effect as `all`, but needs to be quoted in single quotes for the shell to interpret the command properly:

```
$ ansible -i hostgroups-children-ini '*' --list-hosts
  hosts (7):
    loadbalancer.example.com
    frt01.example.com
    frt02.example.com
    app01.example.com
    app02.example.com
    dbms01.example.com
    dbms02.example.com
```

2. Use `:` to specify a logical `OR`, meaning "apply to hosts either in this group or that group," as in this example:

```
$ ansible -i hostgroups-children-ini frontends:apps --list-hosts
  hosts (4):
    frt01.example.com
    frt02.example.com
    app01.example.com
    app02.example.com
```

3. Use `!` to exclude a specific group—you can combine this with other characters such as `:` to show (for example) all hosts except those in the `apps` group. Again, `!` is a special character in the shell and so you must quote your pattern string in single quotes for it to work, as in this example:

```
$ ansible -i hostgroups-children-ini 'all:!apps' --list-hosts
  hosts (5):
    loadbalancer.example.com
    frt01.example.com
    frt02.example.com
    dbms01.example.com
    dbms02.example.com
```

4. Use `:&` to specify a logical AND between two groups, for example, if we want all hosts that are in the `centos` group and the `apps` group (again, you must use single quotes in the shell):

```
$ ansible -i hostgroups-children-ini 'centos:&apps' --list-hosts
  hosts (2):
    app01.example.com
    app02.example.com
```

5. Use `*` wildcards in a similar manner to what you would use in the shell, as in this example:

```
$ ansible -i hostgroups-children-ini 'db*.example.com' --list-hosts
  hosts (2):
    dbms02.example.com
    dbms01.example.com
```

Another way you can limit which hosts a command is run on is to use the `--limit` switch with Ansible. This uses exactly the same syntax and pattern notation as in the preceding but has the advantage that you can use it with the `ansible-playbook` command, where specifying a host pattern on the command line is only supported for the `ansible` command itself. Hence, for example, you could run the following:

```
$ ansible-playbook -i hostgroups-children-ini site.yml --limit
frontends:apps

PLAY [A simple playbook for demonstrating inventory patterns]
******************

TASK [Gathering Facts]
*********************************************************
ok: [frt02.example.com]
ok: [app01.example.com]
ok: [frt01.example.com]
ok: [app02.example.com]

TASK [Ping each host]
*********************************************************
ok: [app01.example.com]
ok: [app02.example.com]
ok: [frt02.example.com]
ok: [frt01.example.com]

PLAY RECAP
*****************************************************************
app01.example.com : ok=2 changed=0 unreachable=0 failed=0 skipped=0
rescued=0 ignored=0
```

```
app02.example.com : ok=2 changed=0 unreachable=0 failed=0 skipped=0
rescued=0 ignored=0
frt01.example.com : ok=2 changed=0 unreachable=0 failed=0 skipped=0
rescued=0 ignored=0
frt02.example.com : ok=2 changed=0 unreachable=0 failed=0 skipped=0
rescued=0 ignored=0
```

Patterns are a very useful and important part of working with inventories, and something you will no doubt find invaluable going forward. That concludes our chapter on Ansible inventories; however, it is hoped that this has given you everything you need to work confidently with Ansible inventories.

Summary

Creating and managing Ansible inventories is a crucial part of your work with Ansible, and hence we have covered this fundamental concept early in this book. They are vital as without them Ansible would have no knowledge of what hosts it is to run automation tasks against, yet they provide so much more than this. They provide an integration point with configuration management systems, they provide a sensible source for host-specific (or group-specific) variables to be stored, and they provide you with a flexible way of running this playbook.

In this chapter, you learned about creating simple static inventory files and adding hosts to them. We then extended this by learning how to add host groups and assign variables to hosts. We also looked at how to organize your inventories and variables when a single flat inventory file becomes too much to handle. We then learned how to make use of dynamic inventory files, before concluding with a look at useful tips and tricks such as combining inventory sources and using patterns to specify hosts, all of which will make how you work with inventories easier and yet simultaneously more powerful.

In the next chapter, we will learn how to develop playbooks and roles to configure, deploy, and manage remote machines using Ansible.

Questions

1. How do you add the `frontends` group variables to your inventory?

    A) `[frontends::]`

    B) `[frontends::values]`

    C) `[frontends:host:vars]`

    D) `[frontends::variables]`

    E) `[frontends:vars]`

2. What enables you to automate Linux tasks such as provisioning DNS, managing DHCP, updating packages, and configuration management?

    A) Playbook

    B) Yum

    C) Cobbler

    D) Bash

    E) Role

3. Ansible allows you to specify an inventory file location by using the `-i` option on the command line.

    A) True

    B) False

Further reading

- All common dynamic inventories of Ansible from the GitHub repository are here: `https://github.com/ansible/ansible/tree/devel/contrib/inventory`.

Playbooks and Roles

4

So far in this book, we have worked mostly with ad hoc Ansible commands for simplicity and to help you to understand the fundamentals. However, the lifeblood of Ansible is most certainly the playbook, which is a logical organization of tasks (think ad hoc commands) in a structure that creates a useful outcome. This might be to deploy a web server on a newly built virtual machine, or it might be to apply a security policy. It might even handle the whole build process for a virtual machine! The possibilities are endless. Ansible playbooks, as we have already covered, are designed to be simple to write and easy to read—they are intended to be self-documenting and, as such, will form a valuable part of your IT processes.

In this chapter, we will explore playbooks in greater depth, from the basics of their creation to more advanced concepts such as running tasks in loops and blocks, performing conditional logic, and—perhaps one of the most important concepts for playbook organization and code re-use—Ansible roles. We will cover roles in more detail later, but please know that this is something you will want to use as much as possible when creating manageable playbook code.

Specifically, in this chapter, we will cover the following topics:

- Understanding the playbook framework
- Understanding roles—the playbook organizer
- Using conditions in your code
- Repeating tasks with loops
- Grouping tasks using blocks
- Configuring play execution via strategies
- Using `ansible-pull`

Technical requirements

This chapter assumes that you have set up your control host with Ansible, as detailed in Chapter 1, *Getting Started with Ansible,* and are using the most recent version available—the examples in this chapter were tested with Ansible 2.9. This chapter also assumes that you have at least one additional host to test against, and ideally this should be Linux based. Although we will give specific examples of hostnames in this chapter, you are free to substitute them with your own hostname and/or IP addresses, and details of how to do this will be provided in the appropriate places.

The code bundle for this chapter is available here: https://github.com/PacktPublishing/Ansible-2-Cookbook/tree/master/Chapter%204.

Understanding the playbook framework

A playbook allows you to manage multiple configurations and complex deployments on many machines simply and easily. This is one of the key benefits of using Ansible for the delivery of complex applications. With playbooks, you can organize your tasks in a logical structure as tasks are (generally) executed in the order they are written, allowing you to have a good deal of control over your automation processes. With that said, it is possible to perform tasks asynchronously, so where tasks are not executed in sequence, we will highlight this. Our goal is that once you complete this chapter, you will understand the best practices for writing your own Ansible playbooks.

Although YAML format is easy to read and write, it is very pedantic when it comes to spacing. For example, you cannot use tabs to set indentation even though on the screen a tab and four spaces might look identical—in YAML, they are not. We recommend that you adopt an editor with YAML support to aid you in writing your playbooks if you are doing this for the first time, perhaps Vim, Visual Studio Code, or Eclipse, as these will help you to ensure that your indentation is correct. To test the playbooks we develop in this chapter, we will reuse a variant of an inventory created in Chapter 3, *Defining Your Inventory* (unless stated otherwise):

```
[frontends]
frt01.example.com https_port=8443
frt02.example.com http_proxy=proxy.example.com

[frontends:vars]
ntp_server=ntp.frt.example.com
proxy=proxy.frt.example.com

[apps]
```

```
app01.example.com
app02.example.com

[webapp:children]
frontends
apps

[webapp:vars]
proxy_server=proxy.webapp.example.com
health_check_retry=3
health_check_interal=60
```

Let's dive right in and get started writing a playbook. In the section entitled *Breaking down the Ansible components* in Chapter 2, *Understanding the Fundamentals of Ansible,* we covered some of the basic aspects of a playbook so we won't repeat these in detail here, but rather build on them to show you what playbook development is all about:

1. Create a simple playbook to run on the hosts in the frontends host group defined in our inventory file. We can set the user that will access the hosts using the remote_user directive in the playbook as demonstrated in the following (you can also use the --user switch on the command line, but as this chapter is about playbook development, we'll ignore that for now):

    ```
    ---
    - hosts: frontends
      remote_user: danieloh

      tasks:
      - name: simple connection test
        ping:
        remote_user: danieloh
    ```

2. Add another task below the first to run the shell module (that will, in turn, run the ls command on the remote hosts). We'll also add the ignore_errors directive to this task to ensure that our playbook doesn't fail if the ls command fails (for example, if the directory we're trying to list doesn't exist). Be careful with the indentation and ensure it matches that of the first part of the file:

    ```
    - name: run a simple command
      shell: /bin/ls -al /nonexistent
      ignore_errors: True
    ```

Let's see how our newly created playbook behaves when we run it:

```
$ ansible-playbook -i hosts myplaybook.yaml

PLAY [frontends]
***************************************************************

TASK [Gathering Facts]
***********************************************************
ok: [frt02.example.com]
ok: [frt01.example.com]

TASK [simple connection test]
******************************************************
ok: [frt01.example.com]
ok: [frt02.example.com]

TASK [run a simple command]
*******************************************************
fatal: [frt02.example.com]: FAILED! => {"changed": true, "cmd": "/bin/ls -
al /nonexistent", "delta": "0:00:00.015687", "end": "2020-04-10
16:37:56.895520", "msg": "non-zero return code", "rc": 2, "start":
"2020-04-10 16:37:56.879833", "stderr": "/bin/ls: cannot access
/nonexistent: No such file or directory", "stderr_lines": ["/bin/ls: cannot
access /nonexistent: No such file or directory"], "stdout": "",
"stdout_lines": []}
...ignoring
fatal: [frt01.example.com]: FAILED! => {"changed": true, "cmd": "/bin/ls -
al /nonexistent", "delta": "0:00:00.012160", "end": "2020-04-10
16:37:56.930058", "msg": "non-zero return code", "rc": 2, "start":
"2020-04-10 16:37:56.917898", "stderr": "/bin/ls: cannot access
/nonexistent: No such file or directory", "stderr_lines": ["/bin/ls: cannot
access /nonexistent: No such file or directory"], "stdout": "",
"stdout_lines": []}
...ignoring

PLAY RECAP
*****************************************************************************
frt01.example.com : ok=3 changed=1 unreachable=0 failed=0 skipped=0
rescued=0 ignored=1
frt02.example.com : ok=3 changed=1 unreachable=0 failed=0 skipped=0
rescued=0 ignored=1
```

From the output of the playbook run, you can see that our two tasks were executed in the order in which they were specified. We can see that the `ls` command failed because we tried to list a directory that did not exist, but the playbook did not register any `failed` tasks because we set `ignore_errors` to `true` for this task (and only this task).

Most Ansible modules (with the exception of those that run user-defined commands such as `shell`, `command`, and `raw`) are coded to be idempotent, that is to say, if you run the same task twice, the results will be the same, and the task will not make the same change twice—if it detects that the action it is being requested to perform has been completed, then it does not perform it a second time. This, of course, is not possible for the aforementioned modules as they could be used to perform just about any conceivable task—hence, how could the module know it was being performed twice?

Every module returns a set of results and among these results is the task status. You can see these summarized at the bottom of the preceding playbook run output, and their meaning is as follows:

- `ok`: The task ran successfully and no changes were made.
- `changed`: The task ran successfully and a change was made.
- `failed`: The task failed to run.
- `unreachable`: The host was unreachable to run the task on.
- `skipped`: This task was skipped.
- `ignored`: This task was ignored (for example, in the case of `ignore_errors`).
- `rescued`: We will see an example of this later when we look at blocks and rescue tasks.

These statuses can be very useful—for example, if we have a task to deploy a new Apache configuration file from a template, we know we must restart the Apache service for the changes to be picked up. However, we only want to do this if the file was actually changed—if no changes were made, we don't want to needlessly restart Apache as it would interrupt people who might be using the service. Hence, we can use the `notify` action, which tells Ansible to call a `handler` when (and only when) the result from a task is `changed`. In brief, a handler is a special type of task that is run as a result of a `notify`. However, unlike Ansible playbook tasks, which are performed in sequence, handlers are all grouped together and run at the very end of the play. Also, they can be notified more than once but will only be run once regardless, again preventing needless service restarts. Consider the following playbook:

```
---
- name: Handler demo 1
  hosts: frt01.example.com
  gather_facts: no
  become: yes

  tasks:
    - name: Update Apache configuration
      template:
```

```
          src: template.j2
          dest: /etc/httpd/httpd.conf
      notify: Restart Apache

  handlers:
    - name: Restart Apache
      service:
        name: httpd
        state: restarted
```

To keep the output concise, I've turned off fact-gathering for this playbook (we won't use them in any of the tasks). I'm also running this on just one host again for conciseness, but you are welcome to expand the demo code as you wish. If we run this task a first time, we will see the following results:

```
$ ansible-playbook -i hosts handlers1.yml

PLAY [Handler demo 1]
********************************************************

TASK [Update Apache configuration]
*********************************************
changed: [frt01.example.com]

RUNNING HANDLER [Restart Apache]
***********************************************
changed: [frt01.example.com]

PLAY RECAP
*******************************************************************
frt01.example.com : ok=2 changed=2 unreachable=0 failed=0 skipped=0
rescued=0 ignored=0
```

Notice how the handler was run at the end, as the configuration file was updated. However, if we run this playbook a second time without making any changes to the template or configuration file, we will see something like this:

```
$ ansible-playbook -i hosts handlers1.yml

PLAY [Handler demo 1]
********************************************************

TASK [Update Apache configuration]
*********************************************
ok: [frt01.example.com]

PLAY RECAP
*******************************************************************
```

```
frt01.example.com : ok=1 changed=0 unreachable=0 failed=0 skipped=0
rescued=0 ignored=0
```

This time, the handler was not called as the result from the configuration task as OK. All handlers should have a globally unique name so that the notify action can call the correct handler. You could also call multiple handlers by setting a common name for using the `listen` directive—this way, you can call either the handler `name` or the `listen` string—as demonstrated in the following example:

```
---
- name: Handler demo 1
  hosts: frt01.example.com
  gather_facts: no
  become: yes

  handlers:
    - name: restart chronyd
      service:
        name: chronyd
        state: restarted
      listen: "restart all services"
    - name: restart apache
      service:
        name: httpd
        state: restarted
      listen: "restart all services"

  tasks:
    - name: restart all services
      command: echo "this task will restart all services"
      notify: "restart all services"
```

We only have one task in the playbook, but when we run it, both handlers are called. Also, remember that we said earlier that `command` was among a set of modules that were a special case because they can't detect whether a change has occurred—as a result, they always return the `changed` value, and so, in this demo playbook, the handlers will always be notified:

```
$ ansible-playbook -i hosts handlers2.yml

PLAY [Handler demo 1]
*********************************************************

TASK [restart all services]
*********************************************************
changed: [frt01.example.com]
```

```
RUNNING HANDLER [restart chronyd]
***********************************************
changed: [frt01.example.com]

RUNNING HANDLER [restart apache]
***********************************************
changed: [frt01.example.com]

PLAY RECAP
*************************************************************************
frt01.example.com : ok=3 changed=3 unreachable=0 failed=0 skipped=0
rescued=0 ignored=0
```

These are some of the fundamentals that you need to know to start writing your own playbooks. With these under your belt, let's run through a comparison of ad hoc commands and playbooks in the next section.

Comparing playbooks and ad hoc tasks

Ad hoc commands allow you to quickly create and execute one-off commands, without keeping any record of what was done (other than perhaps your shell history). These serve an important purpose and can be very valuable in getting small changes made quickly and for learning Ansible and its modules.

Playbooks, by contrast, are logically organized sets of tasks (each could conceivably be an ad hoc command), put together in a sequence that performs one bigger action. The addition of conditional logic, error handling, and so on means that, very often, the benefits of playbooks outweigh the usefulness of ad hoc commands. In addition, provided you keep them organized, you will have copies of all previous playbooks that you run and so you will be able to refer back (if ever you need to) to see what you ran and when.

Let's develop a practical example—suppose you want to install Apache 2.4 on CentOS. There are a number of steps involved even if the default configuration is sufficient (which is unlikely, but for now, we'll keep the example simple). If you were to perform the basic installation by hand, you would need to install the package, open up the firewall, and ensure the service is running (and runs at boot time).

To perform these commands in the shell, you might do the following:

```
$ sudo yum install httpd
$ sudo firewall-cmd --add-service=http --permanent
$ sudo firewall-cmd --add-service=https --permanent
$ sudo firewall-cmd --reload
$ sudo systemctl enable httpd.service
$ sudo systemctl restart httpd.service
```

Now, for each of these commands, there is an equivalent ad hoc Ansible command that you could run. We won't go through all of them here in the interests of space; however, let's say you want to restart the Apache service—in this case, you could run an ad hoc command similar to the following (again, we will perform it only on one host for conciseness):

```
$ ansible -i hosts frt01* -m service -a "name=httpd state=restarted"
```

When run successfully, you will see pages of shell output containing all of the variable data returned from running the service module in this way. A snippet of this is shown in the following for you to check yours against—the key thing being that the command resulted in the changed status, meaning that it ran successfully and that the service was indeed restarted:

```
frt01.example.com | CHANGED => {
    "ansible_facts": {
        "discovered_interpreter_python": "/usr/bin/python"
    },
    "changed": true,
    "name": "httpd",
    "state": "started",
```

You could create and execute a series of ad hoc commands to replicate the six shell commands given in the preceding and run them all individually. With a bit of cleverness, you should reduce this from six commands (for example, the Ansible service module can both enable a service at boot time and restart it in one ad hoc command). However, you would still ultimately end up with at least three or four ad hoc commands, and if you want to run these again later on another server, you will need to refer to your notes to figure out how you did it.

A playbook is hence a far more valuable way to approach this—not only will it perform all of the steps in one go, but it will also give you a record of how it was done for you to refer to later on. There are multiple ways to do this, but consider the following as an example:

```
---
- name: Install Apache
  hosts: frt01.example.com
  gather_facts: no
  become: yes

  tasks:
    - name: Install Apache package
      yum:
        name: httpd
        state: latest
    - name: Open firewall for Apache
      firewalld:
        service: "{{ item }}"
        permanent: yes
        state: enabled
        immediate: yes
      loop:
        - "http"
        - "https"
    - name: Restart and enable the service
      service:
        name: httpd
        state: restarted
        enabled: yes
```

Now, when you run this, you should see that all of our installation requirements have been completed by one fairly simple and easy to read playbook. There is a new concept here, loops, which we haven't covered yet, but don't worry, we will cover this later in this chapter:

```
$ ansible-playbook -i hosts installapache.yml

PLAY [Install Apache]
********************************************************

TASK [Install Apache package]
**************************************************
changed: [frt01.example.com]

TASK [Open firewall for Apache]
************************************************
changed: [frt01.example.com] => (item=http)
```

```
changed: [frt01.example.com] => (item=https)

TASK [Restart and enable the service]
*******************************************
changed: [frt01.example.com]

PLAY RECAP
*****************************************************************
frt01.example.com : ok=2 changed=3 unreachable=0 failed=0 skipped=0
rescued=0 ignored=0
```

As you can see, this is far better for capturing what was actually done and documenting it in a format that someone else could easily pick up. Even though we will cover loops later on in the book, it's fairly easy to see from the preceding how they might be working. With this set out, let's proceed in the next section to look in more detail at a couple of terms we have used several times to ensure you are clear on their meanings: **plays** and **tasks**.

Defining plays and tasks

So far when we have worked with playbooks, we have been creating one single play per playbook (which logically is the minimum you can do). However, you can have more than one play in a playbook, and a "play" in Ansible terms is simply a set of tasks (and roles, handlers, and other Ansible facets) associated with a host (or group of hosts). A task is the smallest possible element of a play and is responsible for running a single module with a set of arguments to achieve a specific goal. Of course, in theory, this sounds quite complex, but when backed up by a practical example, it becomes quite simple to understand.

If we refer to our example inventory, this describes a simple two-tier architecture (we've left out the database tier for now). Now, suppose we want to write a single playbook to configure both the frontend servers and the application servers. We could use two separate playbooks to configure the front end and application servers, but this risks fragmenting your code and making it difficult to organize. However, front end servers and application servers are going to be (by their very nature) fundamentally different and so are unlikely to be configured with the same set of tasks.

The solution to this problem is to create a single playbook with two plays in it. The start of each play can be identified by the line at the lowest indentation (that is, zero spaces in front of it). Let's get started with building up our playbook:

1. Add the first play to the playbook and define some simple tasks to set up the Apache server on the front end, as shown here:

```
---
- name: Play 1 - configure the frontend servers
  hosts: frontends
  become: yes

  tasks:
  - name: Install the Apache package
    yum:
      name: httpd
      state: latest
  - name: Start the Apache server
    service:
      name: httpd
      state: started
```

2. Immediately below this, in the same file, add the second play to configure the application tier servers:

```
- name: Play 2 - configure the application servers
  hosts: apps
  become: true

  tasks:
  - name: Install Tomcat
    yum:
      name: tomcat
      state: latest
  - name: Start the Tomcat server
    service:
      name: tomcat
      state: started
```

Now, you have two plays: one to install web servers in the frontends group and one to install application servers in the apps group, all combined into one simple playbook.

When we run this playbook, we'll see the two plays performed sequentially, in the order they appear in the playbook. Note the presence of the PLAY keyword, which denotes the start of each play:

```
$ ansible-playbook -i hosts playandtask.yml

PLAY [Play 1 - configure the frontend servers]
*********************************

TASK [Gathering Facts]
**************************************************************
changed: [frt02.example.com]
changed: [frt01.example.com]

TASK [Install the Apache package]
**********************************************
changed: [frt01.example.com]
changed: [frt02.example.com]

TASK [Start the Apache server]
***************************************************
changed: [frt01.example.com]
changed: [frt02.example.com]

PLAY [Play 2 - configure the application servers]
******************************

TASK [Gathering Facts]
*************************************************************
changed: [app01.example.com]
changed: [app02.example.com]

TASK [Install Tomcat]
************************************************************
changed: [app02.example.com]
changed: [app01.example.com]

TASK [Start the Tomcat server]
***************************************************
changed: [app02.example.com]
changed: [app01.example.com]

PLAY RECAP
*********************************************************************
app01.example.com : ok=3 changed=2 unreachable=0 failed=0 skipped=0
rescued=0 ignored=0
app02.example.com : ok=3 changed=2 unreachable=0 failed=0 skipped=0
rescued=0 ignored=0
```

```
frt01.example.com : ok=3 changed=2 unreachable=0 failed=0 skipped=0
rescued=0 ignored=0
frt02.example.com : ok=3 changed=2 unreachable=0 failed=0 skipped=0
rescued=0 ignored=0
```

There we have it—one playbook, yet two distinct plays operating on different sets of hosts from the provided inventories. This is very powerful, especially when combined with roles (which will be covered later in this book). Of course, you can have just one play in your playbook—you don't have to have multiple ones, but it is important to be able to develop multi-play playbooks as you will almost certainly find them useful as your environment gets more complex.

Playbooks are the lifeblood of Ansible automation—they extend it beyond single task/commands (which in themselves are incredibly powerful) to a whole series of tasks organized in a logical fashion. As you extend your library of playbooks, however, how do you keep your work organized? How do you efficiently reuse the same blocks of code? In the preceding example, we installed Apache, and this might be a requirement on a number of your servers. However, should you attempt to manage them all from one playbook? Or should you perhaps keep copying and pasting the same block of code over and over again? There is a better way, and in Ansible terms, we need to start looking at roles, which we shall do in the very next section.

Understanding roles – the playbook organizer

Roles are designed to enable you to efficiently and effectively reuse Ansible code. They always follow a known structure and often will include sensible default values for variables, error handling, handlers, and so on. Taking our Apache installation example from the previous chapter, we know that this is something that we might want to do over and over again, perhaps with a different configuration file each time, and perhaps with a few other tweaks on a per-server (or per inventory group) basis. In Ansible, the most efficient way to support the reuse of this code in this way would be to create it as a role.

The process of creating roles is in fact very simple—Ansible will (by default) look within the same directory as you are running your playbook from for a `roles/` directory, and in here, you will create one subdirectory for each role. The role name is derived from the subdirectory name—there is no need to create complex metadata or anything else—it really is that simple. Within each subdirectory goes a fixed directory structure that tells Ansible what the tasks, default variables, handlers, and so on are for each role.

The `roles/` directory is not the only play Ansible will look for roles—this is the first directory it will look in, but it will then look in `/etc/ansible/roles` for any additional roles. This can be further customized through the Ansible configuration file, as discussed in `Chapter 2`, *Understanding the Fundamentals of Ansible*.

Let's explore this in a little more detail. Consider the following directory structure:

```
site.yml
frontends.yml
dbservers.yml
roles/
    installapache/
      tasks/
      handlers/
      templates/
      vars/
      defaults/
    installtomcat/
      tasks/
      meta/
```

The preceding directory structure shows two roles defined in our hypothetical playbook directory, called `installapache` and `installtomcat`. Within each of these directories, you will notice a series of subdirectories. These subdirectories do not need to exist (more on what they mean in a minute, but for example, if your role has no handlers, then `handlers/` does not need to be created). However, where you do require such a directory, you should populate it with a YAML file named `main.yml`. Each of these `main.yml` files will be expected to have certain contents, depending on the directory that contained them.

The subdirectories that can exist inside of a role are as follows:

- `tasks`: This is the most common directory to find in a role, and it contains all of the Ansible tasks that the role should perform.
- `handlers`: All handlers used in the role should go into this directory.
- `defaults`: All default variables for the role go in here.
- `vars`: These are other role variables—these override those declared in the `defaults/` directory as they are higher up the precedence order.
- `files`: Files needed by the role should go in here—for example, any configuration files that need to be deployed to the target hosts.

- `templates`: Distinct from the `files/` directory, this directory should contain all templates used by the role.
- `meta`: Any metadata needed for the role goes in here. For example, roles are normally executed in the order they are called from the parent playbook—however, sometimes a role will have dependency roles that need to be run first, and if this is the case, they can be declared within this directory.

For the examples we will develop in this part of this chapter, we will need an inventory, so let's reuse the inventory we used in the previous section (included in the following for convenience):

```
[frontends]
frt01.example.com https_port=8443
frt02.example.com http_proxy=proxy.example.com

[frontends:vars]
ntp_server=ntp.frt.example.com
proxy=proxy.frt.example.com

[apps]
app01.example.com
app02.example.com

[webapp:children]
frontends
apps

[webapp:vars]
proxy_server=proxy.webapp.example.com
health_check_retry=3
health_check_interal=60
```

Let's get started with some practical exercises to help you to learn how to create and work with roles. We'll start by creating a role called `installapache`, which will handle the Apache installation process we looked at in the previous section. However, here, we will expand it to cover the installation of Apache on both CentOS and Ubuntu. This is good practice, especially if you are looking to submit your roles back to the community as the more general purpose they are (and the wider the range of systems they will work on), the more useful they will be to people. Step through the following process to create your first role:

1. Create the directory structure for the `installapache` role from within your chosen playbook directory—this is as simple as this:

   ```
   $ mkdir -p roles/installapache/tasks
   ```

2. Now, let's create the mandatory `main.yml` inside the `tasks` directory we just created. This won't actually perform the Apache installation—rather, it will call one of two external tasks files, depending on the operating system detected on the target host during the fact-gathering stage. We can use this special variable, `ansible_distribution`, in a `when` condition to determine which of the tasks files to import:

```
---
- name: import a tasks based on OS platform
  import_tasks: centos.yml
  when: ansible_distribution == 'CentOS'
- import_tasks: ubuntu.yml
  when: ansible_distribution == 'Ubuntu'
```

2. Create `centos.yml` in `roles/installapache/tasks` to install the latest version of the Apache web server via the `yum` package manager. This should contain the following content:

```
---
- name: Install Apache using yum
  yum:
    name: "httpd"
    state: latest
- name: Start the Apache server
  service:
    name: httpd
    state: started
```

3. Create a file called `ubuntu.yml` in `roles/installapache/tasks` to install the latest version of the Apache web server via the `apt` package manager on Ubuntu. Notice how the content differs between CentOS and Ubuntu hosts:

```
---
- name: Install Apache using apt
  apt:
    name: "apache2"
    state: latest
- name: Start the Apache server
  service:
    name: apache2
    state: started
```

For now, we're keeping our role code really simple—however, you can see that the preceding tasks files are just like an Ansible playbook, except that they lack the play definition. As they do not come under a play, they are also at a lower indentation level than in a playbook, but apart from this difference, the code should look very familiar to you. In fact, this is part of the beauty of roles: as long as you pay attention to getting the indentation level right, you can more or less use the same code in a playbook or a role.

Now, roles don't run by themselves—we have to create a playbook to call them, so let's write a simple playbook to call our newly created role. This has a play definition just like we saw before, but then rather than having a `tasks:` section within the play, we have a `roles:` section where the roles are declared instead. Convention dictates that this file be called `site.yml`, but you are free to call it whatever you like:

```
---
- name: Install Apache using a role
  hosts: frontends
  become: true

  roles:
    - installapache
```

For clarity, your final directory structure should look like this:

```
.
├── roles
│   └── installapache
│       └── tasks
│           ├── centos.yml
│           ├── main.yml
│           └── ubuntu.yml
└── site.yml
```

With this completed, you can now run your `site.yml` playbook using `ansible-playbook` in the normal way—you should see output similar to this:

```
$ ansible-playbook -i hosts site.yml

PLAY [Install Apache using a role]
*********************************************

TASK [Gathering Facts]
***************************************************************
ok: [frt01.example.com]
ok: [frt02.example.com]

TASK [installapache : Install Apache using yum]
```

```
********************************
changed: [frt02.example.com]
changed: [frt01.example.com]

TASK [installapache : Start the Apache server]
********************************
changed: [frt01.example.com]
changed: [frt02.example.com]

TASK [installapache : Install Apache using apt]
********************************
skipping: [frt01.example.com]
skipping: [frt02.example.com]

TASK [installapache : Start the Apache server]
********************************
skipping: [frt01.example.com]
skipping: [frt02.example.com]

PLAY RECAP
*******************************************************************
frt01.example.com : ok=3 changed=2 unreachable=0 failed=0 skipped=2
rescued=0 ignored=0
frt02.example.com : ok=3 changed=2 unreachable=0 failed=0 skipped=2
rescued=0 ignored=0
```

That's it—you have created, at the simplest possible level, your first role. Of course (as we discussed earlier), there is much more to a role than just simple tasks as we have added here, and we will see expanded examples as we work through this chapter. However, the preceding example is intended to show you how quick and easy it is to get started with roles.

Before we look at some of the other aspects relating to roles, let's take a look at some other ways to call your role. Ansible allows you to statically import or dynamically include roles when you write a playbook. The syntax between these importing or including a role is subtly different, and notably, both go in the tasks section of your playbook rather than in the roles section. The following is a hypothetical example that shows both options in a really simple playbook. The roles directory structure including both the common and approle roles would have been created in a similar manner as in the preceding example:

```
---
- name: Play to import and include a role
  hosts: frontends
  tasks:
  - import_role:
      name: common
```

```
- include_role:
    name: approle
```

These features were not available in versions of Ansible earlier than 2.3, and their usage changed slightly in version 2.4 for consistency with the way that some other Ansible features work. We will not worry about the details of this here as Ansible is now on release 2.9, so unless you absolutely have to run a much earlier version of Ansible, it is sufficient to assume that these two statements work as we shall outline in the following.

Fundamentally, the `import_role` statement performs a static import of the role you specify at the time when all playbook code is parsed. Hence, roles brought into your playbook using the `import_role` statement are treated just as any other code in a play or role is when Ansible begins parsing. Using `import_role` is basically the same as declaring your roles after the `roles:` statement in `site.yml`, just as we did in the preceding example.

`include_role` is subtly but fundamentally different in that the role you specify is not evaluated when the playbook is parsed initially—rather, it is processed dynamically during the playbook run, at the point at which `include_role` is encountered.

Probably the most fundamental reason to choose between the `include` or `import` statements given in the preceding is looping—if you need to run a role within a loop, you cannot do so with `import_role` and so must use `include_role`. There are, however, both benefits and limitations to both, and you will need to choose the most appropriate one for your scenario—the official Ansible documentation (https://docs.ansible.com/ansible/latest/user_guide/playbooks_reuse.html#dynamic-vs-static) will help you to make the right decision.

As we have seen in this section, roles are incredibly simple to get started with and yet offer an incredibly powerful way in which to organize and reuse your Ansible code. In the next section, we will expand upon our simple task-based example by looking at adding role-specific variables and dependencies into your code.

Setting up role-based variables and dependencies

Variables are at the heart of making Ansible playbooks and roles reusable, as they allow the same code to be repurposed with slightly different values or configuration data. The Ansible role directory structure allows for role-specific variables to be declared in two locations. Although, at first, the difference between these two locations may not seem obvious, it is of fundamental importance.

Roles based variables can go in one of two locations:

- `defaults/main.yml`
- `vars/main.yml`

The difference between these two locations is their position in Ansible's variable order of precedence (https://docs.ansible.com/ansible/latest/user_guide/playbooks_variables.html#variable-precedence-where-should-i-put-a-variable). Variables that go in the `defaults/` directory are one of the lowest in terms of precedence and so are easily overwritten. This location is where you would put variables that you want to override easily, but where you don't want to leave a variable undefined. For example, if you are installing Apache Tomcat, you might build a role to install a specific version. However, you don't want the role to exit with an error if someone forgets to set the version—rather, you would prefer to set a sensible default such as `7.0.76`, which can then be overridden with inventory variables or on the command line (using the `-e` or `--extra-vars` switches). In this way, you know the role will work even without someone explicitly setting this variable, but it can easily be changed to a newer Tomcat version if desired.

Variables that go in the `vars/` directory, however, come much higher up on Ansible's variable precedence ordering. This will not be overridden by inventory variables, and so should be used for variable data that it is more important to keep static. Of course, this is not to say they can't be overridden—the `-e` or `--extra-vars` switches are the highest order of precedence in Ansible and so will override anything else that you define.

Most of the time, you will probably make use of the `defaults/` based variables alone, but there will doubtless be times when having the option of variables higher up the precedence ordering becomes valuable to your automation, and so it is vital to know that this option is available to you.

In addition to the role-based variables described previously, there is also the option to add metadata to a role using the `meta/` directory. As before, to make use of this, simply add a file called `main.yml` into this directory. To explain how you might make use of the `meta/` directory, let's build and run a practical example that will show how it can be used. Before we get started though, it is important to note that, by default, the Ansible parser will only allow you to run a role once. This is somewhat similar to the way in which we discussed handlers earlier, which can be called multiple times but ultimately are only run once at the end of the play. Roles are the same in that they can be or referred to multiple times but will only actually get run once. There are two exceptions to this—the first is if the role is called more than once but with different variables or parameters, and the other is if the role being called has `allow_duplicates` set to `true` in its `meta/` directory. We shall see examples of both of these as we build our example:

1. At the top level of our practical example, we will have a copy of the same inventory we have been using throughout this chapter. We will also create a simple playbook called `site.yml`, which contains the following code:

```
---
- name: Role variables and meta playbook
  hosts: frt01.example.com

  roles:
    - platform
```

Notice that we are simply calling one role called `platform` from this playbook—nothing else is called from the playbook itself.

2. Let's go ahead and create the `platform` role—unlike our previous role, this will not contain any tasks or even any variable data; instead, it will just contain a `meta` directory:

```
$ mkdir -p roles/platform/meta
```

Inside this directory, create a file called `main.yml` with the following contents:

```
---
dependencies:
- role: linuxtype
  vars:
    type: centos
- role: linuxtype
  vars:
    type: ubuntu
```

This code will tell Ansible that the platform role is dependent on the `linuxtype` role. Notice that we are specifying the dependency twice, but each type we specify it, we are passing it a variable called `type` with a different value—in this way, the Ansible parser allows us to call the role twice because a different variable value has been passed to it each time it is referred to as a dependency.

3. Let's now go ahead and create the `linuxtype` role—again, this will contain no tasks, but more dependency declarations:

```
$ mkdir -p roles/linuxtype/meta/
```

Again, create a `main.yml` file in the `meta` directory, but this time containing the following:

```
---
dependencies:
- role: version
- role: network
```

Once again, we are creating more dependencies—this time, when the `linuxtype` role is called, it, in turn, is declaring dependencies on roles called `version` and `network`.

4. Let's create the `version` role first—this will have both `meta` and `tasks` directories in it:

```
$ mkdir -p roles/version/meta
$ mkdir -p roles/version/tasks
```

In the `meta` directory, we'll create a `main.yml` file with the following contents:

```
---
allow_duplicates: true
```

This declaration is important in this example—as discussed earlier, normally Ansible will only allow a role to be executed once, even if it is called multiple times. Setting `allow_duplicates` to `true` tells Ansible to allow the execution of the role more than once. This is required because, in the `platform` role, we call (via a dependency) the `linuxtype` role twice, which means, in turn, we will call the `version` role twice.

We'll also create a simple `main.yml` file in the tasks directory, which prints the value of the `type` variable that gets passed to the role:

```
---

- name: Print type variable
  debug:
    var: type
```

5. We will now repeat the process with the `network` role—to keep our example code simple, we'll define it with the same contents as the `version` role:

```
$ mkdir -p roles/network/meta
$ mkdir -p roles/network/tasks
```

In the `meta` directory, we'll again create a `main.yml` file with the following contents:

```
---

allow_duplicates: true
```

Again, we'll create a simple `main.yml` file in the `tasks` directory, which prints the value of the `type` variable that gets passed to the role:

```
---

- name: Print type variable
  debug:
    var: type
```

At the end of this process, your directory structure should look like this:

```
.
├── hosts
├── roles
│   ├── linuxtype
│   │   └── meta
│   │       └── main.yml
│   ├── network
│   │   ├── meta
│   │   │   └── main.yml
│   │   └── tasks
│   │       └── main.yml
│   ├── platform
│   │   └── meta
│   │       └── main.yml
│   └── version
│       ├── meta
│       │   └── main.yml
│       └── tasks
```

```
|                     └── main.yml
└── site.yml

11 directories, 8 files
```

Let's see what happens when we run this playbook. Now, you might think that the playbook is going to run like this: with the dependency structure we created in the preceding code, our initial playbook statically imports the `platform` role. The `platform` role then states that it depends upon the `linuxtype` role, and the dependency is declared twice with a different value in a variable called `type` each time. The `linuxtype` role then states that it depends upon both the `network` and `version` roles, which are allowed to run more than once and print the value of `type`. Hence, you could be forgiven for thinking that we'll see the `network` and `version` roles called twice, printing `centos` once and `ubuntu` the second time (as this is how we originally specified the dependencies in the `platform` role). However, when we run it, we actually see this:

```
$ ansible-playbook -i hosts site.yml

PLAY [Role variables and meta playbook]
*****************************************

TASK [Gathering Facts]
**********************************************************
ok: [frt01.example.com]

TASK [version : Print type variable]
*******************************************
ok: [frt01.example.com] => {
    "type": "ubuntu"
}

TASK [network : Print type variable]
*******************************************
ok: [frt01.example.com] => {
    "type": "ubuntu"
}

TASK [version : Print type variable]
*******************************************
ok: [frt01.example.com] => {
    "type": "ubuntu"
}

TASK [network : Print type variable]
*******************************************
ok: [frt01.example.com] => {
```

```
        "type": "ubuntu"
    }

    PLAY RECAP
    **********************************************************************
    frt01.example.com : ok=5 changed=0 unreachable=0 failed=0 skipped=0
    rescued=0 ignored=0
```

What happened? Although we see that the `network` and `version` roles are called twice (as expected), the value of the `type` variable is always `ubuntu`. This highlights an important point about the way the Ansible parser works and the difference between static imports (which we are doing here) and dynamic includes (which we discussed in the previous section).

With static imports, role variables are scoped as if they were defined at the play level rather than the role level. The roles themselves are all parsed and merged into the play we created in our `site.yml` playbook at parsing time—hence, the Ansible parser creates (in memory) one big playbook that contains all of the merged variable and role content from our directory structure. There is nothing wrong with doing this, but what it means is that the `type` variable gets overwritten each time it is declared, and so the last value we declare (which, in this case, was `ubuntu`) is the value that gets used for the playbook run.

So, how do we get this playbook to run as we originally intended—to load our dependent roles but with the two different values we defined for the `type` variable?

The answer to this question is if we are to continue using statically imported roles, then we should not use role variables when we declare the dependencies. Instead, we should pass over `type` as a role parameter. This is a small but crucial difference—role parameters remain scoped at the role level even when the Ansible parser is run, hence we can declare our dependency twice without the variable getting overwritten. To do this, change the contents of the `roles/platform/meta/main.yml` file to the following:

```
    ---
    dependencies:
    - role: linuxtype
      type: centos
    - role: linuxtype
      type: ubuntu
```

Do you notice the subtle change? The `vars:` keyword has gone, and the declaration of `type` is now at a lower indentation level, meaning it is a role parameter. Now, when we run the playbook, we get the results that we had hoped for:

```
    $ ansible-playbook -i hosts site.yml
```

```
PLAY [Role variables and meta playbook]
****************************************

TASK [Gathering Facts]
********************************************************
ok: [frt01.example.com]

TASK [version : Print type variable]
*******************************************
ok: [frt01.example.com] => {
    "type": "centos"
}

TASK [network : Print type variable]
*******************************************
ok: [frt01.example.com] => {
    "type": "centos"
}

TASK [version : Print type variable]
*******************************************
ok: [frt01.example.com] => {
    "type": "ubuntu"
}

TASK [network : Print type variable]
*******************************************
ok: [frt01.example.com] => {
    "type": "ubuntu"
}

PLAY RECAP
*****************************************************************************
frt01.example.com : ok=5 changed=0 unreachable=0 failed=0 skipped=0
rescued=0 ignored=0
```

This is quite an advanced example of Ansible role dependencies but it has been provided to you to demonstrate the importance of knowing a little about variable precedence (that is, where the variable is scoped) and how the parser works. If you write simple, sequentially parsed tasks, then you may never need to know this, but I recommend that you make extensive use of the debug statement and test your playbook design to make sure that you don't fall foul of this during your playbook development.

Having look in great detail at a number of aspects of roles, let's take a look in the following section at a centralized store for publicly available Ansible roles — Ansible Galaxy.

Ansible Galaxy

No section on Ansible roles would be complete without a mention of Ansible Galaxy. Ansible Galaxy is a community-driven collection of Ansible roles, hosted by Ansible at `https://galaxy.ansible.com/`. It contains a great many community-contributed Ansible roles, and if you can conceive of an automation task, there is a good chance someone has already written a role to do exactly what you want it to do. It is well worth exploring and can get your automation project off the ground quickly as you can start work with a set of ready-made roles.

In addition to the web site, the `ansible-galaxy` client is included in Ansible, and this provides a quick and convenient way for you to download and deploy roles into your playbook structure. Let's say that you want to update the **message of the day** (**MOTD**) on your target hosts—this is surely something that somebody has already figured out. A quick search on the Ansible Galaxy website returns (at the time of writing) 106 roles for setting the MOTD. If we want to use one of these, we could download it into our roles directory using the following command:

```
$ ansible-galaxy role install -p roles/ arillso.motd
```

That's all you need to do—once the download is complete, you can import or include the role in your playbook just as you would for the manually created roles we have discussed in this chapter. Note that if you don't specify `-p roles/`, `ansible-galaxy` installs the roles into `~/.ansible/roles`, the central roles directory for your user account. This might be what you want, of course, but if you want the role downloaded directly into your playbook directory structure, you would add this parameter.

Another neat trick is to use `ansible-galaxy` to create an empty role directory structure for you to create your own roles in—this saves all of the manual directory and file creation we have been undertaking in this chapter, as in this example:

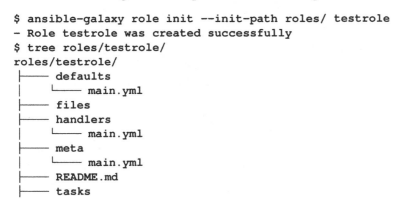

```
$ ansible-galaxy role init --init-path roles/ testrole
- Role testrole was created successfully
$ tree roles/testrole/
roles/testrole/
├── defaults
│   └── main.yml
├── files
├── handlers
│   └── main.yml
├── meta
│   └── main.yml
├── README.md
├── tasks
```

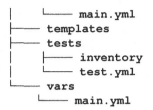

```
│      └────    main.yml
├────    templates
├────    tests
│      ├────    inventory
│      └────    test.yml
└────    vars
         └────    main.yml
```

That should give you enough information to get started on your journey into Ansible roles. I cannot stress highly enough how important it is to develop your code as roles—it might not seem important initially, but as your automation use cases expand, and your requirement to reuse code grows, you will be glad that you did. In the next section, let's expand our look at Ansible playbooks with a discussion of the ways in which conditional logic can be used in your Ansible code.

Using conditions in your code

In most of our examples so far, we have created simple sets of tasks that always run. However, as you generate tasks (whether in roles or playbooks) that you want to apply to a wider array of hosts, sooner or later, you will want to perform some kind of conditional action. This might be to only perform a task in response to the results of a previous task. Or it might be to only perform a task in response to a specific fact gathered from an Ansible system. In this section, we will provide some practical examples of conditional logic to apply to your Ansible tasks to demonstrate how to use this feature.

As ever, we'll need an inventory to get started, and we'll reuse the inventory we have used throughout this chapter:

```
[frontends]
frt01.example.com https_port=8443
frt02.example.com http_proxy=proxy.example.com

[frontends:vars]
ntp_server=ntp.frt.example.com
proxy=proxy.frt.example.com

[apps]
app01.example.com
app02.example.com

[webapp:children]
frontends
apps
```

```
[webapp:vars]
proxy_server=proxy.webapp.example.com
health_check_retry=3
health_check_interal=60
```

Suppose that you want to perform an Ansible task only on certain operating systems. We have already discussed Ansible facts, and these provide the perfect platform to start exploring conditional logic in your playbooks. Consider this: an urgent patch has been released for all of your CentOS systems, and you want to apply it immediately. You could, of course, go through and create a special inventory (or host group) for CentOS hosts, but this is additional work that you don't necessarily need to do.

Instead, let's define the task that will perform our update but add a when clause containing a Jinja 2 expressions to it in a simple example playbook:

```
---

- name: Play to patch only CentOS systems
  hosts: all
  become: true

  tasks:
  - name: Patch CentOS systems
    yum:
      name: httpd
      state: latest
    when: ansible_facts['distribution'] == "CentOS"
```

Now, when we run this task, if your test system(s) are CentOS-based (and mine are), you should see output similar to the following:

```
$ ansible-playbook -i hosts condition.yml

PLAY [Play to patch only CentOS systems]
****************************************

TASK [Gathering Facts]
***********************************************************
ok: [frt02.example.com]
ok: [app01.example.com]
ok: [frt01.example.com]
ok: [app02.example.com]

TASK [Patch CentOS systems]
*********************************************************
ok: [app01.example.com]
changed: [frt01.example.com]
ok: [app02.example.com]
```

```
ok: [frt02.example.com]

PLAY RECAP
***********************************************************************
app01.example.com : ok=2 changed=0 unreachable=0 failed=0 skipped=0
rescued=0 ignored=0
app02.example.com : ok=2 changed=0 unreachable=0 failed=0 skipped=0
rescued=0 ignored=0
frt01.example.com : ok=2 changed=1 unreachable=0 failed=0 skipped=0
rescued=0 ignored=0
frt02.example.com : ok=2 changed=0 unreachable=0 failed=0 skipped=0
rescued=0 ignored=0
```

The preceding output shows that all of our systems were CentOS-based, but that only frt01.example.com needed the patch applying. Now we can make our logic more precise—perhaps it is only our legacy systems that are running on CentOS 6 that need the patch applying. In this case, we can expand the logic in our playbook to check both the distribution and major version, as follows:

```
---
- name: Play to patch only CentOS systems
  hosts: all
  become: true

  tasks:
  - name: Patch CentOS systems
    yum:
      name: httpd
      state: latest
    when: (ansible_facts['distribution'] == "CentOS" and
ansible_facts['distribution_major_version'] == "6")
```

Now, if we run our modified playbook, depending on the systems you have in your inventory, you might see output similar to the following. In this case, my app01.example.com server was based on CentOS 6 so had the patch applied. All other systems were skipped because they did not match my logical expression:

```
$ ansible-playbook -i hosts condition2.yml

PLAY [Play to patch only CentOS systems]
***************************************

TASK [Gathering Facts]
************************************************************
ok: [frt01.example.com]
ok: [app02.example.com]
ok: [app01.example.com]
```

```
ok: [frt02.example.com]

TASK [Patch CentOS systems]
***************************************************
changed: [app01.example.com]
skipping: [frt01.example.com]
skipping: [frt02.example.com]
skipping: [app02.example.com]

PLAY RECAP
***********************************************************************
app01.example.com : ok=2 changed=1 unreachable=0 failed=0 skipped=0
rescued=0 ignored=0
app02.example.com : ok=1 changed=0 unreachable=0 failed=0 skipped=1
rescued=0 ignored=0
frt01.example.com : ok=1 changed=0 unreachable=0 failed=0 skipped=1
rescued=0 ignored=0
frt02.example.com : ok=1 changed=0 unreachable=0 failed=0 skipped=1
rescued=0 ignored=0
```

Of course, this conditional logic is not limited to Ansible facts and can be incredibly valuable when using the shell or command modules. When you run any Ansible module (be it shell, command, yum, copy, or otherwise), the module returns data detailing the results of its run. You can capture this in a standard Ansible variable using the register keyword and then process it further later on in the playbook.

Consider the following playbook code. It contains two tasks, the first of which is to obtain the listing of the current directory and capture the output of the shell module in a variable called shellresult. When then print a simple debug message, but only on the condition that the hosts string is in the output of the shell command:

```
---
- name: Play to patch only CentOS systems
  hosts: localhost
  become: true

  tasks:
    - name: Gather directory listing from local system
      shell: "ls -l"
      register: shellresult

    - name: Alert if we find a hosts file
      debug:
        msg: "Found hosts file!"
      when: '"hosts" in shellresult.stdout'
```

Now, when we run this in the current directory, which if you are working from the GitHub repository that accompanies this book will contain a file named `hosts`, then you should see output similar to the following:

```
$ ansible-playbook condition3.yml
[WARNING]: provided hosts list is empty, only localhost is available. Note
that
the implicit localhost does not match 'all'

PLAY [Play to patch only CentOS systems]
****************************************

TASK [Gathering Facts]
*********************************************************
ok: [localhost]

TASK [Gather directory listing from local system]
*****************************
changed: [localhost]

TASK [Alert if we find a hosts file]
********************************************
ok: [localhost] => {
    "msg": "Found hosts file!"
}

PLAY RECAP
***********************************************************************
localhost : ok=3 changed=1 unreachable=0 failed=0 skipped=0 rescued=0
ignored=0
```

Yet, if the file doesn't exist, then you'll see that the `debug` message gets skipped:

```
$ ansible-playbook condition3.yml
[WARNING]: provided hosts list is empty, only localhost is available. Note
that
the implicit localhost does not match 'all'

PLAY [Play to patch only CentOS systems]
****************************************

TASK [Gathering Facts]
*********************************************************
ok: [localhost]

TASK [Gather directory listing from local system]
*****************************
changed: [localhost]
```

```
TASK [Alert if we find a hosts file]
*****************************************
skipping: [localhost]

PLAY RECAP
*****************************************************************
localhost : ok=2 changed=1 unreachable=0 failed=0 skipped=1 rescued=0
ignored=0
```

You can also create complex conditions for IT operational tasks in production; however, remember that, in Ansible, variables are not cast to any particular type by default, and hence even though the contents of a variable (or fact) might look like a number, Ansible will by default treat it as a string. If you need to perform an integer comparison instead, you must first cast the variable to an integer type. For example, here is a fragment of a playbook that will run a task only on Fedora 25 and newer:

```
tasks:
  - name: Only perform this task on Fedora 25 and later
    shell: echo "only on Fedora 25 and later"
    when: ansible_facts['distribution'] == "Fedora" and
ansible_facts['distribution_major_version']|int >= 25
```

There are many different types of conditionals you can apply to your Ansible tasks, and this section is just scratching the surface; however, it should give you a sound basis on which to expand your knowledge of applying conditions to your tasks in Ansible. Not only can you apply conditional logic to Ansible tasks, but you can also run them in loops over a set of data, and we shall explore this in the next section.

Repeating tasks with loops

Oftentimes, we will want to perform a single task, but use that single task to iterate over a set of data. For example, you might not want to create one user account but 10. Or you might want to install 15 packages to a system. The possibilities are endless, but the point remains the same—you would not want to write 10 individual Ansible tasks to create 10 user accounts. Fortunately, Ansible supports looping over datasets to ensure that you can perform large scale operations using tightly defined code. In this section, we will explore how to make practical use of loops in your Ansible playbooks.

As ever, we must start with an inventory to work against, and we will use our by-now familiar inventory, which we have consistently used throughout this chapter:

```
[frontends]
frt01.example.com https_port=8443
frt02.example.com http_proxy=proxy.example.com

[frontends:vars]
ntp_server=ntp.frt.example.com
proxy=proxy.frt.example.com

[apps]
app01.example.com
app02.example.com

[webapp:children]
frontends
apps

[webapp:vars]
proxy_server=proxy.webapp.example.com
health_check_retry=3
health_check_interal=60
```

Let's start with a really simple playbook to show you how to loop over a set of data in a single task. Although this is quite a contrived example, it is intended to be simple to show you the fundamentals of how loops work in Ansible. We will define a single task that runs the command module on a single host from the inventory and uses the command module to echo the numbers 1 through 6 in turn on the remote system (with some imagination, this could easily be extended to adding user accounts or creating a sequence of files).

Consider the following code:

```
---
- name: Simple loop demo play
  hosts: frt01.example.com

  tasks:
    - name: Echo a value from the loop
      command: echo "{{ item }}"
      loop:
        - 1
        - 2
        - 3
        - 4
        - 5
        - 6
```

The `loop:` statement defines the start of the loop, and the items in the loop are defined as a YAML list. Also, note the higher indentation level, which tells the parser they are part of the loop. When working with the loop data, we use a special variable called `item`, which contains the current value from the loop iteration to be echoed. Hence, if we run this playbook, we should see output similar to the following:

```
$ ansible-playbook -i hosts loop1.yml


PLAY [Simple loop demo play]
***************************************************

TASK [Gathering Facts]
******************************************************
ok: [frt01.example.com]

TASK [Echo a value from the loop]
*********************************************
changed: [frt01.example.com] => (item=1)
changed: [frt01.example.com] => (item=2)
changed: [frt01.example.com] => (item=3)
changed: [frt01.example.com] => (item=4)
changed: [frt01.example.com] => (item=5)
changed: [frt01.example.com] => (item=6)

PLAY RECAP
******************************************************************
frt01.example.com : ok=2 changed=1 unreachable=0 failed=0 skipped=0
rescued=0 ignored=0
```

You can combine the conditional logic we discussed in the preceding section with loops, to make the loop operate on just a subset of its data. For example, consider the following iteration of the playbook:

```
---
- name: Simple loop demo play
  hosts: frt01.example.com

  tasks:
    - name: Echo a value from the loop
      command: echo "{{ item }}"
      loop:
        - 1
        - 2
        - 3
        - 4
        - 5
```

```
      - 6
    when: item|int > 3
```

Now, when we run this, we see that the task is skipped until we reach the integer value of 4 and higher in the loop contents:

```
$ ansible-playbook -i hosts loop2.yml

PLAY [Simple loop demo play]
*************************************************

TASK [Gathering Facts]
****************************************************
ok: [frt01.example.com]

TASK [Echo a value from the loop]
********************************************
skipping: [frt01.example.com] => (item=1)
skipping: [frt01.example.com] => (item=2)
skipping: [frt01.example.com] => (item=3)
changed: [frt01.example.com] => (item=4)
changed: [frt01.example.com] => (item=5)
changed: [frt01.example.com] => (item=6)

PLAY RECAP
*********************************************************************
frt01.example.com : ok=2 changed=1 unreachable=0 failed=0 skipped=0
rescued=0 ignored=0
```

You can, of course, combine this with the conditional logic based on Ansible facts and other variables in the manner we discussed previously. Just as we captured the results of a module's execution using the `register` keyword before, we can do so with loops. The only difference is that the results will now be stored in a dictionary, with one dictionary entry for each iteration of the loop rather than just one set of results.

Hence, let's see what happens if we further enhance the playbook, as follows:

```
---
- name: Simple loop demo play
  hosts: frt01.example.com

  tasks:
    - name: Echo a value from the loop
      command: echo "{{ item }}"
      loop:
        - 1
        - 2
```

```
            - 3
            - 4
            - 5
            - 6
         when: item|int > 3
         register: loopresult

      - name: Print the results from the loop
        debug:
          var: loopresult
```

Now, when we run the playbook, you will see pages out output containing the dictionary with the contents of `loopresult`. The following output is truncated in the interests of space but demonstrates the kind of results you should expect from running this playbook:

```
$ ansible-playbook -i hosts loop3.yml

PLAY [Simple loop demo play]
*************************************************

TASK [Gathering Facts]
****************************************************
ok: [frt01.example.com]

TASK [Echo a value from the loop]
*********************************************
skipping: [frt01.example.com] => (item=1)
skipping: [frt01.example.com] => (item=2)
skipping: [frt01.example.com] => (item=3)
changed: [frt01.example.com] => (item=4)
changed: [frt01.example.com] => (item=5)
changed: [frt01.example.com] => (item=6)

TASK [Print the results from the loop]
*****************************************
ok: [frt01.example.com] => {
    "loopresult": {
        "changed": true,
        "msg": "All items completed",
        "results": [
            {
                "ansible_loop_var": "item",
                "changed": false,
                "item": 1,
                "skip_reason": "Conditional result was False",
                "skipped": true
            },
            {
```

```
        "ansible_loop_var": "item",
        "changed": false,
        "item": 2,
        "skip_reason": "Conditional result was False",
        "skipped": true
},
```

As you can see, the results section of the output is a dictionary, and we can clearly see that the first two items in the list were `skipped` because the result of our `when` clause (`Conditional`) was `false`.

Hence, we can see so far that loops are easy to define and work with—but you may be asking, *can you create nested loops?* The answer to that question is *yes*, but there is a catch—the special variable named `item` would clash as both the inner and outer loops would use the same variable name. This would mean the results from your nested loop run would be, at best, unexpected.

Fortunately, there is a `loop` parameter called `loop_control`, which allows you to change the name of the special variable containing the data from the current `loop` iteration from `item` to something of your choosing. Let's create a nested loop to see how this works.

First of all, we'll create a playbook in the usual manner, with a single task to run in a loop. To generate our nested loop, we'll use the `include_tasks` directory to dynamically include a single task from another YAML file that will also contain a loop. As we're intending to use this playbook in a nested loop, we'll use the `loop_var` directive to change the name of the special loop contents variable from `item` to `second_item`:

```
---
- name: Play to demonstrate nested loops
  hosts: localhost

  tasks:
    - name: Outer loop
      include_tasks: loopsubtask.yml
      loop:
        - a
        - b
        - c
      loop_control:
        loop_var: second_item
```

Then, we'll create a second file called `loopsubtask.yml`, which contains the inner loop and is included in the preceding playbook. As we're already changed the loop item variable name in the outer loop, we don't need to change it again here. Note that the structure of this file is very much like a tasks file in a role—it is not a complete playbook, but rather simply a list of tasks:

```
---
- name: Inner loop
  debug:
    msg: "second item={{ second_item }} first item={{ item }}"
  loop:
    - 100
    - 200
    - 300
```

Now you should be able to run the playbook, and you will see Ansible iterate over the outer loop first and then process the inner loop over the data defined by the outer loop. As the loop variable names do not clash, all works exactly as we would expect:

```
$ ansible-playbook loopmain.yml
[WARNING]: provided hosts list is empty, only localhost is available. Note
that
the implicit localhost does not match 'all'

PLAY [Play to demonstrate nested loops]
*****************************************

TASK [Gathering Facts]
*********************************************************
ok: [localhost]

TASK [Outer loop]
*************************************************************
included: /root/Practical-Ansible-2/Chapter 4/loopsubtask.yml for localhost
included: /root/Practical-Ansible-2/Chapter 4/loopsubtask.yml for localhost
included: /root/Practical-Ansible-2/Chapter 4/loopsubtask.yml for localhost

TASK [Inner loop]
*************************************************************
ok: [localhost] => (item=100) => {
    "msg": "second item=a first item=100"
}
ok: [localhost] => (item=200) => {
    "msg": "second item=a first item=200"
}
ok: [localhost] => (item=300) => {
    "msg": "second item=a first item=300"
```

```
}

TASK [Inner loop]
**************************************************************
ok: [localhost] => (item=100) => {
    "msg": "second item=b first item=100"
}
ok: [localhost] => (item=200) => {
    "msg": "second item=b first item=200"
}
ok: [localhost] => (item=300) => {
    "msg": "second item=b first item=300"
}

TASK [Inner loop]
**************************************************************
ok: [localhost] => (item=100) => {
    "msg": "second item=c first item=100"
}
ok: [localhost] => (item=200) => {
    "msg": "second item=c first item=200"
}
ok: [localhost] => (item=300) => {
    "msg": "second item=c first item=300"
}

PLAY RECAP
*********************************************************************
localhost : ok=7 changed=0 unreachable=0 failed=0 skipped=0 rescued=0
ignored=0
```

Loops are simple to work with, and yet very powerful as they allow you to easily use one task to iterate over a large set of data. In the next section, we'll look at another construct of the Ansible language for controlling playbook flow—blocks.

Grouping tasks using blocks

Blocks in Ansible allow you to logically group a set of tasks together, primarily for one of two purposes. One might be to apply conditional logic to an entire set of tasks; in this example, you could apply an identical when clause to each of the tasks, but this is cumbersome and inefficient—far better to place all of the tasks in a block and apply the conditional logic to the block itself. In this way, the logic only needs to be declared once. Blocks are also valuable when it comes to error handling and especially when it comes to recovering from an error condition. We shall explore both of these through simple practical examples in this chapter to get you up to speed with blocks in Ansible.

As ever, let's ensure we have an inventory to work from:

```
[frontends]
frt01.example.com https_port=8443
frt02.example.com http_proxy=proxy.example.com

[frontends:vars]
ntp_server=ntp.frt.example.com
proxy=proxy.frt.example.com

[apps]
app01.example.com
app02.example.com

[webapp:children]
frontends
apps

[webapp:vars]
proxy_server=proxy.webapp.example.com
health_check_retry=3
health_check_interal=60
```

Now, let's dive straight in and look at an example of how you would use blocks to apply conditional logic to a set of tasks. At a high level, suppose we want to perform the following actions on all of our Fedora Linux hosts:

- Install the package for the Apache web server.
- Install a templated configuration.
- Start the appropriate service.

We could achieve this with three individual tasks, all with a when clause associated with them, but blocks provide us with a better way. The following example playbook shows the three tasks discussed contained in a block (notice the additional level of indentation required to denote their presence in the block):

```
---
- name: Conditional block play
  hosts: all
  become: true

  tasks:
  - name: Install and configure Apache
    block:
      - name: Install the Apache package
        dnf:
          name: httpd
          state: installed
      - name: Install the templated configuration to a dummy location
        template:
          src: templates/src.j2
          dest: /tmp/my.conf
      - name: Start the httpd service
        service:
          name: httpd
          state: started
          enabled: True
    when: ansible_facts['distribution'] == 'Fedora'
```

When you run this playbook, you should find that the Apache-related tasks are only run on any Fedora hosts you might have in your inventory; you should see that either all three tasks are run or are skipped—depending on the makeup and contents of your inventory, it might look something like this:

```
$ ansible-playbook -i hosts blocks.yml

PLAY [Conditional block play]
****************************************************

TASK [Gathering Facts]
**********************************************************
ok: [app02.example.com]
ok: [frt01.example.com]
ok: [app01.example.com]
ok: [frt02.example.com]

TASK [Install the Apache package]
********************************************
```

```
changed: [frt01.example.com]
changed: [frt02.example.com]
skipping: [app01.example.com]
skipping: [app02.example.com]

TASK [Install the templated configuration to a dummy location]
******************
changed: [frt01.example.com]
changed: [frt02.example.com]
skipping: [app01.example.com]
skipping: [app02.example.com]

TASK [Start the httpd service]
************************************************
changed: [frt01.example.com]
changed: [frt02.example.com]
skipping: [app01.example.com]
skipping: [app02.example.com]

PLAY RECAP
*****************************************************************
app01.example.com : ok=1 changed=0 unreachable=0 failed=0 skipped=3
rescued=0 ignored=0
app02.example.com : ok=1 changed=0 unreachable=0 failed=0 skipped=3
rescued=0 ignored=0
frt01.example.com : ok=4 changed=3 unreachable=0 failed=0 skipped=3
rescued=0 ignored=0
frt02.example.com : ok=4 changed=3 unreachable=0 failed=0 skipped=3
rescued=0 ignored=0
```

This is very simple to construct, but very powerful in terms of the effect it has on your ability to control the flow over large sets of tasks.

This time, let's build a different example to demonstrate how blocks can be utilized to help Ansible to handle error conditions gracefully. So far, you should have experienced that if your playbooks encounter any errors, they are likely to stop executing at the point of failure. This is in some situations far from ideal, and you might want to perform some kind of recovery actions in this event rather than simply halting the playbook.

Let's create a new playbook, this time with the following contents:

```
---
- name: Play to demonstrate block error handling
  hosts: frontends

  tasks:
    - name: block to handle errors
```

```
block:
  - name: Perform a successful task
    debug:
      msg: 'Normally executing....'
  - name: Deliberately create an error
    command: /bin/whatever
  - name: This task should not run if the previous one results in an
error
    debug:
      msg: 'Never print this message if the above command fails!!!!'
rescue:
  - name: Catch the error (and perform recovery actions)
    debug:
      msg: 'Caught the error'
  - name: Deliberately create another error
    command: /bin/whatever
  - name: This task should not run if the previous one results in an
error
    debug:
      msg: 'Do not print this message if the above command fails!!!!'
always:
  - name: This task always runs!
    debug:
      msg: "Tasks in this part of the play will be ALWAYS
executed!!!!"
```

Notice that in the preceding play, we now have additional sections to block—as well as the tasks in block itself, we have two new parts labeled rescue and always. The flow of execution is as follows:

1. All tasks in the block section are executed normally, in the sequence in which they are listed.

2. If a task in the block results in an error, no further tasks in the block are run:
   - Tasks in the rescue section start to run in the order they are listed.
   - Tasks in the rescue section do not run if no errors result from the block tasks.

3. If an error results from a task being run in the rescue section, no further rescue tasks are executed and execution moves on to the always section.

4. Tasks in the always section are always run, regardless of any errors in either the block or rescue sections. They even run when no errors are encountered.

With this flow of execution in mind, you should see output similar to the following when you execute this playbook, noting that we have deliberately created two error conditions to demonstrate the flow:

```
$ ansible-playbook -i hosts blocks-error.yml

PLAY [Play to demonstrate block error handling]
*******************************

TASK [Gathering Facts]
**********************************************************
ok: [frt02.example.com]
ok: [frt01.example.com]

TASK [Perform a successful task]
***********************************************
ok: [frt01.example.com] => {
    "msg": "Normally executing...."
}
ok: [frt02.example.com] => {
    "msg": "Normally executing...."
}

TASK [Deliberately create an error]
*********************************************
fatal: [frt01.example.com]: FAILED! => {"changed": false, "cmd":
"/bin/whatever", "msg": "[Errno 2] No such file or directory", "rc": 2}
fatal: [frt02.example.com]: FAILED! => {"changed": false, "cmd":
"/bin/whatever", "msg": "[Errno 2] No such file or directory", "rc": 2}

TASK [Catch the error (and perform recovery actions)]
*************************
ok: [frt01.example.com] => {
    "msg": "Caught the error"
}
ok: [frt02.example.com] => {
    "msg": "Caught the error"
}

TASK [Deliberately create another error]
****************************************
fatal: [frt01.example.com]: FAILED! => {"changed": false, "cmd":
"/bin/whatever", "msg": "[Errno 2] No such file or directory", "rc": 2}
fatal: [frt02.example.com]: FAILED! => {"changed": false, "cmd":
"/bin/whatever", "msg": "[Errno 2] No such file or directory", "rc": 2}

TASK [This task always runs!]
***************************************************
```

```
ok: [frt01.example.com] => {
    "msg": "Tasks in this part of the play will be ALWAYS executed!!!!"
}
ok: [frt02.example.com] => {
    "msg": "Tasks in this part of the play will be ALWAYS executed!!!!"
}

PLAY RECAP
********************************************************************
frt01.example.com : ok=4 changed=0 unreachable=0 failed=1 skipped=0
rescued=1 ignored=0
frt02.example.com : ok=4 changed=0 unreachable=0 failed=1 skipped=0
rescued=1 ignored=0
```

Ansible has two special variables, which contain information you might find useful in the rescue block to perform your recovery actions:

- `ansible_failed_task`: This is a dictionary containing details of the task from `block` that failed, causing us to enter the `rescue` section. You can explore this by displaying its contents using `debug`, but for example, the name of the failing task can be obtained from `ansible_failed_task.name`.
- `ansible_failed_result`: This is the result of the failed task and behaves the same as if you had added the `register` keyword to the failing task. This saves you having to add `register` to every single task in the block in case it fails.

As your playbooks get more complex and error handling gets more and more important (or indeed conditional logic becomes more vital), blocks will become an important part of your arsenal in writing good, robust playbooks. Let's proceed in the next section to explore execution strategies to gain further control of your playbook runs.

Configuring play execution via strategies

As your playbooks become increasingly complex, it becomes more and more important that you have robust ways to debug any issues that might arise. For example, is there a way you can check the contents of a given variable (or variables) during execution without the need to insert `debug` statements throughout your playbook? Similarly, we have so far seen that Ansible will ensure that a particular task runs to completion on all inventory hosts that it applies to before moving on to the next task—is there a way to vary this?

When you are getting started with Ansible, the execution strategy that you see by default (and we have seen this so far in every playbook we have executed, even though we have not mentioned it by name) is known as `linear`. This does exactly what it describes—each task is executed in turn on all applicable hosts before the next task is started. However, there is another, less commonly used strategy called `free`, which allows all tasks to be completed as fast as they can on each host, without waiting for other hosts.

The most useful strategy when you are starting work with Ansible, however, is going to be the `debug` strategy, and this enables Ansible to drop you straight into its integrated debug environment if an error should occur in the playbook. Let's demonstrate this by creating a playbook that has a deliberate error in it. Note the `strategy:  debug` and `debugger:  on_failed` statements in the play definition:

```
---
- name: Play to demonstrate the debug strategy
  hosts: frt01.example.com
  strategy: debug
  debugger: on_failed
  gather_facts: no
  vars:
    username: daniel

  tasks:
    - name: Generate an error by referencing an undefined variable
      ping: data={{ mobile }}
```

Now if you execute this playbook, you should see that it starts to run, but then drops you into the integrated debugger when it encounters the deliberate error it contains. The start of the output should be similar to the following:

```
$ ansible-playbook -i hosts debug.yml

PLAY [Play to demonstrate the debug strategy]
**********************************

TASK [Generate an error by referencing an undefined variable]
******************
fatal: [frt01.example.com]: FAILED! => {"msg": "The task includes an option
with an undefined variable. The error was: 'mobile' is undefined\n\nThe
error appears to be in '/root/Practical-Ansible-2/Chapter 4/debug.yml':
line 11, column 7, but may\nbe elsewhere in the file depending on the exact
syntax problem.\n\nThe offending line appears to be:\n\n tasks:\n - name:
Generate an error by referencing an undefined variable\n ^ here\n"}
[frt01.example.com] TASK: Generate an error by referencing an undefined
variable (debug)>
```

```
[frt02.prod.com] TASK: make an error with refering incorrect variable
(debug)> p task_vars
{'ansible_check_mode': False,
 'ansible_current_hosts': [u'frt02.prod.com'],
 'ansible_diff_mode': False,
 'ansible_facts': {},
 'ansible_failed_hosts': [],
 'ansible_forks': 5,
...
[frt02.prod.com] TASK: make an error with refering incorrect variable
(debug)> quit
User interrupted execution
$
```

Notice that the playbook starts executing but fails on the first task with an error as the
variable is undefined. However, rather than exiting back to the shell, it enters an interactive
debugger. An exhaustive guide to the use of the debugger is beyond the scope of this book,
but further details are available here if you are interested in learning: `https://docs.`
`ansible.com/ansible/latest/user_guide/playbooks_debugger.html`.

To take you through a very simple, practical debugging example, however, enter the `p`
`task` command at the prompt—this will cause the Ansible debugger to print the name of
the failing task; this is very useful if you are in the midst of a large playbook:

```
[frt01.example.com] TASK: Generate an error by referencing an undefined
variable (debug)> p task
TASK: Generate an error by referencing an undefined variable
```

Now we know where the play failed, so let's dig a little deeper by issuing the `p task.args`
command, which will show us the arguments that were passed to the module in the task:

```
[frt01.example.com] TASK: Generate an error by referencing an undefined
variable (debug)> p task.args
{u'data': u'{{ mobile }}'}
```

So, we can see that our module was passed the argument called `data`, with the argument
value being a variable (denoted by the pairs of curly braces) called `mobile`. Hence, it might
be logical to have a look at the variables available to the task, to see whether this variable
exists, and if so whether the value is sensible (use the `p task_vars` command to do this):

```
[frt01.example.com] TASK: Generate an error by referencing an undefined
variable (debug)> p task_vars
{'ansible_check_mode': False,
 'ansible_current_hosts': [u'frt01.example.com'],
 'ansible_dependent_role_names': [],
 'ansible_diff_mode': False,
```

```
'ansible_facts': {},
'ansible_failed_hosts': [],
'ansible_forks': 5,
```

The preceding output is truncated, and you will find a great many variables associated with the task—this is because any gathered facts, and internal Ansible variables, are all available to the task. However, if you scroll through the list, you will be able to confirm that there is no variable called `mobile`.

Hence, this should be enough information to fix your playbook. Enter `q` to quit the debugger:

```
[frt01.example.com] TASK: Generate an error by referencing an undefined
variable (debug)> q
User interrupted execution
$
```

The Ansible debugger is an incredibly powerful tool and you should learn to make effective use of it, especially as your playbook complexity grows. This concludes our practical look at the various aspects of playbook design—in the next section, we'll take a look at the ways in which you can integrate Git source code management into your playbooks.

Using ansible-pull

The `ansible-pull` command is a special feature of Ansible that allows you to, all in one go, pull a playbook from a Git repository (for example, GitHub) and then execute it, hence saving the usual steps such as cloning (or updating the working copy of) the repository, then executing the playbook. The great thing about `ansible-pull` is that it allows you to centrally store and version control your playbooks and then execute them with a single command, hence enabling them to be executed using the `cron` scheduler without the need to even install the Ansible playbooks on a given box.

An important thing to note, however, is that, while the `ansible` and `ansible-playbook` commands can both operate over an entire inventory and run the playbooks against one or more remote hosts, the `ansible-pull` command is only intended to run the playbooks it obtains from your source control system on the localhost. Hence, if you want to use `ansible-pull` throughout your infrastructure, you must install it onto every host that needs it.

Nonetheless, let's see how this might work. We'll simply run the command by hand to explore its application, but in reality, you would almost certainly install it into your `crontab` so that it runs on a regular basis, picking up any changes you make to your playbook in the version control system.

As `ansible-pull` is only intended to run the playbook on the local system, an inventory file is somewhat redundant—instead, we'll use a little-used inventory specification whereby you can simply specify inventory hosts directory as a comma-separated list on the command line. If you only have one host, you simply specify its name followed by a comma.

Let's use a simple playbook from GitHub that sets the message of the day based on variable content. To do this, we will run the following command (which we'll break down in a minute):

```
$ ansible-pull -d /var/ansible-set-motd -i ${HOSTNAME}, -U
https://github.com/jamesfreeman959/ansible-set-motd.git site.yml -e
"ag_motd_content='MOTD generated by ansible-pull'" >> /tmp/ansible-pull.log
2>&1
```

This command breaks down as follows:

- `-d /var/ansible-set-motd`: This sets the working directory that will contain the checkout of the code from GitHub.
- `-i ${HOSTNAME},`: This runs only on the current host, specified by its hostname from the appropriate shell variable.
- `-U https://github.com/jamesfreeman959/ansible-set-motd.git`: We use this URL to obtain the playbooks.
- `site.yml`: This is the name of the playbook to run.
- `-e "ag_motd_content='MOTD generated by ansible-pull'"`: This sets the appropriate Ansible variable to generate the MOTD content.
- `>> /tmp/ansible-pull.log 2>&1`: This redirects the output of the command to a log file in case we need to analyze it later—especially useful if running the command in a `cron job` where the output would never be printed to the user's terminal.

When you run this command, you should see some output similar to the following (note that log redirection has been removed to make it easier to see the output):

```
$ ansible-pull -d /var/ansible-set-motd -i ${HOSTNAME}, -U
https://github.com/jamesfreeman959/ansible-set-motd.git site.yml -e
"ag_motd_content='MOTD generated by ansible-pull'"
Starting Ansible Pull at 2020-04-14 17:26:21
```

```
/usr/bin/ansible-pull -d /var/ansible-set-motd -i cookbook, -U
https://github.com/jamesfreeman959/ansible-set-motd.git site.yml -e
ag_motd_content='MOTD generated by ansible-pull'
cookbook |[WARNING]: SUCCESS = Your git > {
    "aversion isfter": "7d too old t3a191ecb2do fully suebe7f84f4fpport the
a5817b0f1bdepth argu49c4cd54",ment.
Fall
    "ansing back tible_factso full che": {
     ckouts.
    "discovered_interpreter_python": "/usr/bin/python"
    },
    "before": "7d3a191ecb2debe7f84f4fa5817b0f1b49c4cd54",
    "changed": false,
    "remote_url_changed": false
}


PLAY [Update the MOTD on hosts]
*************************************************

TASK [Gathering Facts]
****************************************************
ok: [cookbook]

TASK [ansible.motd : Add 99-footer file]
**************************************
skipping: [cookbook]

TASK [ansible.motd : Delete 99-footer file]
**************************************
ok: [cookbook]

TASK [ansible.motd : Delete /etc/motd file]
**************************************
skipping: [cookbook]

TASK [ansible.motd : Check motd tail supported]
*******************************
fatal: [cookbook]: FAILED! => {"changed": true, "cmd": "test -f
/etc/update-motd.d/99-footer", "delta": "0:00:00.004444", "end":
"2020-04-14 17:26:25.489793", "msg": "non-zero return code", "rc": 1,
"start": "2020-04-14 17:26:25.485349", "stderr": "", "stderr_lines": [],
"stdout": "", "stdout_lines": []}
...ignoring

TASK [ansible.motd : Add motd tail]
*********************************************
skipping: [cookbook]
```

```
TASK [ansible.motd : Add motd]
***************************************************
changed: [cookbook]

PLAY RECAP
*********************************************************************
cookbook : ok=4 changed=2 unreachable=0 failed=0 skipped=3 rescued=0
ignored=1
```

This command can be a very powerful part of your overall Ansible solution, especially as it means you don't have to worry too greatly about running all of your playbooks centrally, or ensuring that they are all up to date every time you run them. The ability to schedule this in `cron` is especially powerful in a large infrastructure where, ideally, automation means things should take care of themselves.

This concludes our practical look at playbooks and how to author your own code—with a little research into Ansible modules, you should now have enough to write your own robust playbooks with ease.

Summary

Playbooks are the lifeblood of Ansible automation, providing a robust framework within which to define logical collections of tasks and handle error conditions cleanly and robustly. The addition of roles into this mix is valuable in terms of not only organizing your code but also in terms of supporting code reuse as your automation requirements grow. Ansible playbooks provide a truly complete automation solution for your technology needs.

In this chapter, you learned about the playbook framework and how to start building your own playbooks. You then learned how to organize your code into roles and design your code to effectively and efficiently support reuse. We then explored some of the more advanced playbook writing topics such as working with conditional logic, blocks, and loops. Finally, we looked at playbook execution strategies, especially with a view to being able to debug your playbooks effectively, and we wrapped up with a look at how you can run Ansible playbooks on a local machine directly from GitHub.

In the next chapter, we will learn how to consume and create our very own modules, providing you with the skills you need to expand the capabilities of Ansible to suit your own bespoke environments, and to contribute back to the community.

Questions

1. How do you restart the Apache web server in the `frontends` host group via an ad hoc command?

    A) `ansible frontends -i hosts -a "name=httpd state=restarted"`

    B) `ansible frontends -i hosts -b service -a "name=httpd state=restarted"`

    C) `ansible frontends -i hosts -b -m service -a "name=httpd state=restarted"`

    D) `ansible frontends -i hosts -b -m server -a "name=httpd state=restarted"`

    E) `ansible frontends -i hosts -m restart -a "name=httpd"`

2. Do blocks allow you to logically make a group of tasks, or perform error handling?

    A) True

    B) False

3. Default strategies are intended via the relevant modules in the playbook.

    A) True

    B) False

Further reading

`ansible-galaxy` and the documentation can be found here: `https://galaxy.ansible.com/docs/`.

Section 2: Expanding the Capabilities of Ansible

In this section, we will cover the important concepts of Ansible plugins and modules. We will cover both their effective use and how to expand Ansible's capabilities by writing your own plugins and modules. We'll even look at the requirements for submitting your modules and plugins back to the official Ansible project. We'll also look at coding best practices, as well as some advanced Ansible techniques that allow you to safely automate your infrastructure even when you are working with a clustered environment.

This section contains the following chapters:

- Chapter 5, *Consuming and Creating Modules*
- Chapter 6, *Consuming and Creating Plugins*
- Chapter 7, *Coding Best Practices*
- Chapter 8, *Advanced Ansible Topics*

Consuming and Creating Modules

5

Throughout this book, we have almost constantly referred to and made use of Ansible modules. We have treated these as "black boxes" – that is to say, we have just accepted that they exist and that they will work in a certain documented manner. However, one of the many great things about Ansible is that it is an open source product, and as such, not only can you view and modify its source code, but you can also write your own additions. To date, there are literally thousands of modules available for Ansible, handling everything from simple commands such as copying files and installing packages, through to configuring highly complex and bespoke networking equipment. This large array of modules has grown out of a genuine need to solve problems with Ansible, and the number included with each release of Ansible increases every time.

Sooner or later, you will come across a specific piece of functionality that doesn't exist in any of the current Ansible modules. Of course, you could attempt to fill this gap in functionally, either by writing your own module or by contributing enhancements to one of the existing modules back to the Ansible project for everyone else to benefit from. In this chapter, you will learn the basics of creating your own modules, as well as how to contribute your code back to the upstream Ansible project if you wish.

Specifically, in this chapter, you will cover the following topics:

- Executing multiple modules using the command line
- Reviewing the module index
- Accessing module documentation from the command line
- Module return values
- Developing custom modules

Let's get started!

Technical requirements

This chapter assumes that you have set up your control host with Ansible, as detailed in `Chapter 1`, *Getting Started with Ansible,* and are using the most recent version available – the examples in this chapter were tested with Ansible 2.9. This chapter also assumes that you have at least one additional host to test against. Ideally, this should be Linux-based. Although we will give specific examples of hostnames in this chapter, you are free to substitute them with your own hostname and/or IP addresses. Details of how to do this will be provided in the appropriate places.

The module development work that will be covered in this chapter assumes the presence of a Python 2 or Python 3 development environment on your computer and that you are running either Linux, FreeBSD, or macOS. Where additional Python modules are needed, their installation is documented. The task of building module documentation has some very specific requirements around Python 3.5 or later, so you will need to install a suitable Python environment if you wish to attempt this.

The code bundle for this chapter is available here: `https://github.com/PacktPublishing/Ansible-2-Cookbook/tree/master/Chapter%205`.

Executing multiple modules using the command line

As this chapter is all about modules and how to create them, let's recap how to use modules. We've done this throughout this book, but we have not drawn attention to some of the specifics related to how they work. One of the key things we have not discussed is how the Ansible engine talks to its modules and vice versa, so let's explore this now.

As ever, when working with Ansible commands, we need an inventory to run our commands against. For this chapter, as our focus is on the modules themselves, we will use a very simple and small inventory, as shown here:

```
[frontends]
frt01.example.com

[appservers]
app01.example.com
```

Now, for the first part of our recap, you can run a module very easily via an ad hoc command and use the $-m$ switch to tell Ansible which module you want to run. Hence, one of the simplest commands you can run is the Ansible `ping` command, as shown here:

```
$ ansible -i hosts appservers -m ping
```

Now, one thing we have not previously looked at is the communication between Ansible and its modules; however, let's examine the output of the preceding command:

```
$ ansible -i hosts appservers -m ping
app01.example.com | SUCCESS => {
    "ansible_facts": {
        "discovered_interpreter_python": "/usr/bin/python"
    },
    "changed": false,
    "ping": "pong"
}
```

Did you notice the structure of the output – the curly braces, colons, and commas? Yes, Ansible uses JSON-formatted data to talk to its modules, and the modules report their data back to Ansible in JSON as well. The preceding output is, in fact, a subset of the JSON-formatted data returned to the Ansible engine by the `ping` module.

Of course, we never have to worry about this as we work with the modules using either `key=value` pairs on the command line or YAML in playbooks and roles. Hence, the JSON is shielded from us, but this is an important fact to bear in mind as we head into the world of module development later in this chapter.

Ansible modules are just like functions in a high-level programming language, in that they take a well-defined list of arguments as input, perform their function, and then provide a set of output data, which is also well-defined and documented. We'll look at this in more detail later in this chapter. Of course, the preceding command didn't include any arguments, so this was the simplest possible invocation of a module via Ansible.

Now, let's run another command that takes an argument and passes that data to the module:

```
$ ansible -i hosts appservers -m command -a "/bin/echo 'hello modules'"
```

In this case, we provided a single string as an argument to the command module, which Ansible, in turn, converts into JSON and passes down to the command module when it's invoked. When you run this ad hoc command, you will see an output similar to the following:

```
$  ansible -i hosts appservers -m command -a "/bin/echo 'hello modules'"
app01.example.com | CHANGED | rc=0 >>
hello modules
```

In this instance, the output data does not appear to be JSON formatted; however, what Ansible prints to the Terminal when you run a module is only a subset of the data that each module returns – for example, both the CHANGED status and rc=0 exit code from our command were passed back to Ansible in a JSON-formatted data structure – this was just hidden from us.

This point doesn't need to be labored too much, but it is important to set a context. It is this context that we shall build upon throughout this chapter, so simply remember these key points:

- Communication between Ansible and its modules is done through JSON-formatted data structures.
- Modules take input data that controls how they function (arguments).
- Modules always return data – at the very least, the status of the module's execution (for example, changed, ok, or failed).

Of course, before you start coding your own modules, it makes sense to check whether a module that can perform all (or some) of the functionality you need already exists. We will explore this in the next section.

Reviewing the module index

As discussed in the preceding section, Ansible provides thousands of modules to make it fast and easy to develop playbooks and run them across multiple host machines. How do you go about finding the right module to begin with, though, when there are so many? Fortunately, the Ansible documentation features a well-organized, categorized list of modules that you can consult to find your desired module – this is available here: https://docs.ansible.com/ansible/latest/modules/modules_by_category.html.

Let's suppose you want to see whether there is a native Ansible module that can help you configure and manage your Amazon Web Services S3 buckets. That's a fairly precise, well-defined need, so let's approach this in a logical manner:

1. Begin by opening the categorized module index in your web browser, as discussed previously:

   `https://docs.ansible.com/ansible/latest/modules/modules_by_category.html`

2. Now, we know that Amazon Web Services is almost certainly going to feature in the `Cloud` modules category, so let's open that in our browser.

3. There are still hundreds, if not thousands, of modules listed on this page! So, let's use the **Find** function (*Ctrl + F*) in the browser to see whether the `s3` keyword appears anywhere:

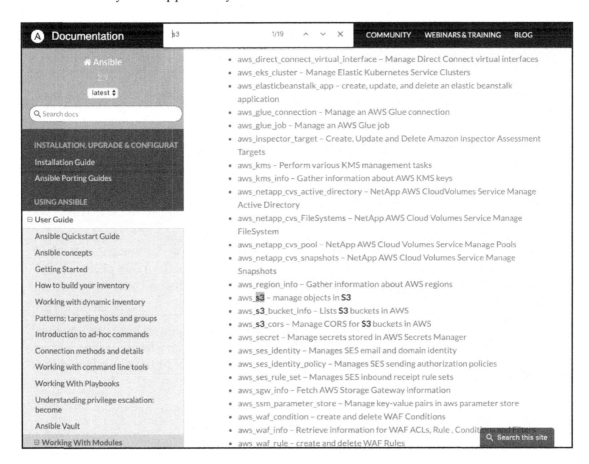

We're in luck – it does, and there are several more listings further down the page:

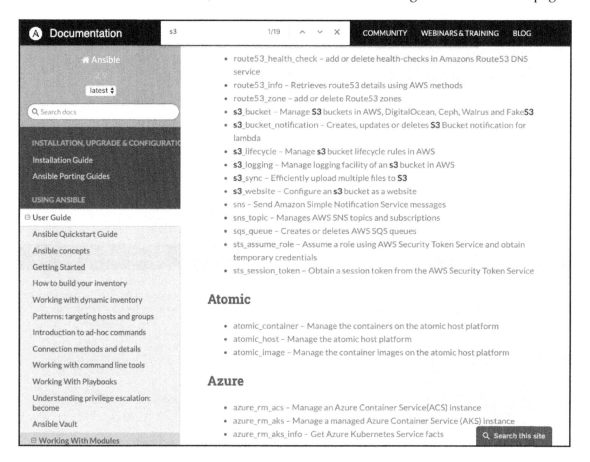

We now have a shortlist of modules to work with – granted, there are several, so we still need to work out which one (or ones) we will need for our playbook. As shown from the preceding short descriptions, this will depend on what your intended task is.

4. The short descriptions should be enough to give you some clues about whether the module will suit your needs or not. Once you have an idea, you can click on the appropriate document links to view more details about the module and how to work with it:

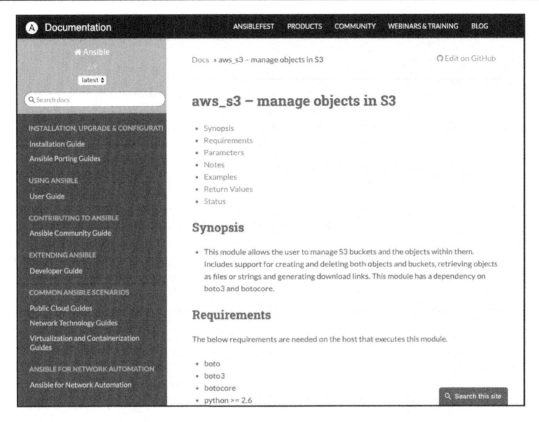

As you can see, the documentation page for each module provides a great deal of information, including a longer description. If you scroll down the page, you will see a list of the possible arguments that you can provide the module with, some practical examples of how to use them, and some details about the outputs from the module. Also, note the **Requirements** section in the preceding screenshot – some modules, especially cloud-related ones, require additional Python modules before they will work, and if you attempt to run the `aws_s3` module from a playbook without installing the `boto`, `boto3`, and `botocore` modules on Python 2.6 or later, you will simply receive an error.

All modules must have documentation like this created before they will be accepted as part of the Ansible project, so you must keep this in mind if you intend to submit your own modules. This is also one of the reasons for Ansible's popularity – with easy-to-maintain and well-documented standards, it is the perfect community platform for automation. The official Ansible website isn't the only place you can obtain documentation, however, as it is even available on the command line. We shall look at how to retrieve documentation via this route in the next section.

Accessing module documentation from the command line

As discussed in the preceding section, the Ansible project prides itself on its documentation, and making this documentation readily accessible is an important part of the project itself. Now, suppose you are working on an Ansible task (in a playbook, role, or even an ad hoc command) and you are in a data center environment where you only have access to the shell of the machine you are working on. How would you get access to the Ansible documentation?

Fortunately, part of the Ansible installation that we have not discussed yet is the `ansible-doc` tool, which is installed as standard along with the familiar `ansible` and `ansible-playbook` executables. The `ansible-doc` command includes a complete (text-based) library of documentation for all the modules that ship with the version of Ansible you have installed. This means that the very information you need in order to work with modules is at your fingertips, even if you are in the middle of a data center and without a working internet connection!

The following are some examples to show you how to interact with the `ansible-doc` tool:

- You can list all of the modules that there's documentation for on your Ansible control machine by simply issuing the following command:

```
$ ansible-doc -l
```

You should see an output similar to the following:

```
fortios_router_community_list          Configure community lists in
Fortinet's FortiOS ...
azure_rm_devtestlab_info               Get Azure DevTest Lab facts
ecs_taskdefinition                     register a task definition
in ecs
avi_alertscriptconfig                  Module for setup of
AlertScriptConfig Avi RESTfu...
tower_receive                          Receive assets from Ansible
Tower
netapp_e_iscsi_target                  NetApp E-Series manage iSCSI
target configuratio...
azure_rm_acs                           Manage an Azure Container
Service(ACS) instance
fortios_log_syslogd2_filter            Filters for remote system
server in Fortinet's F...
junos_rpc                              Runs an arbitrary RPC over
NetConf on an Juniper...
```

```
na_elementsw_vlan                         NetApp Element Software
Manage VLAN
pn_ospf                                   CLI command to add/remove
ospf protocol to a vRo...
pn_snmp_vacm                              CLI command to
create/modify/delete snmp-vacm
cp_mgmt_service_sctp                      Manages service-sctp objects
on Check Point over...
onyx_ospf                                 Manage OSPF protocol on
Mellanox ONYX network de.
```

There are many pages of output, which just shows you how many modules there are! In fact, you can count them:

```
$ ansible-doc -l | wc -l
3387
```

That's right – 3,387 modules ship with Ansible 2.9.6!

- As before, you can search for specific modules using your favorite shell tools to process the index; for example, you could grep for s3 to find all of the S3-related modules, as we did interactively in the web browser in the previous section:

```
$ ansible-doc -l | grep s3
s3_bucket_notification                    Creates, upda...
purefb_s3user                             Create or del...
purefb_s3acc                              Create or del...
aws_s3_cors                               Manage CORS f...
s3_sync                                   Efficiently u...
s3_logging                                Manage loggin...
s3_website                                Configure an ...
s3_bucket                                 Manage S3 buc...
s3_lifecycle                              Manage s3 buc...
aws_s3_bucket_info                        Lists S3 buck...
aws_s3                                    manage object...
```

- Now, we can easily look up the specific documentation for the module that interests us. Say we want to learn more about the aws_s3 module – just as we did on the website, simply run the following:

```
$ ansible-doc aws_s3
```

This should produce an output similar to the following:

```
$ ansible-doc aws_s3
> AWS_S3 (/usr/lib/python2.7/site-
packages/ansible/modules/cloud/amazon/aws_s
```

```
                    This module allows the user to manage S3 buckets and the
                    objects within them. Includes support for creating and
                    deleting both objects and buckets, retrieving objects as
       files
                    or strings and generating download links. This module has a
                    dependency on boto3 and botocore.

                 * This module is maintained by The Ansible Core Team
                 * note: This module has a corresponding action plugin.

       OPTIONS (= is mandatory):

       - aws_access_key
                    AWS access key id. If not set then the value of the
                    AWS_ACCESS_KEY environment variable is used.
                    (Aliases: ec2_access_key, access_key)[Default: (null)]
                    type: str
       ....
```

Although the formatting is somewhat different, `ansible-doc` tells us about the module, provides a list of all of the arguments (`OPTIONS`) that we can pass it, and as we scroll down, even gives some working examples and possible return values. We shall explore the topic of return values in the next section as they are important to understand, especially as we approach the topic of developing our own modules.

Module return values

As we discussed earlier in this chapter, Ansible modules return their results as structured data, formatted behind the scenes in JSON. You came across this return data in the previous example, both in the form of exit code and where we used the `register` keyword to capture the results of a task in an Ansible variable. In this section, we shall explore how to discover the return values for an Ansible module so that we can work with them later on in a playbook, for example, with conditional processing (see Chapter 4, *Playbooks and Roles*).

Due to conserving space, we shall choose what is perhaps one of the simplest Ansible modules to work with when it comes to return values – the `ping` module.

Without further ado, let's use the `ansible-doc` tool that we learned about in the previous section and see what this says about the return values for this module:

```
$ ansible-doc ping
```

If you scroll to the bottom of the output from the preceding command, you should see something like this:

```
$ ansible-doc ping
...

RETURN VALUES:

ping:
    description: value provided with the data parameter
    returned: success
    type: str
    sample: pong
```

Hence, we can see that the `ping` module will only return one value, and that is called `ping`. `description` tells us what we should expect this particular return value to contain, while the `returned` field tells us that it will only be returned on `success` (if it would be returned on other conditions, these would be listed here). The `type` return value is a string (denoted by `str`), and although you can change the value with an argument provided to the `ping` module, the default return value (and hence `sample`) is `pong`.

Now, let's see what that looks like in practice. For example, there's nothing contained in those return values that would tell us whether the module ran successfully and whether anything was changed; however, we know that these are fundamental pieces of information about every module run.

Let's put a very simple playbook together. We're going to run the `ping` module with no arguments, capture the return values using the `register` keyword, and then use the `debug` module to dump the return values onto the Terminal:

```
---
- name: Simple play to demonstrate a return value
  hosts: localhost

  tasks:
    - name: Perform a simple module based task
      ping:
      register: pingresult

    - name: Display the result
      debug:
        var: pingresult
```

Now, let's see what happens when we run this playbook:

```
$ ansible-playbook retval.yml
[WARNING]: provided hosts list is empty, only localhost is available. Note
that
the implicit localhost does not match 'all'

PLAY [Simple play to demonstrate a return value]
*******************************

TASK [Gathering Facts]
**********************************************************
ok: [localhost]

TASK [Perform a simple module based task]
*************************************
ok: [localhost]

TASK [Display the result]
*****************************************************
ok: [localhost] => {
    "pingresult": {
        "changed": false,
        "failed": false,
        "ping": "pong"
    }
}

PLAY RECAP
*******************************************************************
localhost : ok=3 changed=0 unreachable=0 failed=0 skipped=0 rescued=0
ignored=0
```

Notice that the ping module does indeed return a value called ping, which contains the pong string (as the ping was successful). However, you can see that there are, in fact, two additional return values that were not listed in the Ansible documentation. These accompany every single task run, and are hence implicit – that is to say, you can assume they will be among the data that's returned from every module. The changed return value will be set to true if the module run resulted in a change on the target host, while the failed return value will be set to true if the module run failed for some reason.

Using the debug module to print the output from a module run is an incredibly useful trick if you want to gather more information about a module, how it works, and what sort of data is returned. At this point, we've covered just about all of the fundamentals of working with modules, so in the next section, we'll make a start on developing our very own (simple) module.

Developing custom modules

Now that we're familiar with modules, how to call them, how to interpret their results, and how to find documentation on them, we can make a start on writing our own simple module. Although this will not include the deep and intricate functionality of many of the modules that ship with Ansible, it is hoped that this will give you enough information to proceed with confidence when you build out your own, more complex, ones.

One important point to note is that Ansible is written in Python, and as such, so are its modules. As a result, you will need to write your module in Python, and to get started with developing your own module, you will need to make sure you have Python and a few essential tools installed. If you are already running Ansible on your development machine, you probably have the required packages installed, but if you are starting from scratch, you will need to install Python, the Python package manager (`pip`), and perhaps some other development packages. The exact process will vary widely between operating systems, but here are some examples to get you started:

- On Fedora, you would run the following command to install the required packages:

  ```
  $ sudo dnf install python python-devel
  ```

- Similarly, on CentOS, you would run the following command to install the required packages:

  ```
  $ sudo yum install python python-devel
  ```

- On Ubuntu, you would run the following commands to install the packages you need:

  ```
  $ sudo apt-get update
  $ sudo apt-get install python-pip python-dev build-essential
  ```

- If you are working on macOS and are using the Homebrew packaging system, the following command will install the packages you need:

  ```
  $ sudo brew install python
  ```

Once you have the required packages installed, you will need to clone the Ansible Git repository to your local machine as there are some valuable scripts in there that we will need later on in the module development process. Use the following command to clone the Ansible repository to your current directory on your development machine:

```
$ git clone https://github.com/ansible/ansible.git
```

Finally (although optionally), it is good practice to develop your Ansible modules in a virtual environment (`venv`) as this means any Python packages you need to install go in here, rather than in with your global system Python modules. Installing modules for the entire system in an uncontrolled manner can, at times, cause compatibility issues or even break local tools, and so although this is not a required step, it is highly recommended.

The exact command to create a virtual environment for your Python module development work will depend on both the operating system you are running and the version of Python you are using. You should refer to the documentation for your Linux distribution for more information; however, the following commands were tested on CentOS 7.7 with the default Python 2.7.5 to create a virtual environment called `moduledev` inside the Ansible source code directory you just cloned from GitHub:

```
$ cd ansible
$  python -m virtualenv moduledev
New python executable in /home/james/ansible/moduledev/bin/python
Installing setuptools, pip, wheel...done.
```

With our development environment set up, let's start writing our first module. This module will be very simple as it's beyond the scope of this book to provide an in-depth discussion around how to write large amounts of Python code. However, we will code something that can use a function from a Python library to copy a file locally on the target machine.

Obviously, this overlaps heavily with existing module functionality, but it will serve as a nice concise example of how to write a simple Python program in a manner that allows Ansible to make use of it as a module. Now, let's start coding our first module:

1. In your preferred editor, create a new file called (for example) `remote_filecopy.py`:

   ```
   $ vi remote_filecopy.py
   ```

2. Start with a shebang to indicate that this module should be executed with Python:

   ```
   #!/usr/bin/python
   ```

3. Although not mandatory, it is good practice to add copyright information, as well as your details, in the headers of your new module. By doing this, anyone using it will understand the terms under which they can use, modify, or redistribute it. The text given here is merely an example; you should investigate the various appropriate licenses for yourself and determine which is the best for your module:

```
# Copyright: (c) 2018, Jesse Keating <jesse.keating@example.org>
# GNU General Public License v3.0+ (see COPYING or
https://www.gnu.org/licenses/gpl-3.0.txt)
```

4. It is also good practice to add an Ansible metadata section that includes `metadata_version`, `status`, and `supported_by` information immediately after the copyright section. Note that the `metadata_version` field represents the Ansible metadata version (which, at the time of writing, should be `1.1`) and is not related to the version of your module, nor the Ansible version you are using. The values suggested in the following code will be fine for just getting started, but if your module gets accepted into the official Ansible source code, they are likely to change:

```
ANSIBLE_METADATA = {'metadata_version': '1.1',
                    'status': ['preview'],
                    'supported_by': 'community'}
```

5. Remember `ansible-doc` and that excellent documentation that is available on the Ansible documentation website? That all gets automatically generated from special sections you add to this file. Let's get started by adding the following code to our module:

```
DOCUMENTATION = '''
---
module: remote_filecopy
version_added: "2.9"
short_description: Copy a file on the remote host
description:
  - The remote_copy module copies a file on the remote host from a
given source to a provided destination.
options:
  source:
    description:
      - Path to a file on the source file on the remote host
    required: True
  dest:
    description:
      - Path to the destination on the remote host for the copy
```

```
        required: True
author:
- Jesse Keating (@omgjlk)
'''
```

Pay particular attention to the `author` dictionary – to pass the syntax checks for inclusion in the official Ansible codebase, the author's name should be appended with their GitHub ID in brackets. If you don't do this, your module will still work, but it won't pass the test we'll perform later.

 Notice how the documentation is in YAML format, enclosed between triple single quotes? The fields listed should be common to just about all modules, but naturally, if your module takes different options, you would specify these so that they match your module.

6. The examples that you will find in the documentation are also generated from this file – they have their own special documentation section immediately after `DOCUMENTATION` and should provide practical examples on how you might create a task using your module, as shown in the following example:

```
EXAMPLES = '''
    # Example from Ansible Playbooks
    - name: backup a config file
      remote_copy:
        source: /etc/herp/derp.conf
        dest: /root/herp-derp.conf.bak
'''
```

7. The data that's returned by your module to Ansible should also be documented in its own section. Our example module will return the following values:

```
RETURN = '''
source:
  description: source file used for the copy
  returned: success
  type: str
  sample: "/path/to/file.name"
dest:
  description: destination of the copy
  returned: success
  type: str
  sample: "/path/to/destination.file"
gid:
  description: group ID of destination target
  returned: success
  type: int
```

```
      sample: 502
  group:
    description: group name of destination target
    returned: success
    type: str
    sample: "users"
  uid:
    description: owner ID of destination target
    returned: success
    type: int
    sample: 502
  owner:
    description: owner name of destination target
    returned: success
    type: str
    sample: "fred"
  mode:
    description: permissions of the destination target
    returned: success
    type: int
    sample: 0644
  size:
    description: size of destination target
    returned: success
    type: int
    sample: 20
  state:
    description: state of destination target
    returned: success
    type: str
    sample: "file"
  '''
```

8. Immediately after we have finished our documentation section, we should import any Python modules we're going to use. Here, we will include the shutil module, which will be used to perform our file copy:

```
import shutil
```

9. Now that we've built up the module headers and documentation, we can actually start working on the code. Now, you can see just how much effort goes into the documentation of every single Ansible module! Our module should start by defining a `main` function, in which we will create an object of the `AnsibleModule` type and use an `argument_spec` dictionary to obtain the options that the module was called with:

```
def main():
    module = AnsibleModule(
        argument_spec = dict(
            source=dict(required=True, type='str'),
            dest=dict(required=True, type='str')
        )
    )
```

10. At this stage, we have everything we need to write our module's functional code – even the options that it was called with. Hence, we can use the Python `shutil` module to perform the local file copy, based on the arguments provided:

```
shutil.copy(module.params['source'],
            module.params['dest'])
```

11. At this point, we've executed the task our module was designed to complete. However, it is fair to say that we're not done yet – we need to exit the module cleanly and provide our return values to Ansible. Normally, at this point, you would write some conditional logic to detect whether the module was successful and whether it actually performed a change on the target host or not. However, for simplicity, we'll simply exit with the `changed` status every time – expanding this logic and making the return status more meaningful is left as an exercise for you:

```
module.exit_json(changed=True)
```

The `module.exit_json` method comes from `AnsibleModule`, which we created earlier – remember, we said it was important to know that data was passed back and forth using JSON!

12. As we approach the end of our module code, we must now tell Python where it can import the `AnsibleModule` object from. This can be done with the following line of code:

```
from ansible.module_utils.basic import *
```

13. Now for the final two lines of code for the module – this is where we tell the module that it should be running the `main` function when it starts:

```
if __name__ == '__main__':
    main()
```

That's it – with a series of well-documented steps, you can write your own Ansible modules in Python. The next step is, of course, to test it, and before we actually test it in Ansible, let's see whether we can run it manually in the shell. Of course, to make the module think it is being run within Ansible, we must generate some arguments in – you guessed it – JSON format. Create a file with the following contents to provide the arguments:

```
{
    "ANSIBLE_MODULE_ARGS": {
        "source": "/tmp/foo",
        "dest": "/tmp/bar"
    }
}
```

Armed with this little snippet of JSON, you can execute your module directly with Python. If you haven't already done so, you'll need to set up your Ansible development environment as follows. Note that we also manually create the source file, /tmp/foo, so that our module can really perform the file copy:

```
$ touch /tmp/foo
$ . moduledev/bin/activate
(moduledev) $ . hacking/env-setup
running egg_info
creating lib/ansible_base.egg-info
writing requirements to lib/ansible_base.egg-info/requires.txt
writing lib/ansible_base.egg-info/PKG-INFO
writing top-level names to lib/ansible_base.egg-info/top_level.txt
writing dependency_links to lib/ansible_base.egg-info/dependency_links.txt
writing manifest file 'lib/ansible_base.egg-info/SOURCES.txt'
reading manifest file 'lib/ansible_base.egg-info/SOURCES.txt'
reading manifest template 'MANIFEST.in'
warning: no files found matching 'SYMLINK_CACHE.json'
warning: no previously-included files found matching
'docs/docsite/rst_warnings'
warning: no previously-included files matching '*' found under directory
'docs/docsite/_build'
warning: no previously-included files matching '*.pyc' found under
directory 'docs/docsite/_extensions'
warning: no previously-included files matching '*.pyo' found under
directory 'docs/docsite/_extensions'
warning: no files found matching '*.ps1' under directory
'lib/ansible/modules/windows'
```

```
warning: no files found matching '*.psm1' under directory 'test/support'
writing manifest file 'lib/ansible_base.egg-info/SOURCES.txt'

Setting up Ansible to run out of checkout...

PATH=/home/james/ansible/bin:/home/james/ansible/moduledev/bin:/usr/local/s
bin:/usr/local/bin:/usr/sbin:/usr/bin:/home/james/bin
PYTHONPATH=/home/james/ansible/lib
MANPATH=/home/james/ansible/docs/man:/usr/local/share/man:/usr/share/man

Remember, you may wish to specify your host file with -i

Done!
```

Now, you're finally ready to run your module for the first time. You can do this as follows:

```
(moduledev) $ python remote_filecopy.py args.json
{"invocation": {"module_args": {"dest": "/tmp/bar", "source": "/tmp/foo"}},
"changed": true}

(moduledev) $ ls -l /tmp/bar
-rw-r--r-- 1 root root 0 Apr 16 16:24 /tmp/bar
```

Success! Your module works – and it both ingests and produces JSON data, as we discussed earlier in this chapter. Of course, there's much more to add to your module – we've not addressed `failed` or `ok` returns from the module, nor does it support check mode. However, we're off to a flying start, and if you want to learn more about Ansible modules and fleshing out your functionality, you can find more details here: https://docs.ansible.com/ansible/latest/dev_guide/developing_modules_general.html.

Note that when it comes to testing your module, creating arguments in a JSON file is hardly intuitive, although, as we have seen, it does work well. Luckily for us, it is easy to run our Ansible module in a playbook! By default, Ansible will check the playbook directory for a subdirectory called `library/` and will run referenced modules from here. Hence, we might create the following:

```
$ cd ~
$ mkdir testplaybook
$ cd testplaybook
$ mkdir library
$ cp ~/ansible/moduledev/remote_filecopy.py library/
```

Now, create a simple inventory file in this playbook directory, just as we did previously, and add a playbook with the following contents:

```
---
- name: Playbook to test custom module
  hosts: all

  tasks:
    - name: Test the custom module
      remote_filecopy:
        source: /tmp/foo
        dest: /tmp/bar
      register: testresult

    - name: Print the test result data
      debug:
        var: testresult
```

For the purposes of clarity, your final directory structure should look like this:

```
testplaybook
├── hosts
├── library
│   └── remote_filecopy.py
└── testplaybook.yml
```

Now, try running the playbook in the usual manner and see what happens:

```
$ ansible-playbook -i hosts testplaybook.yml

PLAY [Playbook to test custom module]
******************************************

TASK [Gathering Facts]
***********************************************************
ok: [frt01.example.com]
ok: [app01.example.com]

TASK [Test the custom module]
****************************************************
changed: [app01.example.com]
changed: [frt01.example.com]

TASK [Print the test result data]
************************************************
ok: [app01.example.com] => {
    "testresult": {
        "changed": true,
```

```
                "failed": false
        }
    }
    ok: [frt01.example.com] => {
        "testresult": {
            "changed": true,
            "failed": false
        }
    }

    PLAY RECAP
    ************************************************************************
    app01.example.com : ok=3 changed=1 unreachable=0 failed=0 skipped=0
    rescued=0 ignored=0
    frt01.example.com : ok=3 changed=1 unreachable=0 failed=0 skipped=0
    rescued=0 ignored=0
```

Success! Not only have you tested your Python code locally, but you have also successfully run it on two remote servers in an Ansible playbook. That was really easy, which just proves how straightforward it is to get started expanding your Ansible modules to meet your own bespoke needs.

Despite the success of running this piece of code, we've not checked the documentation yet, nor tested its operation from Ansible. Before we address these issues in more detail, in the next section, we'll take a look at some of the common pitfalls of module development and how to avoid them.

Avoiding common pitfalls

It is vital that your modules are well thought out and handle error conditions gracefully – people are going to rely on your module someday to automate a task on perhaps thousands of servers, and so the last thing they want is to spend significant amounts of time debugging errors, especially trivial ones that could have been trapped or handled gracefully. In this section, we'll look specifically at error handling and ways to do this so that playbooks will still run and exit gracefully.

One piece of overall guidance before we get started is that just like documentation receives a high degree of attention in Ansible, so should your error messages. They should be meaningful and easy to interpret, and you should steer clear of meaningless strings such as Error!.

So, right now, if we remove the source file that we're attempting to copy and then rerun our module with the same arguments, I think you'll agree that the output is neither pretty nor meaningful, unless you happen to be a hardened Python developer:

```
(moduledev) $ rm -f /tmp/foo
(moduledev) $ python remote_filecopy.py args.json
Traceback (most recent call last):
  File "remote_filecopy.py", line 99, in <module>
    main()
  File "remote_filecopy.py", line 93, in main
    module.params['dest'])
  File "/usr/lib64/python2.7/shutil.py", line 119, in copy
    copyfile(src, dst)
  File "/usr/lib64/python2.7/shutil.py", line 82, in copyfile
    with open(src, 'rb') as fsrc:
IOError: [Errno 2] No such file or directory: '/tmp/foo'
```

We can, without a doubt, do better. Let's make a copy of our module and add a little code to it. First of all, replace the shutil.copy lines of code with the following:

```
try:
    shutil.copy(module.params['source'], module.params['dest'])
except:
    module.fail_json(msg="Failed to copy file")
```

This is some incredibly basic exception handling in Python, but what it does is allow the code to try the shutil.copy task. However, if this fails and an exception is raised, rather than exiting with a traceback, we exit cleanly using the module.fail_json call. This will tell Ansible that the module failed and cleanly sends a JSON-formatted error message back. Naturally, we could do a lot to improve the error message; for example, we could obtain the exact error message from the shutil module and pass it back to Ansible, but again, this is left as an exercise for you to complete.

Now, when we try and run the module with a non-existent source file, we will see the following cleanly formatted JSON output:

```
(moduledev) $ rm -f /tmp/foo
(moduledev) $ python better_remote_filecopy.py args.json

{"msg": "Failed to copy file", "failed": true, "invocation":
{"module_args": {"dest": "/tmp/bar", "source": "/tmp/foo"}}}
```

However, the module still works in the same manner as before if the copy succeeds:

```
(moduledev) $ touch /tmp/foo
(moduledev) $ python better_remote_filecopy.py args.json

{"invocation": {"module_args": {"dest": "/tmp/bar", "source": "/tmp/foo"}},
"changed": true}
```

With this simple change to our code, we can now cleanly and gracefully handle the failure of the file copy operation and report something more meaningful back to the user rather than using a traceback. Some additional pointers for exception handling and processing in your modules are as follows:

- Fail quickly – don't attempt to keep processing after an error.
- Return the most meaningful possible error messages using the various module JSON return functions.
- Never return a traceback if there's any way you can avoid it.
- Try making errors meaningful in the context of the module and what it does (for example, for our module, `File copy error` is more meaningful than `File error` – and I think you'll easily come up with even better error messages).
- Don't bombard the user with errors; instead, try to focus on reporting the most meaningful ones, especially when your module code is complex.

That completes our brief yet practical look at error handling in Ansible modules. In the next section, we shall return to the documentation we included in our module, including how to build it into HTML documentation so that it can go on the Ansible website (and indeed, if your module gets accepted into the Ansible source code, this is exactly how the web documentation will be generated).

Testing and documenting your module

We have already put a great deal of work into documenting our module, as we discussed earlier in this chapter. However, how can we see it, and how can we check that it compiles correctly into the HTML that would go on the Ansible website if it were accepted as part of the Ansible source code?

Before we get into actually viewing our documentation, we should make use of a tool called `ansible-test`, which was newly added in the 2.9 release. This tool can perform a sanity check on our module code to ensure that our documentation meets all the standards required by the Ansible project team and that the code is structured correctly (for example, the Python `import` statements should always come after the documentation blocks). Let's get started:

1. To run the sanity tests, assuming you have cloned the official repository, change into this directory and set up your environment. Note that if your standard Python binary isn't Python 3, the `ansible-test` tool will not run, so you should ensure Python 3 is installed and, if necessary, set up a virtual environment to ensure you are using Python 3. This can be done as follows:

```
$ cd ansible$ python 3 -m venv venv
$ . venv/bin/activate
(venv) $ source hacking/env-setup
running egg_info
creating lib/ansible.egg-info
writing lib/ansible.egg-info/PKG-INFO
writing dependency_links to lib/ansible.egg-info/dependency_links.txt
writing requirements to lib/ansible.egg-info/requires.txt
writing top-level names to lib/ansible.egg-info/top_level.txt
writing manifest file 'lib/ansible.egg-info/SOURCES.txt'
reading manifest file 'lib/ansible.egg-info/SOURCES.txt'
reading manifest template 'MANIFEST.in'
warning: no files found matching 'SYMLINK_CACHE.json'
writing manifest file 'lib/ansible.egg-info/SOURCES.txt'

Setting up Ansible to run out of checkout...

PATH=/home/james/ansible/bin:/home/james/ansible/venv/bin:/usr/local/sbin:/usr/local/bin:/usr/sbin:/usr/bin:/home/james/bin
PYTHONPATH=/home/james/ansible/lib
MANPATH=/home/james/ansible/docs/man:/usr/local/share/man:/usr/share/man

Remember, you may wish to specify your host file with -i

Done!
```

2. Next, use `pip` to install the Python requirements so that you can run the `ansible-test` tool:

```
(venv) $ pip install -r test/runner/requirements/sanity.txt
```

3. Now, provided you have copied your module code into the appropriate location in the source tree (an example copy command is shown here), you can run the sanity tests as follows:

```
(venv) $ cp ~/moduledev/remote_filecopy.py
./lib/ansible/modules/files/
(venv) $ ansible-test sanity --test validate-modules
remote_filecopy
Sanity check using validate-modules
WARNING: Cannot perform module comparison against the base branch.
Base branch not detected when running locally.
WARNING: Reviewing previous 1 warning(s):
WARNING: Cannot perform module comparison against the base branch.
Base branch not detected when running locally.
```

From the preceding output, you can see that apart from one warning related to us not having a base branch to compare against, the module code that we developed earlier in this chapter has passed all the tests. If you had an issue with the documentation (for example, the author name format was incorrect), this would be given as an error.

Now that we have passed the sanity checks with `ansible-test`, let's see whether the documentation looks right by using the `ansible-doc` command. This is very easy to do. First of all, exit your virtual environment, if you are still in it, and change to the Ansible source code directory you cloned from GitHub earlier. Now, you can manually tell `ansible-doc` where to look for modules instead of the default path. This means that you could run the following:

```
$ cd ~/ansible
$ ansible-doc -M moduledev/ remote_filecopy
```

You should be presented with the textual rendering of the documentation we created earlier – an example of the first page is shown here to give you an idea of how it should look:

```
> REMOTE_FILECOPY (/home/james/ansible/moduledev/remote_filecopy.py)

        The remote_copy module copies a file on the remote host from a
        given source to a provided destination.

  * This module is maintained by The Ansible Community
OPTIONS (= is mandatory):

= dest
        Path to the destination on the remote host for the copy
```

```
= source
        Path to a file on the source file on the remote host
```

Excellent! So, we can already access our module documentation using `ansible-doc` and indeed confirm that it renders correctly in text mode. However, how do we go about building the HTML version? Fortunately, there is a well-defined process for this, which we shall outline here:

1. Under `lib/ansible/modules/`, you will find a series of categorized directories that modules are placed under – ours fits best under the `files` category, so copy it to this location in preparation for the build process to come:

   ```
   $ cp moduledev/remote_filecopy.py lib/ansible/modules/files/
   ```

2. Change to the `docs/docsite/` directory as the next step in the documentation creation process:

   ```
   $ cd docs/docsite/
   ```

3. Build a documentation-based Python file. Use the following command to do so:

   ```
   $ MODULES=hello_module make webdocs
   ```

   Now, in theory, making the Ansible documentation should be this simple; however, unfortunately, at the time of writing, the source code for Ansible v2.9.6 refuses to build `webdocs`. This will no doubt be fixed in due course as, at the time of writing, the documentation build scripts are being ported to Python 3. To get the `make webdocs` command to run at all, I had to clone the source code for Ansible v2.8.10 as a starting point.

   Even in this environment, on CentOS 7, the `make webdocs` command fails unless you have some very specific Python 3 requirements in place. These are not well-documented, but from testing, I can tell you that Sphinx v2.4.4 works. The version supplied with CentOS 7 is too old and fails, while the newest version available from the Python module repositories (v3.0.1, at the time of writing) is not compatible with the build process and fails.

Once I'd started working from the Ansible v2.8.10 source tree, I had to make sure I had removed any preexisting `sphinx` modules from my Python 3 environment (you need Python 3.5 or above to build the documentation locally – if you don't have this installed on your node, please do this before proceeding) and then ran the following commands:

```
$ pip3 uninstall sphinx
$ pip3 install sphinx==2.4.4
$ pip3 install sphinx-notfound-page
```

With this in place, you will be able to successfully run `make webdocs` to build your documentation. You will see pages of output. A successful run should end with something like the output shown here:

```
generating indices... genindex py-modindexdone
writing additional pages...
search/home/james/ansible/docs/docsite/_themes/sphinx_rtd_theme/sea
rch.html:21: RemovedInSphinx30Warning: To modify script_files in
the theme is deprecated. Please insert a <script> tag directly in
your theme instead.
  {% endblock %}
 opensearchdone
copying images... [100%]
dev_guide/style_guide/images/thenvsthan.jpg
copying downloadable files... [ 50%]
network/getting_started/sample_files/first_copying downloadable
files... [100%]
network/getting_started/sample_files/first_playbook_ext.yml
copying static files... ... done
copying extra files... done
dumping search index in English (code: en)... done
dumping object inventory... done
build succeeded, 35 warnings.

The HTML pages are in _build/html.
make[1]: Leaving directory `/home/james/ansible/docs/docsite'
```

Now, notice how, at the end of this process, the `make` command tells us where to look for the compiled documentation. If you look in here, you will find the following:

```
$ find /home/james/ansible/docs/docsite -name remote_filecopy*
/home/james/ansible/docs/docsite/rst/modules/remote_filecopy_module.rst
/home/james/ansible/docs/docsite/_build/html/modules/remote_filecopy_module
.html
/home/james/ansible/docs/docsite/_build/doctrees/modules/remote_filecopy_mo
dule.doctree
```

Try opening up the HTML file in your web browser – you should see that the page renders just like one of the documentation pages from the official Ansible project documentation! This enables you to check that your documentation builds correctly and looks and reads well in the context that it will be viewed in. It also gives you confidence that, when you submit your code to the Ansible project (if you are doing so), you are submitting something consistent with Ansible's documentation quality standards.

More information on building the documentation locally is provided here: `https://docs.ansible.com/ansible/latest/community/documentation_contributions.html#building-the-documentation-locally`. Although this is an excellent document, it does not currently reflect the compatibility issues around Sphinx, nor the build issues regarding Ansible 2.9. Hopefully, however, it will give you all of the other pointers you need to get going with your documentation.

The current process of building the documentation is currently a little fussy around the environments that are supported; however, hopefully, this is something that will be resolved in due course. In the meantime, the process outlined in this section has given you a tested and working process to start from.

The module checklist

In addition to the pointers and good practices that we have covered so far, there are a few more things you should adhere to in your module code to produce something that will be considered of a high standard for potential inclusion with Ansible. The following list is not exhaustive but will give you a good idea of the practices you should adhere to as a module developer:

- Test your modules as much as you can, both in cases that will succeed and in those that cause errors. You can test them using JSON data, as we did in this chapter, or make use of them within a test playbook.
- Try and keep your Python requirements to a minimum. Sometimes, there is no way to avoid the need for additional Python dependencies (such as the `boto` requirements of the AWS-specific modules), but in general, the less you can use, the better.
- Don't cache data for your module – the execution strategies of Ansible across differing hosts mean you are unlikely to get good results from doing this. Expect to gather all of the data you need on each run.
- Modules should be a single Python file – they shouldn't be distributed across multiple files.

- Make sure you investigate and run the Ansible integration tests when you are submitting your module code. More information on these is available here: `https://docs.ansible.com/ansible/latest/dev_guide/testing_integration.html`.
- Make sure you include exception handling at the appropriate points in your module code, as we did in this chapter, to prevent issues.
- Do not use `PSCustomObjects` in Windows modules unless you absolutely cannot avoid it.

Armed with the information you've gained from this chapter, you should have everything you need to start creating your own modules. You may not decide to submit them to the Ansible project, and there is certainly no requirement to do so. However, even if you don't, following the practices outlined in this chapter will ensure that you build a good quality module, regardless of its intended audience. Finally, on the basis that you do want to submit your source code to the Ansible project, in the next section, we'll look at how to do this through a pull request to the Ansible project.

Contributing upstream – submitting a GitHub pull request

When you've worked hard on your module and thoroughly tested and documented it, you might feel that it is time to submit it to the Ansible project for inclusion. Doing this means creating a pull request on the official Ansible repository. Although the intricacies of working with GitHub are beyond the scope of this book, we will give you a practically focused outline of the basic procedures involved.

 Following the process outlined here will generate a real request against the Ansible project on GitHub so that the code you are committing can be merged with their code. *Do not* follow this process unless you genuinely have a new module that is ready for submission to the Ansible codebase.

To submit your module as a pull request of the Ansible repository, you need to fork the `devel` branch of the official Ansible repository. To do this, log into your GitHub account from your web browser (or create an account if you don't already have one), and then navigate to the URL shown in the following screenshot. Click **Fork** in the top-right corner. As a reminder, the official Ansible source code repository URL is `https://github.com/ansible/ansible.git`:

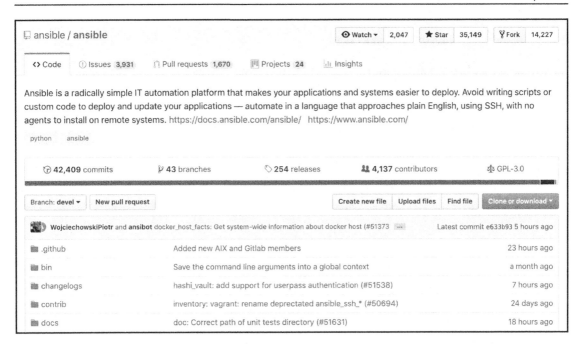

Now that you have forked the repository to your own account, we will walk through the commands you need to run in order to add your module code to it. Then, we'll show you how to create the required **pull requests** (also known as **PRs**) so that you can merge your new module with the upstream Ansible project:

1. Clone the `devel` branch that you've just forked to your local machine. Use a command similar to the following, but be sure to replace the URL with the one that matches your own GitHub account:

   ```
   $ git clone https://github.com/danieloh30/ansible.git
   ```

2. Copy your module code into the appropriate modules directory – the `copy` command given in the following code is just an example to give you a clue as to what to do, but in reality, you should choose the appropriate category subdirectory for your module as it won't necessarily fit into the `files` category. Once you've added your Python file, perform `git add` to make Git aware of the new file, and then commit it with a meaningful commit message. Some example commands are as follows:

   ```
   $ cd ansible
   $ cp ~/ansible-development/moduledev/remote_filecopy.py
   ./lib/ansible/modules/files/
   $ git add lib/ansible/modules/files/remote_filecopy.py
   ```

```
$ git commit -m 'Added tested version of remote_filecopy.py for
pull request creation'
```

3. Now, be sure to push the code to your forked repository using the following command:

```
$ git push
```

4. Return to GitHub in your web browser and navigate to the **Pull Requests** page, as shown here. Click the **New pull request** button:

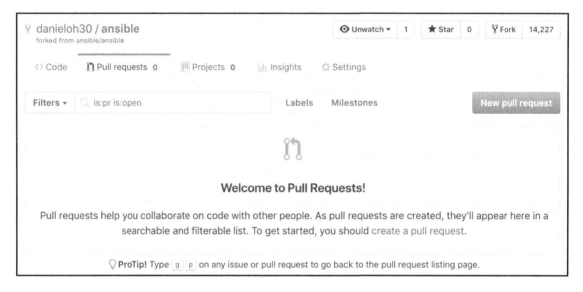

Follow the pull request creation process through, as guided by the GitHub website. Once you have successfully submitted your pull request, you should be able to navigate to the list of pull requests on the official Ansible source code repository and find yours there. An example of the pull requests list is shown here for your reference:

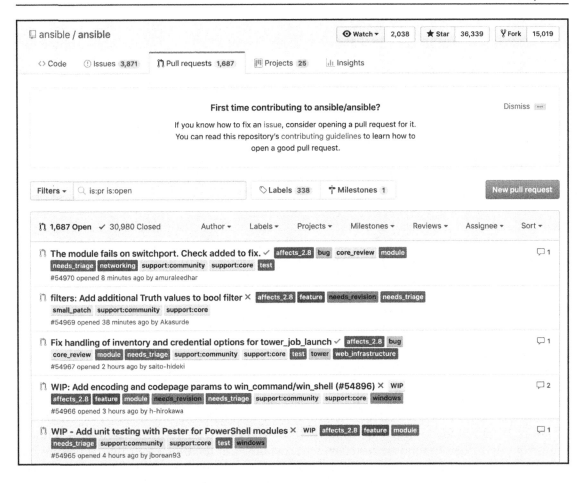

When this screenshot was taken, there were almost 31,000 closed pull requests and nearly 1,700 open for review! By the time you read this book, there will surely be many more, demonstrating how much Ansible relies on the open source community for its continued development and growth. Just think – you could be part of this! Don't be alarmed if it takes a long time for your pull request to get reviewed – this is simply a facet of how many pull requests there are to review and process. You can always use your module code locally by adding it to a local `library/` directory, as we demonstrated earlier, so that the speed of your pull request being processed doesn't hinder your work with Ansible. Further details of where to place your plugin code when working locally can be found here: `https://docs.ansible.com/ansible/latest/dev_guide/developing_locally.html`.

There are many more ways to contribute to the Ansible project other than creating pull requests for custom modules. Here are some examples of other ways you can contribute to the project:

- Review the Ansible documentation and report any bugs you find in it (one was filed in the creation of `Chapter 4`, *Playbooks and Roles*)
- Create a local Ansible MeetUp to spread your knowledge about Ansible. If you are lucky enough to have one in your area already, consider attending it on a regular basis.
- Spread Ansible knowledge and awareness via social media with the appropriate account references and hashtags; for example, `@ansible`, `#ansible`, and so on.

That completes our journey of learning how to create modules, from the very first steps of looking into the theory of module operation, all of the way through to contributing your new module code to the official Ansible project on GitHub. We hope you have found this journey informative and valuable and that it enhances your ability to work with Ansible and extend its functionality where required.

Summary

Modules are the very lifeblood of Ansible – without them, Ansible could not perform all of the complex and varied tasks it performs so well across a wide variety of systems. By virtue of being an open source project, it is incredibly easy to extend the functionality of Ansible by yourself, and in this chapter, we explored how you can, with a little Python knowledge, write your own custom module from scratch. Ansible is, at the time of writing, incredibly feature-rich, but this ease of customization and extension makes Ansible virtually limitless in terms of its potential, especially given the power and popularity of Python as a programming language.

In this chapter, we started with a recap of how to execute multiple modules using the command line. We then explored the process of interrogating the current module index, as well as how to obtain documentation about modules to evaluate their suitability for our needs, regardless of whether we have an active internet connection or not. We then explored module data and its JSON format, before finally going on a journey through which we put together the code for a simple custom module. This provided you with a basis for creating your own modules in the future, if you so desire.

In the next chapter, we will explore the process of using and creating another core Ansible feature, known as plugins.

Questions

1. Which command line can be passed down as a parameter to a module?

    A) `ansible dbservers -m command "/bin/echo 'hello modules'"`

    B) `ansible dbservers -m command -d "/bin/echo 'hello modules'"`

    C) `ansible dbservers -z command -a "/bin/echo 'hello modules'"`

    D) `ansible dbservers -m command -a "/bin/echo 'hello modules'"`

    E) `ansible dbservers -a "/bin/echo 'hello modules'"`

2. Which of the following practices is not recommended when you create a custom module and address exceptions?

    A) Design a custom module simply and never provide a traceback to the user, if you can avoid it.

    B) Fail your module code quickly, and verify that you are providing helpful and understandable exception messages.

    C) Only display error messages for the most relevant exceptions, rather than all possible errors.

    D) Ensure that your module documentation is relevant and easy to understand.

    E) Delete playbooks that result in errors and then recreate them from scratch.

3. True or False: To contribute to the Ansible upstream project, you need to submit your code to the `devel` branch.

    A) True

    B) False

Further reading

- Documentation regarding the common return values of modules in Ansible can be found here: `https://docs.ansible.com/ansible/latest/reference_appendices/common_return_values.html#common`.
- Check out the following documentation for all the existing modules on Windows machines that you can use: `https://docs.ansible.com/ansible/latest/modules/list_of_windows_modules.html#windows-modules`.
- Some of the major module indexes, along with their categorization, can be found at the following links:

  - **Cloud modules**: `https://docs.ansible.com/ansible/latest/modules/list_of_cloud_modules.html`
  - **Clustering modules**: `https://docs.ansible.com/ansible/latest/modules/list_of_clustering_modules.html`
  - **Commands modules**: `https://docs.ansible.com/ansible/latest/modules/list_of_commands_modules.html`
  - **Crypto modules**: `https://docs.ansible.com/ansible/latest/modules/list_of_crypto_modules.html`
  - **Database modules**: `https://docs.ansible.com/ansible/latest/modules/list_of_database_modules.html`
  - **Identity modules**: `https://docs.ansible.com/ansible/latest/modules/list_of_identity_modules.html`
  - **All modules**: `https://docs.ansible.com/ansible/latest/modules/list_of_all_modules.html`

6
Consuming and Creating Plugins

Modules have been a very obvious and key part of our journey through Ansible so far. They are used to execute well-defined tasks and can be used either in one-off commands (using ad hoc commands) or as part of a much larger playbook. Plugins are just as important to Ansible, and we have used them in all of our testings so far without even realizing it! While modules are always used to create some kind of task in Ansible, the way that plugins are used depends on their use case. There are many different types of plugins; we will introduce them to you in this chapter and give you an idea of their purpose. But, as a taster, did you realize that when Ansible connects to a remote server using SSH, functionality is provided by a connection plugin? This demonstrates the important role that plugins play.

In this chapter, we will provide you with an in-depth introduction to plugins, as well as show you how to explore the various plugins that come with Ansible. We'll then expand on this by demonstrating how you can create your own plugins and use them in an Ansible project, in very much the same way as we did with our custom module in the previous chapter. This will hopefully help you to understand the limitless possibilities that open source software such as Ansible provides.

In this chapter, we will cover the following topics:

- Discovering the plugin types
- Finding the included plugins
- Creating custom plugins

Technical requirements

This chapter assumes that you have set up your control host with Ansible, as detailed in Chapter 1, *Getting Started with Ansible,* and that you are using the most recent version available. The examples in this chapter are tested with Ansible 2.9. This chapter also assumes that you have at least one additional host to test against; ideally, this should be Linux-based.

Although we will give specific examples of hostnames in this chapter, you are free to substitute them with your own hostname and/or IP addresses, and details of how to do this are provided at the appropriate places. The plugin development work covered in this chapter assumes the presence of a Python 2 or Python 3 development environment on your computer, and that you are running either Linux, FreeBSD, or macOS. Where additional Python modules are needed, their installation is documented. The task of building module documentation has some very specific requirements in Python 3.5 or later, so it is assumed you can install a suitable Python environment if you wish to attempt this.

The code bundle for this chapter is available at https://github.com/PacktPublishing/Ansible-2-Cookbook/tree/master/Chapter%206.

Discovering the plugin types

Ansible's code has always been designed to be modular—indeed, this is one of its core strengths. Whether that is through the use of modules to perform tasks or through plugins (as we will see shortly), Ansible's modular design allows it to be as versatile and powerful as it has demonstrated itself to be so far in this book. As with modules, Ansible plugins are all written in Python and are expected to ingest and return data in a certain well-defined format (more on this later). Ansible's plugins are often invisible in their function in that you rarely call them by name in your commands or playbooks, yet they are responsible for some of the most important features Ansible has to offer, including SSH connectivity, the ability to parse inventory files (in INI format, YAML, or otherwise), and the ability to run `jinja2` filters on your data.

As ever, let's validate the presence of a suitably installed version of Ansible on your test machine before proceeding further:

```
$ ansible-doc --version
ansible-doc 2.9.6
  config file = /etc/ansible/ansible.cfg
  configured module search path = [u'/root/.ansible/plugins/modules',
u'/usr/share/ansible/plugins/modules']
```

```
ansible python module location = /usr/lib/python2.7/site-packages/ansible
executable location = /usr/bin/ansible-doc
python version = 2.7.5 (default, Aug 7 2019, 00:51:29) [GCC 4.8.5
20150623 (Red Hat 4.8.5-39)]
```

As much work goes into documenting the plugins as it does in documenting the modules, and you will be pleased to know that there is a plugin index available at `https://docs.ansible.com/ansible/latest/plugins/plugins.html`.

You can also use the `ansible-doc` command as we did before, only you need to add the `-t` switch to it, too. Plugins are always placed in an appropriate category as their function is radically different between categories. If you don't specify the `-t` switch with `ansible-doc`, you end up specifying the `ansible-doc -t` module, which returns a list of the available modules.

At the time of writing, the following plugin categories can be found in Ansible:

- `become`: Responsible for enabling Ansible to obtain super-user access (for example, through `sudo`)
- `cache`: Responsible for caching facts retrieved from backend systems to improve automation performance
- `callback`: Allows you to add new behaviors when responding to events—for example, changing the format that data is printed in the output in of an Ansible playbook run
- `cliconf`: Provides abstractions to the command-line interfaces of various network devices, giving Ansible a standard interface to operate on
- `connection`: Provides connectivity from Ansible to remote systems (for example, over SSH, WinRM, Docker, and many more)
- `httpapi`: Tells Ansible how to interact with a remote system's API (for example, for a Fortinet firewall)
- `inventory`: Provides Ansible with the ability to parse various static and dynamic inventory formats
- `lookup`: Allows Ansible to look up data from an external source (for example, by reading a flat text file)
- `netconf`: Provides Ansible with abstractions to enable it to work with NETCONF-enabled networking devices
- `shell`: Provides Ansible with the ability to work with various shells on different systems (for example, `powershell` on Windows versus `sh` on Linux)

- strategy: Provides plugins to Ansible with different execution strategies (for example, the debug strategy we saw in Chapter 4, *Playbooks and Roles*)
- vars: Provides Ansible with the ability to source variables from certain sources, such as the host_vars and group_vars directories we explored in Chapter 3, *Defining Your Inventory*)

We will leave exploring the plugin documentation on the Ansible website as an exercise for you to complete. However, if you want to explore the various plugins using the ansible-doc tool, you would need to run the following commands:

1. To use the ansible-doc command to list all the plugins available in a given category, you can run the following command:

```
$ ansible-doc -t connection -l
```

This will return a textual index of the connection plugins, similar to what we saw when we were looking at the module documentation. The first few lines of the index output are shown here:

```
kubectl             Execute tasks in pods running on Kubernetes
napalm              Provides persistent connection using NAPALM
qubes               Interact with an existing QubesOS AppVM
libvirt_lxc         Run tasks in lxc containers via libvirt
funcd               Use funcd to connect to target
chroot              Interact with local chroot
psrp                Run tasks over Microsoft PowerShell Remoting
Protocol
zone                Run tasks in a zone instance
winrm               Run tasks over Microsoft's WinRM
paramiko_ssh        Run tasks via python ssh (paramiko)
```

2. You can then explore the documentation for a given plugin. For example, if we want to learn about the paramiko_ssh plugin, we can issue the following command:

```
$ ansible-doc -t connection paramiko_ssh
```

You will find that the plugin documentation takes on a very familiar format, similar to what we saw for the modules in Chapter 5, *Consuming and Creating Modules*:

```
> PARAMIKO (/usr/lib/python2.7/site-
packages/ansible/plugins/connection/param

        Use the python ssh implementation (Paramiko) to connect to
```

```
    targets The paramiko transport is provided because many
    distributions, in particular EL6 and before do not support
    ControlPersist in their SSH implementations. This is needed on
    the Ansible control machine to be reasonably efficient with
    connections. Thus paramiko is faster for most users on these
    platforms. Users with ControlPersist capability can consider
    using -c ssh or configuring the transport in the configuration
    file. This plugin also borrows a lot of settings from the ssh
    plugin as they both cover the same protocol.

  * This module is maintained by The Ansible Community
OPTIONS (= is mandatory):

- host_key_auto_add
        TODO: write it
        [Default: (null)]
        set_via:
          env:
          - name: ANSIBLE_PARAMIKO_HOST_KEY_AUTO_ADD
          ini:
          - key: host_key_auto_add
```

Thanks to all the hard work and effort that goes into documenting every area of Ansible, you can easily find out about the plugins that are included with Ansible and how to work with them. So far, we have seen that the documentation for plugins is no less complete than it is for modules. In the next section of this chapter, we'll dive a bit deeper into how to find the plugin code that accompanies your Ansible distribution.

Finding included plugins

As we discussed in the preceding section, plugins are not as apparent in Ansible as their module counterparts are, and yet we have been using them behind the scenes in every single Ansible command we've issued so far! Let's build on our work in the previous section, where we looked at the plugin documentation by looking at where we can find the source code for the plugins. This, in turn, will serve as a precursor to us building a simple plugin of our own.

If you installed Ansible on a Linux system using a package manager (that is, via an RPM or DEB package), then the location of your plugins will depend on your OS. For example, on my test CentOS 7 system where I installed Ansible from the official RPM package, I can see the plugins installed here:

```
$ ls /usr/lib/python2.7/site-packages/ansible/plugins/
action    cliconf    httpapi     inventory    lookup    terminal
```

```
become     connection     __init__.py     loader.py     netconf     test
cache      doc_fragments  __init__.pyc    loader.pyc    shell       vars
callback   filter         __init__.pyo    loader.pyo    strategy
```

Notice how the plugins are separated into subdirectories, all named after their categories. If we want to look up the `paramiko_ssh` plugin that we reviewed the documentation of in the preceding section, we can look in the `connection/` subdirectory:

```
$ ls -l /usr/lib/python2.7/site-
packages/ansible/plugins/connection/paramiko_ssh.py
-rw-r--r-- 1 root root 23544 Mar 5 05:39 /usr/lib/python2.7/site-
packages/ansible/plugins/connection/paramiko_ssh.py
```

However, in general, I do not recommend that you edit or change the files installed from a package as you might all too easily overwrite them when upgrading the package. As one of our goals in this chapter is to write our own simple custom plugin, let's look at how to find the plugins in the official Ansible source code:

1. Clone the official Ansible repository from GitHub, as we did previously, and change the directory to the location of your clone:

   ```
   $ git clone https://github.com/ansible/ansible.git
   $ cd ansible
   ```

2. Within the official source code directory structure, you will find that the plugins are all contained (again, in categorized subdirectories) under `lib/ansible/plugins/`:

   ```
   $ cd lib/ansible/plugins
   ```

3. We can explore the connection-based plugins by looking in the `connection` directory:

   ```
   $ ls -al connection/
   ```

   The exact contents of this directory will depend on the version of Ansible source code that you have cloned. At the time of writing, it looks as follows, with one Python file for each plugin (similar to how we saw one Python file for each module in Chapter 5, *Consuming and Creating Modules*):

   ```
   $ ls -al connection/
   total 176
   drwxr-xr-x 2 root root 109 Apr 15 17:24 .
   drwxr-xr-x 19 root root 297 Apr 15 17:24 ..
   -rw-r--r-- 1 root root 16411 Apr 15 17:24 __init__.py
   -rw-r--r-- 1 root root 6855 Apr 15 17:24 local.py
   ```

```
-rw-r--r-- 1 root root 23525 Apr 15 17:24 paramiko_ssh.py
-rw-r--r-- 1 root root 32839 Apr 15 17:24 psrp.py
-rw-r--r-- 1 root root 55367 Apr 15 17:24 ssh.py
-rw-r--r-- 1 root root 31277 Apr 15 17:24 winrm.py
```

4. You can review the contents of each plugin to learn more about how they work, which is again part of the beauty of open source software:

```
$ less connection/paramiko_ssh.py
```

An example of the beginning of this file is shown in the following code block to give you an idea of the kind of output you should be seeing if this command runs correctly:

```
# (c) 2012, Michael DeHaan <michael.dehaan@gmail.com>
# (c) 2017 Ansible Project
# GNU General Public License v3.0+ (see COPYING or
https://www.gnu.org/licenses/gpl-3.0.txt)
from __future__ import (absolute_import, division, print_function)
__metaclass__ = type

DOCUMENTATION = """
    author: Ansible Core Team
    connection: paramiko
    short_description: Run tasks via python ssh (paramiko)
    description:
        - Use the python ssh implementation (Paramiko) to connect
to targets
        - The paramiko transport is provided because many
distributions, in particular EL6 and before do not support
ControlPersist
            in their SSH implementations.
    ....
```

Notice the DOCUMENTATION block, which is very similar to what we saw when we were working with the module source code. If you explore the source code of each plugin, you will find that the structure bears some similarity to the module code structure. However, rather than simply taking this statement at face value, in the next section, let's get started with building our very own custom plugin to learn, through a practical example, how they are put together.

Creating custom plugins

In this section, we will take you through a practical guide on creating your own plugin. The example will be, by necessity, simple. However, hopefully, it will serve you well in guiding you in the principles and best practices of plugin development and give you a solid foundation to build your own more complex plugins. We will even show you how to integrate these with your own playbooks and, when you're ready, submit them to the official Ansible project for inclusion.

As we noted when we built our own module, Ansible is written in Python, and its plugins are no exception. As a result, you will need to write your plugin in Python; so, to get started on developing your own plugin, you will need to make sure you have Python and a few essential tools installed. If you already have Ansible running on your development machine, you probably have the required packages installed. However, if you are starting from scratch, you will need to install Python, the Python package manager (`pip`), and perhaps some other development packages. The exact process will vary widely between OSes, but here are some examples to get you started:

- On Fedora, you can run the following command to install the required packages:

  ```
  $ sudo dnf install python python-devel
  ```

- Similarly, on CentOS, you can run the following command to install the required packages:

  ```
  $ sudo yum install python python-devel
  ```

- On Ubuntu, you can run the following commands to install the packages you will need:

  ```
  $ sudo apt-get update
  $ sudo apt-get install python-pip python-dev build-essential
  ```

- If you are working on macOS and using the Homebrew packaging system, the following command will install the packages you need:

  ```
  $ sudo brew install python
  ```

Once you have installed the required packages, you will need to clone the Ansible Git repository to your local machine, as there are some valuable scripts in there that we will need later on in the module development process. Use the following command to clone the Ansible repository to your current directory on your development machine:

```
$ git clone https://github.com/ansible/ansible.git
$ cd ansible
```

With all of these prerequisites in place, let's get started with creating your own plugin. Although there are many similarities between coding modules and plugins, there are also fundamental differences. In fact, each of the different types of plugins that Ansible can work with is actually coded slightly differently and has different recommendations. Sadly, we don't have space to go through each one in this book, but you can find out more about the requirements for each plugin type from the official Ansible documentation at https://docs.ansible.com/ansible/latest/dev_guide/developing_plugins.html.

For our simple example, we'll create a filter plugin that replaces a given string with another. If you refer to the preceding documentation link, filter plugins are perhaps some of the easiest ones to code because there isn't a stringent requirement on the documentation in the same way that there is for modules. However, if we were to create a lookup plugin, we would be expected to create the same DOCUMENTATION, EXAMPLES, and RETURN documentation sections that we created in Chapter 5, *Consuming and Creating Modules*. We would also need to test and build our web documentation in the same way.

We have already covered this, so it doesn't serve to repeat the entirety of this process again in this chapter. Instead, we will focus on creating a filter plugin, first. In contrast with other Ansible plugins and modules, you can actually have several filters defined in a single Python plugin file. Filters are, by nature, quite compact to code. They are also numerous, so having one file per filter doesn't scale well. However, if you want to code other types of plugins (such as lookup plugins), you *will* need to create one Python file per plugin.

Let's get started on creating our simple filter plugin. As we are only creating one, it will live in its own single Python file. You could propose a modification to one of the Ansible core filter Python files if you want to submit your code back to the Ansible project; but for now, we'll leave that as a project for you to complete yourself. Our filter file will be called custom_filter.py and it will live in a directory called filter_plugins, which must be in the same directory as your playbook.

Perform the following steps to create and test your plugin code:

1. Start your plugin file with a header so that people will know who wrote the plugin and what license it is released under. Naturally, you should update both the copyright and license fields with values appropriate to your plugin, but the following text is given as an example for you to get started with:

```
# (c) 2020, James Freeman <james.freeman@example.com>
# GNU General Public License v3.0+ (see COPYING or
https://www.gnu.org/licenses/gpl-3.0.txt)
```

2. Next, we'll add a very simple Python function—yours can be as complex as you want it to be, but for ours, we will simply use the Python `.replace` function to replace one string with another inside a `string` variable. The following example looks for instances of `Puppet` and replaces them with `Ansible`:

```
def improve_automation(a):
  return a.replace("Puppet", "Ansible")
```

3. Next, we need to create an object of the `FilterModule` class, which is how Ansible will know that this Python file contains a filter. Within this object, we can create a `filters` definition and return the value of our previously defined filter function to Ansible:

```
class FilterModule(object):
      '''improve_automation filters'''
      def filters(self):
          return {'improve_automation': improve_automation}
```

4. As you can see, this code is all incredibly simple and we're able to use built-in Python functions, such as `replace`, to manipulate the strings. There isn't a specific test harness for plugins in Ansible, so we will test out our plugin code by writing a simple playbook that will implement it. The following playbook code defines a simple string that includes the word `Puppet` in it and prints this to the console using the `debug` module, applying our newly defined filter to the string:

```
---
- name: Play to demonstrate our custom filter
  hosts: frontends
  gather_facts: false
  vars:
    statement: "Puppet is an excellent automation tool!"

  tasks:
    - name: make a statement
```

```
debug:
  msg: "{{ statement | improve_automation }}"
```

Now, before we attempt to run this, let's recap what the directory structure should look like. Just as we were able to utilize the custom module that we created in Chapter 5, *Consuming and Creating Modules*, by creating a `library/` subdirectory to house our module, we can also create a `filter_plugins/` subdirectory for our plugin. Your directory tree structure, when you have finished coding the various file details in the preceding code block, should look something like this:

```
.
├── filter_plugins
│   ├── custom_filter.py
├── hosts
├── myplugin.yml
```

Let's now run our little test playbook and see what output we get. If all goes well, it should look something like the following:

```
$ ansible-playbook -i hosts myplugin.yml

PLAY [Play to demonstrate our custom filter]
**********************************

TASK [make a statement]
*****************************************************
ok: [frt01.example.com] => {
    "msg": "Ansible is an excellent automation tool!"
}

PLAY RECAP
*********************************************************************
frt01.example.com : ok=1 changed=0 unreachable=0 failed=0 skipped=0
rescued=0 ignored=0
```

As you can see, our new filter plugin replaced the `Puppet` string in our variable's contents and replaced it with the `Ansible` string. This, of course, is just a silly test and not one you are likely to contribute back to the Ansible project. However, it shows how, in just six lines of code and with a modicum of Python knowledge, we have created our own filter plugin to manipulate a string. You could come up with something far more complex and useful, I'm sure!

Other plugin types require more effort than this; although we won't go through the process of creating a filter plugin here, you'll find coding a filter plugin more akin to coding a module, as you need to do the following:

- Include the DOCUMENTATION, EXAMPLES, and RETURN sections with the appropriate documentation.
- Ensure you have incorporated appropriate and sufficient error handling in the plugin.
- Test it thoroughly, including both the failure and success cases.

As an example of this, let's repeat the preceding process, but to create a lookup plugin, instead. This plugin will be based heavily on a simplified version of the file lookup plugin. However, we want to adapt our version to return only the first character of a file. You could adapt this example to perhaps read the header from a file, or you could add arguments to the plugin to allow you to extract a substring using character indexes. We will leave this enhancement activity as an exercise for you to carry out yourself. Let's get started! Our new lookup plugin will be called firstchar, and as lookup plugins have a one-to-one mapping with their Python files, the plugin file will be called firstchar.py. (In fact, Ansible will use this filename as the name of the plugin—you won't find a reference to it in the code anywhere!). If you intend to test this from a playbook, as executed previously, you should create this in a directory called lookup_plugins/:

1. Start by adding a header to the plugin file, as before, so that the maintainer and copyright details are clear. We are borrowing a large chunk of the original file.py lookup plugin code for our example, so it is important we include the relevant credit:

```
# (c) 2020, James Freeman <james.freeman@example.com>
# (c) 2012, Daniel Hokka Zakrisson <daniel@hozac.com>
# (c) 2017 Ansible Project
# GNU General Public License v3.0+ (see COPYING or
https://www.gnu.org/licenses/gpl-3.0.txt)
```

2. Next, add in the Python 3 headers—these are an absolute requirement if you intend to submit your plugin via a **Pull Request** (**PR**) to the Ansible project:

```
from __future__ import (absolute_import, division, print_function)
__metaclass__ = type
```

3. Next, add a DOCUMENTATION block to your plugin so that other users can understand how to interact with it:

```
DOCUMENTATION = """
    lookup: firstchar
```

```
author: James Freeman <james.freeman@example.com>
version_added: "2.9"
short_description: read the first character of file contents
description:
    - This lookup returns the first character of the contents
from a file on the Ansible controller's file system.
options:
  _terms:
    description: path(s) of files to read
    required: True
notes:
    - if read in variable context, the file can be interpreted as
YAML if the content is valid to the parser.
    - this lookup does not understand 'globing', use the fileglob
lookup instead.
"""
```

4. Add the relevant EXAMPLES blocks to show how to use your plugin, just as we did for modules:

```
EXAMPLES = """
- debug: msg="the first character in foo.txt is
{{lookup('firstchar', '/etc/foo.txt') }}"

"""
```

5. Also, make sure you document the RETURN values from your plugin:

```
RETURN = """
  _raw:
    description:
      - first character of content of file(s)
"""
```

6. With the documentation complete, we can now start to work on our Python code. We will start by importing all the Python modules we need to make our module work. We'll also set up the display object, which is used in verbose output and debugging. This should be used in place of the print statements in your plugin code if you need to display the debug output:

```
from ansible.errors import AnsibleError, AnsibleParserError
from ansible.plugins.lookup import LookupBase
from ansible.utils.display import Display

display = Display()
```

7. We will now create an object of the `LookupModule` class. Define a default function within this called `run` (this is expected for the Ansible `lookup` plugin framework) and initialize an empty array for our return data:

```
class LookupModule(LookupBase):

    def run(self, terms, variables=None, **kwargs):

        ret = []
```

8. With this in place, we will start a loop to iterate over each of the terms (which, in our simple plugin, will be the filenames passed to the plugin). Although we will only test this on simple use cases, the way that lookup plugins can be used means that they need to support the lists of `terms` to operate on. Within this loop, we display valuable debugging information and, most importantly, define an object with the details of each of the files we will open, called `lookupfile`:

```
for term in terms:
        display.debug("File lookup term: %s" % term)

    lookupfile = self.find_file_in_search_path(variables, 'files',
term)

        display.vvvv(u"File lookup using %s as file" % lookupfile)
```

9. Now, we will read in the file contents. This could be as simple as using one line of Python code, but we know from our work on modules in Chapter 5, *Consuming and Creating Modules*, that we should not take it for granted that we will be passed a file we can actually read. As a result, we will put the statement to read our file contents into a `try` block and implement exception handling to ensure that the behavior of the plugin is sensible, even in error cases, and that easy-to-understand error messages are passed back to the user, rather than to Python tracebacks:

```
try:
            if lookupfile:
            contents, show_data =
self._loader._get_file_contents(lookupfile)
                ret.append(contents.rstrip()[0])
            else:
                raise AnsibleParserError()
        except AnsibleParserError:
            raise AnsibleError("could not locate file in
lookup: %s" % term)
```

Notice that within this, we append the first character of the file contents (denoted by the `[0]` index) to our empty array. We also remove any training spaces using `rstrip`.

10. Finally, we return the character we gathered from the file to Ansible with a `return` statement:

```
return ret
```

11. Once again, we can create a simple test playbook to test out our newly created plugin:

```
---
- name: Play to demonstrate our custom lookup plugin
  hosts: frontends
  gather_facts: false

  tasks:
    - name: make a statement
      debug:
        msg: "{{ lookup('firstchar', 'testdoc.txt')}}"
```

Again, we are using the debug module to print output to the console and referencing our `lookup` plugin to obtain the output.

12. Create the text file referenced in the previous code block, called `testdoc.txt`. This can contain anything you like—mine contains the following simple text:

```
Hello
```

For clarity, your final directory structure should look as follows:

```
.
├── hosts
├── lookup_plugins
│   └── firstchar.py
├── myplugin2.yml
└── testdoc.txt
```

13. Now, when we run our new playbook, we should see an output similar to the following:

```
$ ansible-playbook -i hosts myplugin2.yml

PLAY [Play to demonstrate our custom lookup plugin]
****************************
```

```
TASK [make a statement]
**********************************************************
ok: [frt01.example.com] => {
    "msg": "H"
}

PLAY RECAP
************************************************************
**
frt01.example.com : ok=1 changed=0 unreachable=0 failed=0 skipped=0
rescued=0 ignored=0
```

If all goes well, your playbook should return the first character of the text file you created. Naturally, there is a lot we could do to enhance this code, but this serves as a nice, simple example to get you started.

With this foundation in place, you should now have a reasonable idea of how to get started with writing your own plugins for Ansible. The next logical step for us is to look in greater depth at how we can test our newly written plugins, which we will do in the next section.

Learning to integrate custom plugins with Ansible source code

So far, we have only tested our plugin in a standalone manner. This is all well and good, but what if you actually wanted to add it either to your own fork of the Ansible source code—or, better yet, submit it back to the Ansible project for inclusion with a PR? Fortunately, this process is very similar to the one we covered in Chapter 5, *Consuming and Creating Modules*, only with slightly different folder structures.

As before, your first task will be to obtain a copy of the official Ansible project source code—for example, by cloning the GitHub repository to your local machine:

```
$ git clone https://github.com/ansible/ansible.git
$ cd ansible
```

Next, you will need to copy your plugin code into one of the appropriate plugin directories.

1. For example, our example filter would be copied to the following directory in the source code you just cloned:

```
$ cp ~/custom_filter.py ./lib/ansible/plugins/filter/
```

2. Similarly, our custom lookup plugin would go in the lookup plugin's directory, using a command such as the following:

```
$ cp ~/firstchar.py ./lib/ansible/plugins/lookup/
```

With your code copied into place, you need to test the documentation (that is, whether your plugin includes it) as before. You can build the webdocs documentation in exactly the same way as we did in Chapter 5, *Consuming and Creating Modules*, so we will not recap this here. However, as a refresher, we can quickly check whether the documentation renders correctly using the ansible-doc command, as follows:

```
$ . hacking/env-setup
running egg_info
creating lib/ansible.egg-info
writing requirements to lib/ansible.egg-info/requires.txt
writing lib/ansible.egg-info/PKG-INFO
writing top-level names to lib/ansible.egg-info/top_level.txt
writing dependency_links to lib/ansible.egg-info/dependency_links.txt
writing manifest file 'lib/ansible.egg-info/SOURCES.txt'
reading manifest file 'lib/ansible.egg-info/SOURCES.txt'
reading manifest template 'MANIFEST.in'
warning: no files found matching 'SYMLINK_CACHE.json'
writing manifest file 'lib/ansible.egg-info/SOURCES.txt'

Setting up Ansible to run out of checkout...

PATH=/home/james/ansible/bin:/usr/local/sbin:/usr/local/bin:/usr/sbin:/usr/
bin:/root/bin
PYTHONPATH=/home/james/ansible/lib
MANPATH=/home/james/ansible/docs/man:/usr/local/share/man:/usr/share/man

Remember, you may wish to specify your host file with -i

Done!

$ ansible-doc -t lookup firstchar
> FIRSTCHAR (/home/james/ansible/lib/ansible/plugins/lookup/firstchar.py)

        This lookup returns the first character of the contents from a
        file on the Ansible controller's file system.
```

```
      * This module is maintained by The Ansible Community
OPTIONS (= is mandatory):

= _terms
        path(s) of files to read
```

As you have seen so far, there is a great deal of overlap between plugin development and module development in Ansible. It is especially important to pay attention to error handling with exceptions to produce good quality, easy-to-understand error messages and to adhere to and uphold Ansible's high documentation standards. One additional item that we have not covered here is the plugin output. All plugins must return strings in Unicode; this ensures that they can run through the jinja2 filters correctly. Further guidance can be found in the official Ansible documentation at https://docs.ansible.com/ansible/ latest/dev_guide/developing_plugins.html.

Armed with this knowledge, you should now be well placed to begin your own plugin development work, and even to submit your code back to the community, if you desire. We'll offer a brief recap of this in the next section.

Sharing plugins with the community

You may wish to submit your new plugin to the Ansible project, just as we considered for our custom modules in Chapter 5, *Consuming and Creating Modules*. The process for doing this with plugins is almost identical to what you do for modules, which this section will recap.

Using the following process will submit a real request to the Ansible project on GitHub to merge the code you submit with their code. Do *not* follow this process unless you genuinely have a new module that is ready for submission to the Ansible codebase.

In order to submit your plugin as a PR of the Ansible repository, you first need to fork the devel branch of the official Ansible repository. To do this, log into your GitHub account on your web browser (or create an account if you don't already have one), and then navigate to https://github.com/ansible/ansible.git. Click on **Fork** at the top-right corner of the page:

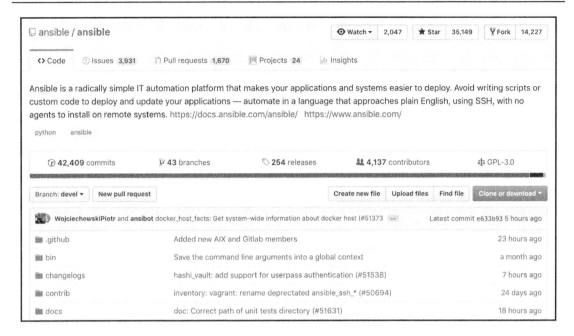

Once you have forked the repository to your own account, we will walk you through the commands you need to run to add your module code to it and then to create the required PRs in order to merge your new module with the upstream Ansible project:

1. Clone the `devel` branch that you just forked to your local machine. Use a command similar to the following, but be sure to replace the URL with one that matches your own GitHub account:

```
$ git clone https://github.com/<your GitHub account>/ansible.git
```

2. Copy your module code into the appropriate `plugins/` directory. The `copy` command used in the following code block is just an example to give you an idea as to what to do—in reality, you should choose the appropriate category subdirectory for your plugin as it won't necessarily fit into the `lookup` category. Once you've added your Python file, perform a `git add` command to make Git aware of the new file, and then commit it with a meaningful `commit` message. Some example commands are shown here:

```
$ cd ansible
$ cp ~/ansible-development/plugindev/firstchar.py
./lib/ansible/plugins/lookup
$ git add lib/ansible/plugins/lookup/firstchar.py
$ git commit -m 'Added tested version of firstchar.py for pull
request creation'
```

3. Now, be sure to push the code to your forked repository using the following command:

```
$ git push
```

4. Return to GitHub in your web browser and navigate to the **Pull Requests** page, as in the following screenshot. Click on the **New pull request** button:

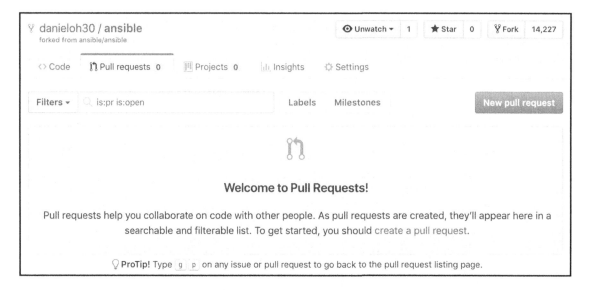

Follow the PR creation process, as guided by the GitHub website. Once you have successfully submitted your PR, you should be able to navigate to the list of PRs on the official Ansible source code repository and find yours there. An example of the PR list is shown in the following screenshot for your reference:

As discussed previously, don't be alarmed if it takes a long time for your PR to be reviewed—this is simply due to how many PRs there are to review and process. You can always use your plugin code locally by adding it to a local `*_plugins/` directory, as we demonstrated earlier, so that the processing speed of your PR doesn't hinder your work with Ansible. Further details of where to place your plugin code when working locally can be found at `https://docs.ansible.com/ansible/latest/dev_guide/developing_locally.html`.

That completes our look at the creation of plugins, including two working examples. Hopefully, you have found this journey informative and valuable and it has enhanced your ability to work with Ansible and extend its functionality where required.

Summary

Ansible plugins are a core part of Ansible's functionality and we discovered, in this chapter, that we have been working with them throughout this book without even realizing it! Ansible's modular design makes it easy to extend and add functionality to, regardless of whether you are working with modules or the various types of plugins that are currently supported. Whether it's to add a new filter for string processing or a new way of looking up data (or perhaps even a new connection mechanism to new technology), Ansible plugins provide a complete framework that can extend Ansible far beyond its already extensive capabilities.

In this chapter, we learned about the various types of plugins that are supported by Ansible, before exploring them in greater detail and looking at how you can obtain documentation and information on the existing ones. We then completed two practical examples to create two different types of plugin for Ansible while looking at the best practices for plugin development and how this overlaps with module development. We finished off by recapping how to submit our new plugin code as a PR back to the Ansible project.

In the next chapter, we will explore the best practices that you should adhere to when writing your Ansible playbooks to ensure that you produce manageable, high-quality automation code.

Questions

1. Which of the following `ansible-doc` commands can you use to list the names of all the cache plugins?

   A) `ansible-doc -a cache -l`

   B) `ansible-doc cache -l`

   C) `ansible-doc -a cache`

   D) `ansible-doc -t cache -l`

   E) `ansible-doc cache`

2. Which class do you need to add to your `lookup` plugin's code to include the bulk of the plugin code, including `run()`, the `items` loop, `try`, and `except`?

A) `LookupModule`

B) `RunModule`

C) `StartModule`

D) `InitModule`

E) `LoadModule`

3. True or false – in order to create custom plugins using Python, you need to install Python with the relevant dependencies on your OS:

A) True

B) False

Further reading

You can find all of the plugins on Ansible by accessing the Ansible repository directly at `https://github.com/ansible/ansible/tree/devel/lib/ansible/plugins`.

Coding Best Practices

7

Ansible can help you automate just about all of your daily IT tasks, from mundane tasks, such as applying patches or deploying configuration files, to deploying entirely new infrastructure as code. The use of, and engagement with, Ansible has been growing year by year as more and more people come to realize both its power and simplicity. You will find many example Ansible playbooks, roles, blog articles, and so on across the internet, and combined with resources such as this book, you will become proficient at writing your own Ansible playbooks.

Yet, how do you know what the best approaches for writing your automation code in Ansible are? How can you tell whether an example you found on the internet is actually a good way of doing things? In this chapter, we will take you through a practical guide of the best practices in Ansible, showing you what is currently considered good practice when it comes to directory structure and playbook layout, how to make effective use of inventories (especially on the cloud), and how best to differentiate your environments. By the end of this chapter, you should be able to proceed with confidence in writing everything from small single-task playbooks to large-scale playbooks for complex environments.

In this chapter, we will cover the following topics:

- The preferred directory layout
- The best approach to cloud inventories
- Differentiating between different environment types
- The proper approach to defining group and host variables
- Using top-level playbooks
- Leveraging version control tools
- Setting OS and distribution variances
- Porting between Ansible versions

Technical requirements

This chapter assumes that you have set up your control host with Ansible, as in Chapter 1, *Getting Started with Ansible,* and that you are using the most recent version available; the examples in this chapter were tested on Ansible 2.9. This chapter also assumes that you have at least one additional host to test against; ideally, this should be Linux-based. Although we will give specific examples of hostnames in this chapter, you are welcome to substitute them with your own hostname and/or IP addresses, and details of how to do this are provided in the appropriate places.

The code bundle used in this chapter is available at https://github.com/ PacktPublishing/Ansible-2-Cookbook/tree/master/Chapter%207.

The preferred directory layout

As we have explored Ansible throughout this book, we have shown many times that the more your playbook grows in size and scale, the more likely you are to want to divide it up into multiple files and directories. A great example of this is roles, which we covered in Chapter 4, *Playbooks and Roles,* where we defined roles to not only enable us to reuse common automation code but also to split up what could potentially be a massive, single playbook into smaller, logically organized, manageable chunks. We also looked, in Chapter 3, *Defining Your Inventory,* at the process of defining your inventory file and how you can also split this up across multiple files and directories. What we have not looked at, however, is how we can put all of this together. All of this is documented in the official Ansible documentation at https://docs.ansible.com/ansible/latest/user_guide/ playbooks_best_practices.html#content-organization.

However, in this chapter, let's get started with a practical example of this to show you a great way of setting up your directory structure for a simple role-based playbook that has two different inventories—one for a development environment and one for a production environment (you would want to keep these separate in any real-world use case, although ideally, you should be able to execute the same plays on both for consistency and for testing purposes).

Let's get started by building the directory structure:

1. Create a directory tree for your development inventory with the following commands:

```
$ mkdir -p inventories/development/group_vars
$ mkdir -p inventories/development/host_vars
```

2. Next, we'll define an INI-formatted inventory file for our development inventory—in our example, we'll keep this really simple with just two servers. The file to create is `inventories/development/hosts`:

```
[app]
app01.dev.example.com
app02.dev.example.com
```

3. To further our example, we'll add a group variable to our app group. As discussed in `Chapter 3`, *Defining Your Inventory*, create a file called `app.yml` in the `group_vars` directory we created in the previous step:

```
---
http_port: 8080
```

4. Next, create a `production` directory structure using the same method:

```
$ mkdir -p inventories/production/group_vars
$ mkdir -p inventories/production/host_vars
```

5. Create an inventory file called `hosts` in the newly created `production` directory with the following contents:

```
[app]
app01.prod.example.com
app02.prod.example.com
```

6. Now, we'll define a different value to the `http_port` group variable for our production inventory. Add the following contents to `inventories/production/group_vars/app.yml`:

```
---
http_port: 80
```

That completes our inventory definition. Next, we will add in any custom modules or plugins that we might find useful for our playbook. Suppose we want to use the `remote_filecopy.py` module we created in `Chapter 5`, *Consuming and Creating Modules*. Just as we discussed in this chapter, we first create the directory for this module:

```
$ mkdir library
```

Then, add the `remote_filecopy.py` module to this library. We won't relist the code here to save space, but you can copy it from the section called *Developing custom modules* from `Chapter 5`, *Consuming and Creating Modules*, or take advantage of the example code that accompanies this book on GitHub.

The same can be done for the plugins; if we also want to use our `filter` plugin that we created in Chapter 6, *Consuming and Creating Plugins*, we would create an appropriately named directory:

```
$ mkdir filter_plugins
```

Then, copy the `filter` plugin code into this directory.

Finally, we'll create a role to use in our new playbook structure. Naturally, you will have many roles, but we'll create one as an example and then you can repeat the process for each role. We'll call our role `installapp` and use the `ansible-galaxy` command (covered in Chapter 4, *Playbooks and Roles*) to create the directory structure for us:

```
$ mkdir roles
$ ansible-galaxy role init --init-path roles/ installapp
- Role installapp was created successfully
```

Then, in our `roles/installapp/tasks/main.yml` file, we'll add the following contents:

```
---
- name: Display http_port variable contents
  debug:
    var: http_port

- name: Create /tmp/foo
  file:
    path: /tmp/foo
    state: file

- name: Use custom module to copy /tmp/foo
  remote_filecopy:
    source: /tmp/foo
    dest: /tmp/bar

- name: Define a fact about automation
  set_fact:
    about_automation: "Puppet is an excellent automation tool"

- name: Tell us about automation with a custom filter applied
  debug:
    msg: "{{ about_automation | improve_automation }}"
```

In the preceding code, we've reused a number of examples from earlier chapters of this book. You can also define the handlers, variables, default values, and so on to the role, as discussed previously, but for our example, this will suffice.

The final stage in creating our best practice directory structure is to add a top-level playbook to run. By convention, this will be called `site.yml` and it will have the following simple contents (note that the directory structure we have built takes care of many things, allowing the top-level playbook to be incredibly simple):

```
---
- name: Play using best practise directory structure
  hosts: all

  roles:
    - installapp
```

For the purpose of clarity, your resulting directory structure should look as follows:

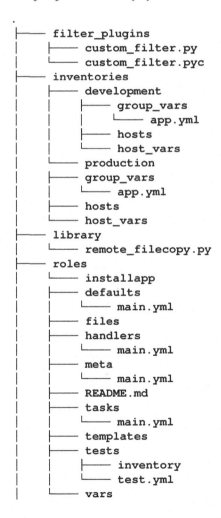

```
|       └──── main.yml
└──── site.yml
```

Now, we can simply run our playbook in the normal manner. For example, to run it on the development inventory, execute the following:

```
$ ansible-playbook -i inventories/development/hosts site.yml

PLAY [Play using best practise directory structure]
***************************

TASK [Gathering Facts]
********************************************************
ok: [app02.dev.example.com]
ok: [app01.dev.example.com]

TASK [installapp : Display http_port variable contents]
***********************
ok: [app01.dev.example.com] => {
    "http_port": 8080
}
ok: [app02.dev.example.com] => {
    "http_port": 8080
}

TASK [installapp : Create /tmp/foo]
******************************************
changed: [app02.dev.example.com]
changed: [app01.dev.example.com]

TASK [installapp : Use custom module to copy /tmp/foo]
************************
changed: [app02.dev.example.com]
changed: [app01.dev.example.com]

TASK [installapp : Define a fact about automation]
*****************************
ok: [app01.dev.example.com]
ok: [app02.dev.example.com]

TASK [installapp : Tell us about automation with a custom filter applied]
******
ok: [app01.dev.example.com] => {
    "msg": "Ansible is an excellent automation tool"
}
ok: [app02.dev.example.com] => {
    "msg": "Ansible is an excellent automation tool"
}
```

```
PLAY RECAP
***********************************************************************
app01.dev.example.com : ok=6 changed=2 unreachable=0 failed=0 skipped=0
rescued=0 ignored=0
app02.dev.example.com : ok=6 changed=2 unreachable=0 failed=0 skipped=0
rescued=0 ignored=0
```

Similarly, run the following for the production inventory:

```
$ ansible-playbook -i inventories/production/hosts site.yml

PLAY [Play using best practise directory structure]
****************************

TASK [Gathering Facts]
*********************************************************
ok: [app02.prod.example.com]
ok: [app01.prod.example.com]

TASK [installapp : Display http_port variable contents]
************************
ok: [app01.prod.example.com] => {
    "http_port": 80
}
ok: [app02.prod.example.com] => {
    "http_port": 80
}

TASK [installapp : Create /tmp/foo]
*********************************************
changed: [app01.prod.example.com]
changed: [app02.prod.example.com]

TASK [installapp : Use custom module to copy /tmp/foo]
************************
changed: [app02.prod.example.com]
changed: [app01.prod.example.com]

TASK [installapp : Define a fact about automation]
****************************
ok: [app01.prod.example.com]
ok: [app02.prod.example.com]

TASK [installapp : Tell us about automation with a custom filter applied]
******
ok: [app01.prod.example.com] => {
    "msg": "Ansible is an excellent automation tool"
}
```

```
ok: [app02.prod.example.com] => {
    "msg": "Ansible is an excellent automation tool"
}

PLAY RECAP
***********************************************************************
app01.prod.example.com : ok=6 changed=2 unreachable=0 failed=0 skipped=0
rescued=0 ignored=0
app02.prod.example.com : ok=6 changed=2 unreachable=0 failed=0 skipped=0
rescued=0 ignored=0
```

Notice how the appropriate hosts and associated variables are picked up for each inventory and how tidy and well organized our directory structure is. This is the ideal way for you to lay out your playbooks and will ensure that they can be scaled up to whatever size you need them to be, without them becoming unwieldy and difficult to manage or troubleshoot. In the next section of this chapter, we will explore the best approaches for working with cloud inventories.

The best approach to cloud inventories

In Chapter 3, *Defining Your Inventory*, we looked at a simple example of how you can work with a dynamic inventory, and we walked you through a practical example using the Cobbler provisioning system. However, when it comes to working with cloud inventories (which are simply a form of dynamic inventory, but specifically focused on the cloud), they might, at first, seem somewhat confusing and you may find it difficult to get them up and running. If you follow the high-level procedure outlined in this section, this will become an easy and straightforward task.

As this is a practically focused book, we will choose an example to work with. Sadly, we don't have space to provide practical examples for all of the cloud providers, but if you follow the high-level process we will outline for Amazon EC2 and apply it to your desired cloud provider (for example, Microsoft Azure or Google Cloud Platform), you will find that the process of getting up and running is actually quite straightforward.

An important note before we start, however, is that in Ansible versions up to and including 2.8.x, the dynamic inventory scripts are part of the Ansible source code itself and can be obtained from the main Ansible repository that we examined and cloned previously in this book. With the ever-growing and expanding nature of Ansible, it has become necessary, in the version 2.9.x releases (and beyond), to separate the dynamic inventory scripts into a new distribution mechanism called Ansible collections, which will become mainstream in the 2.10 version (not yet released at the time of writing). You can learn more about Ansible collections and what they are at `https://www.ansible.com/blog/getting-started-with-ansible-collections`.

> The way you download and work with dynamic inventory scripts is likely to change radically with the 2.10 release of Ansible, yet sadly, very little has been revealed, at the time of writing, of what this will look like. As a result, we will guide you through the process of downloading your required dynamic inventory provider scripts for the current 2.9 release, and advise you to consult the Ansible documentation when the 2.10 release comes out for the download location of the relevant scripts. Once you have downloaded them, it is my understanding that you will be able to continue working with them as outlined in this chapter.

If you are working with the 2.9 release of Ansible, you can find and download all of the latest dynamic inventory scripts from the stable-2.9 branch on GitHub, at `https://github.com/ansible/ansible/tree/stable-2.9/contrib/inventory`.

Although the official Ansible documentation has been updated, most guides on the internet still reference the old GitHub locations of these scripts and you will find that they no longer work. Do bear this in mind when working with dynamic inventories! Let's now proceed to cover at the process for working with a dynamic inventory script for a cloud provider; we will use the following Amazon EC2 dynamic inventory script as a working example, but the principles we apply here can equally be used with any other cloud inventory scripts:

1. Having established that we are going to work with Amazon EC2, our first task is to obtain the dynamic inventory script and its associated configuration file. As cloud technologies move fast, it is probably safest to download the latest version of these files directly from the official Ansible project on GitHub. The following three commands will download the dynamic inventory script and make it executable, as well as downloading the template configuration file:

```
$ wget
https://raw.githubusercontent.com/ansible/ansible/stable-2.9/contrib/inventory/ec2.py
$ chmod +x ec2.py
$ wget
```

```
https://raw.githubusercontent.com/ansible/ansible/stable-2.9/contri
b/inventory/ec2.ini
```

2. With the files successfully downloaded, let's take a look inside them. Unfortunately, Ansible dynamic inventories do not have the same neat documentation system that we have seen in modules and plugins. Fortunately for us, however, the authors of these dynamic inventory scripts have put lots of helpful comments at the top of these files to get us started. Let's take a look inside ec2.py:

```
#!/usr/bin/env python

'''
EC2 external inventory script
=================================

Generates inventory that Ansible can understand by making API
request to
AWS EC2 using the Boto library.

NOTE: This script assumes Ansible is being executed where the
environment
variables needed for Boto have already been set:
    export AWS_ACCESS_KEY_ID='AK123'
    export AWS_SECRET_ACCESS_KEY='abc123'

Optional region environment variable if region is 'auto'

This script also assumes that there is an ec2.ini file alongside
it. To specify
 a
different path to ec2.ini, define the EC2_INI_PATH environment
variable:

    export EC2_INI_PATH=/path/to/my_ec2.ini
```

There are pages of documentation to read, but some of the most pertinent information is contained within those first few lines. First of all, we need to ensure that the Boto library is installed. Secondly, we need to set the AWS access parameters for Boto. The author of this document has given us the quickest way to get started (indeed, it is not their job to replicate the Boto documentation).

However, if you refer to the official documentation for Boto, you'll see that there are lots of ways of configuring it with your AWS credentials—setting the environment variables is just one. You can read more about configuring the Boto authentication at https://boto3.amazonaws.com/v1/documentation/api/latest/guide/configuration.html.

3. Before we go ahead and install Boto, let's take a look at the sample ec2.ini file:

```
# Ansible EC2 external inventory script settings
#

[ec2]

# to talk to a private eucalyptus instance uncomment these lines
# and edit edit eucalyptus_host to be the host name of your cloud
controller
#eucalyptus = True
#eucalyptus_host = clc.cloud.domain.org

# AWS regions to make calls to. Set this to 'all' to make request
to all regions
# in AWS and merge the results together. Alternatively, set this to
a comma
# separated list of regions. E.g. 'us-east-1,us-west-1,us-west-2'
and do not
# provide the 'regions_exclude' option. If this is set to 'auto',
AWS_REGION or
# AWS_DEFAULT_REGION environment variable will be read to determine
the region.
regions = all
regions_exclude = us-gov-west-1, cn-north-1
```

Again, you can see pages of well-documented options in this file, and if you scroll all the way to the bottom, you'll even see that you can specify your credentials in this file as an alternative to the methods discussed previously. The default settings for this file are, however, sufficient if you just want to get started.

4. Let's now make sure the Boto library is installed; exactly how you do this will depend on your chosen OS and your version of Python. You might be able to install it through a package; on CentOS 7, you can do this as follows:

```
$ sudo yum -y install python-boto python-boto3
```

Alternatively, you can use `pip` for this purpose. For example, to install it as part of your Python 3 environment, you can run the following command:

```
$ sudo pip3 install boto3
```

5. Once you have `Boto` installed, let's go ahead and set our AWS credentials using the environment variables suggested to us in the preceding documentation:

```
$ export AWS_ACCESS_KEY_ID='<YOUR_DATA>'
$ export AWS_SECRET_ACCESS_KEY='<YOUR_DATA>'
```

6. With these steps complete, you can now use your dynamic inventory script in the usual way—you simply reference the executable inventory script with the `-i` parameter in the same way you do with static inventories. For example, if you want to run the Ansible `ping` module as an ad hoc command against all the hosts you have running in Amazon EC2, you would need to run the following command. Make sure you substitute the user account specified by the `-u` switch with the one you connect to your EC2 instances with. Also, reference your private SSH key file:

```
$ ansible -i ec2.py -u ec2-user --private-key /home/james/my-ec2-
id_rsa -m ping all
```

That's all there is to it—if you approach all dynamic inventory scripts in this same methodical manner, you will have no problem getting them up and running. Just remember that the documentation is normally embedded in both the script file and its accompanying configuration file, and make sure you read both before you attempt to use the scripts.

One thing to note is that many of the dynamic inventory scripts, `ec2.py` included, cache the results of their API calls to the cloud provider to speed up repeated runs and avoid excessive API calls. However, you might find that in a fast-moving development environment, changes to your cloud infrastructure are not picked up fast enough. For most scripts, there are two ways around this—most feature cache configuration parameters in their configuration file, such as the `cache_path` and `cache_max_age` parameters in `ec2.ini`. If you don't want to set these for every single run, you can also refresh the cache manually by calling the dynamic inventory script directly with a special switch—for example, in `ec2.py`:

```
$ ./ec2.py --refresh-cache
```

That concludes our practical introduction to cloud inventory scripts. As we discussed, provided you consult the documentation (both on the internet and embedded within each dynamic inventory script) and follow the simple methodology we described, you should have no problems and should be able to get up and running with dynamic inventories in minutes. In the next section, we'll revert back to looking at static inventories and the best ways to differentiate your various technology environments.

Differentiating between different environment types

In almost every business, you will need to split your technology environment by type. For example, you will almost certainly have a development environment, where all the testing and development work is performed, and a production environment, where all of the stable test code is run. The environments should (in a best-case scenario) make use of the same Ansible playbooks—after all, the logic is that if you can successfully deploy and test an application in your development environment, then you should be able to deploy it in the same way in a production environment and have it work just as well. However, there are always differences between the two environments, not just in the hostnames, but also sometimes in the parameters, the load balancer names, the port numbers, and so on—the list can seem endless.

In the *The preferred directory layout* section of this chapter, we covered a way of differentiating between a development and production environment using two separate inventory directory trees. This is how you should proceed when it comes to differentiating these environments; so, obviously, we won't repeat the examples, but it's important to note that when working with multiple environments, your goals should be as follows:

- Try and reuse the same playbooks for all of your environments that run the same code. For example, if you deploy a web app in your development environment, you should be confident that your playbooks will deploy the same app in the production environment (and your **Quality Assurance (QA)** environment, as well as any others that it might need to be deployed in).
- This means that not only are you testing your application deployments and code, you are also testing your Ansible playbooks and roles as part of your overall testing process.

- Your inventories for each environment should be kept in separate directory trees (as we saw in the *The preferred directory layout* section of this chapter), but all roles, playbooks, plugins, and modules (if used) should be in the same directory structure (this should be the case for both environments).
- It is normal for different environments to require different authentication credentials; you should keep these separate not only for security but also to ensure that playbooks are not accidentally run in the wrong environment.
- Your playbooks should be in your version control system, just as your code is. This enables you to track changes over time and ensure that everyone is working from the same copy of the automation code.

If you pay attention to these simple pointers, you will find that your automation workflow becomes a real asset to your business and ensures reliability and consistency across all of your deployments. Conversely, failure to follow these pointers puts you at risk of experiencing the dreaded, *it worked in development but it doesn't work in production* deployment failures that so often plague the technology industry. Let's now build on this discussion in the next section by looking at best practices when handling host and group variables, something that, as we saw in *The preferred directory layout* section, you need to apply, especially when working with multiple environments.

The proper approach to defining group and host variables

When working with group and host variables, you can split them up using the directory-based approach we used in the *The preferred directory layout* section. However, there are a few additional pointers to managing this that you should be aware of. First and foremost, you should always pay attention to variable precedence. A detailed list of variable precedence order can be found at `https://docs.ansible.com/ansible/latest/user_guide/playbooks_variables.html#variable-precedence-where-should-i-put-a-variable`. However, the key takeaways for working with multiple environments are as follows:

- Host variables are always of a higher order of precedence than group variables; so, you can override any group variable with a host variable. This behavior is useful if you take advantage of it in a controlled manner, but can yield unexpected results if you are not aware of it.
- There is a special group variables definition called `all`, which is applied to all inventory groups. This has a lower order of precedence than specifically defined group variables.

- What happens if you define the same variable twice in two groups? If this happens, both groups have the same order of precedence, so which one wins? To demonstrate this (and our earlier examples), we will create a simple practical example for you to follow.

To get started, let's create a directory structure for our inventories. To keep this example as concise as possible, we will only create a development environment. However, you are free to expand on these concepts by building on the more complete example we covered in the *The preferred directory layout* section of this chapter:

1. Create an inventory directory structure with the following commands:

```
$ mkdir -p inventories/development/group_vars
$ mkdir -p inventories/development/host_vars
```

2. Create a simple inventory file with two hosts in a single group in the `inventories/development/hosts` file; the contents should be as follows:

```
[app]
app01.dev.example.com
app02.dev.example.com
```

3. Now, let's create a special group variable file for all the groups in the inventory; this file will be called `inventories/development/group_vars/all.yml` and should contain the following content:

```
---
http_port: 8080
```

4. Finally, let's create a simple playbook called `site.yml` to query and print the value of the variable we just created:

```
---
- name: Play using best practise directory structure
  hosts: all

  tasks:
    - name: Display the value of our inventory variable
      debug:
        var: http_port
```

5. Now, if we run this playbook, we'll see that the variable (which we only defined in one place) takes the value we would expect:

```
$ ansible-playbook -i inventories/development/hosts site.yml

PLAY [Play using best practise directory structure]
***************************

TASK [Gathering Facts]
********************************************************
ok: [app01.dev.example.com]
ok: [app02.dev.example.com]

TASK [Display the value of our inventory variable]
***************************
ok: [app01.dev.example.com] => {
    "http_port": 8080
}
ok: [app02.dev.example.com] => {
    "http_port": 8080
}

PLAY RECAP
****************************************************************
**
app01.dev.example.com : ok=2 changed=0 unreachable=0 failed=0
skipped=0 rescued=0 ignored=0
app02.dev.example.com : ok=2 changed=0 unreachable=0 failed=0
skipped=0 rescued=0 ignored=0
```

6. So far, so good! Now, let's add a new file to our inventory directory structure, with the all.yml file remaining unchanged. Let's also create a new file located in inventories/development/group_vars/app.yml, which will contain the following content:

```
---
http_port: 8081
```

7. We have now defined the same variable twice—once in a special group called all and once in the app group (which both servers in our development inventory belong to). So, what happens if we now run our playbook? The output should appear as follows:

```
$ ansible-playbook -i inventories/development/hosts site.yml

PLAY [Play using best practise directory structure]
***************************
```

```
TASK [Gathering Facts]
***********************************************************
ok: [app02.dev.example.com]
ok: [app01.dev.example.com]

TASK [Display the value of our inventory variable]
***************************
ok: [app01.dev.example.com] => {
    "http_port": 8081
}
ok: [app02.dev.example.com] => {
    "http_port": 8081
}

PLAY RECAP
******************************************************************************
**
app01.dev.example.com : ok=2 changed=0 unreachable=0 failed=0
skipped=0 rescued=0 ignored=0
app02.dev.example.com : ok=2 changed=0 unreachable=0 failed=0
skipped=0 rescued=0 ignored=0
```

8. As expected, the variable definition in the specific group won, which is in line with the order of precedence documented for Ansible. Now, let's see what happens if we define the same variable twice in two specifically named groups. To complete this example, we'll create a child group, called `centos`, and another group that could notionally contain hosts built to a new build standard, called `newcentos`, which both application servers will be a member of. This means modifying `inventories/development/hosts` so that it now looks as follows:

```
[app]
app01.dev.example.com
app02.dev.example.com

[centos:children]
app

[newcentos:children]
app
```

9. Now, let's redefine the `http_port` variable for the `centos` group by creating a file called `inventories/development/group_vars/centos.yml`, which contains the following content:

```
---
http_port: 8082
```

10. Just to add to the confusion, let's also define this variable for the `newcentos` group in `inventories/development/group_vars/newcentos.yml`, which will contain the following content:

```
---
http_port: 8083
```

11. We've now defined the same variable four times at the group level! Let's rerun our playbook and see which value comes through:

```
$ ansible-playbook -i inventories/development/hosts site.yml

PLAY [Play using best practise directory structure]
***************************

TASK [Gathering Facts]
**********************************************************
ok: [app01.dev.example.com]
ok: [app02.dev.example.com]

TASK [Display the value of our inventory variable]
***************************
ok: [app01.dev.example.com] => {
    "http_port": 8083
}
ok: [app02.dev.example.com] => {
    "http_port": 8083
}

PLAY RECAP
*****************************************************************
**
app01.dev.example.com : ok=2 changed=0 unreachable=0 failed=0
skipped=0 rescued=0 ignored=0
app02.dev.example.com : ok=2 changed=0 unreachable=0 failed=0
skipped=0 rescued=0 ignored=0
```

The value we entered in `newcentos.yml` won—but why? The Ansible documentation states that where identical variables are defined at the group level in the inventory (the one place you can do this), the one from the last-loaded group wins. Groups are processed in alphabetical order and `newcentos` is the group with the name beginning furthest down the alphabet—so, its value of `http_port` was the value that won.

12. Just for completeness, we can override all of this by leaving the `group_vars` directory untouched, but adding a file called `inventories/development/host_vars/app01.dev.example.com.yml`, which will contain the following content:

    ```
    ---
    http_port: 9090
    ```

13. Now, if we run our playbook one final time, we will see that the value we defined at the host level completely overrides any value that we set at the group level for `app01.dev.example.com`. `app02.dev.example.com` is unaffected as we did not define a host variable for it, so the next highest level of precedence—the group variable from the `newcentos` group—won:

    ```
    $ ansible-playbook -i inventories/development/hosts site.yml

    PLAY [Play using best practise directory structure]
    ***************************

    TASK [Gathering Facts]
    ********************************************************
    ok: [app01.dev.example.com]
    ok: [app02.dev.example.com]

    TASK [Display the value of our inventory variable]
    ****************************
    ok: [app01.dev.example.com] => {
        "http_port": 9090
    }
    ok: [app02.dev.example.com] => {
        "http_port": 8083
    }

    PLAY RECAP
    **************************************************************************
    **
    app01.dev.example.com : ok=2 changed=0 unreachable=0 failed=0
    skipped=0 rescued=0 ignored=0
    app02.dev.example.com : ok=2 changed=0 unreachable=0 failed=0
    skipped=0 rescued=0 ignored=0
    ```

With this knowledge, you can now make advanced decisions about how to structure your variables within your inventory to make sure you achieve the desired results at both a host and group level. It's important to know about variable precedence ordering, as these examples have demonstrated, but following the documented order will also allow you to produce powerful, flexible playbook inventories that work well across multiple environments. Now, you may have noticed that, throughout this chapter, we have used a top-level playbook in our directory structure called `site.yml`. We will look at this playbook in greater detail in the next section.

Using top-level playbooks

In all of the examples so far, we have built out using the best practice directory structure recommended by Ansible and continually referred to a top-level playbook, typically called `site.yml`. The idea behind this playbook, and, indeed, its common name across all of our directory structures, is so that it can be used across your entire server estate—that is to say, your **site**.

This, of course, is not to say that you have to use the same set of playbooks across every server in your infrastructure or for every single function; rather, it means only you can make the best decision as to what suits your environment best. However, the whole aim of Ansible automation is that the created solution is simple to run and operate. Imagine handing a playbook directory structure with 100 different playbooks to a new system administrator—how would they know which ones to run and in which circumstances? The task of training someone to use the playbooks would be immense and would simply move complexity from one area to another.

At the other the end of the spectrum, you could make use of the `when` clauses with facts and inventory grouping, such that your playbook knows exactly what to run on each server in every possible circumstance. This, of course, is unlikely to happen and the truth is that your automation solution will end up somewhere in the middle.

The most important thing is that, on receipt of a new playbook directory structure, a new operator at least knows what the starting point for both running the playbooks, and understanding the code is. If the top-level playbook they encounter is always `site.yml`, then at least everyone knows where to start. Through the clever use of roles and the `import_*` and `include_*` statements, you can split your playbook up into logical portions of reusable code, as we previously discussed, all from one playbook file.

Now that you have learned about the importance of top-level playbooks, let's take a look, in the next section, at how to take advantage of version control tools to ensure good practices are adhered to when it comes to centralizing and maintaining your automation code.

Leveraging version control tools

As we discussed earlier in this chapter, it is vital that you version control and test not only your code but also your Ansible automation code. This should include inventories (or dynamic inventory scripts), any custom modules, plugins, roles, and playbook code. The reason for this is simple—the ultimate goal of Ansible automation is likely to be to deploy an entire environment using a playbook (or set of playbooks). This might even involve deploying infrastructure as code, especially if you are deploying to a cloud environment.

Any changes to your Ansible code could mean big changes to your environment, and possibly even whether an important production service works or not. As a result, it is vital that you maintain a version history of your Ansible code and that everyone works from the same version. You are free to choose the version control system that suits you best; most corporate environments will already have some kind of version control system in place. However, if you haven't worked with version control systems before, we recommend that you sign up for a free account on somewhere such as GitHub or GitLab, which both offer version control repositories for free, along with more advanced paid-for plans.

A complete discussion of version control with Git is beyond the scope of this book; there are, indeed, entire books devoted to the subject. However, we will take you through the simplest possible use case. It is assumed, in the following examples, that you are using a free account on GitHub, but if you are using a different provider, simply change the URLs to match those given to you by your version control repository host.

In addition to this, you will need to install the command-line Git tools on your Linux host. On CentOS, you would install these as follows:

```
$ sudo yum install git
```

On Ubuntu, the process is similarly straightforward:

```
$ sudo apt-get update
$ sudo apt-get install git
```

Once the tools are installed and your account is set up, your next task is to clone a Git repository to your machine. If you want to start working with your own repository, you will need to set this up with your provider—excellent documentation is provided by both GitHub and GitLab and you should follow this to set up your first repository.

Once it is set up and initialized, you can clone a copy to your local machine to make changes to your code. This local copy is called a working copy, and you can work through the process of cloning it and making changes as follows (note that these are purely hypothetical examples to give you an idea of the commands you will need to run; you should adapt them for your own use case):

1. Clone your `git` repository to your local machine to create a working copy using a command such as the following:

```
$ git clone https://github.com/<YOUR_GIT_ACCOUNT>/<GIT_REPO>.git
Cloning into '<GIT_REPO>'...
remote: Enumerating objects: 7, done.
remote: Total 7 (delta 0), reused 0 (delta 0), pack-reused 7
Unpacking objects: 100% (7/7), done.
```

2. Change to the directory of the code you cloned (the working copy) and make any code changes you need to make:

```
$ cd <GIT_REPO>
$ vim myplaybook.yml
```

3. Be sure to test your code and, when you are happy with it, add the changed files that are ready for committing a new version using a command such as the following:

```
$ git add myplaybook.yml
```

4. The next step is to commit the changes you have made. A commit is basically a new version of code within the repository, so it should be accompanied by a meaningful `commit` message (specified in quotes after the –m switch), as follows:

```
$ git commit -m 'Added new spongle-widget deployment to
myplaybook.yml'
[master ed14138] Added new spongle-widget deployment to
myplaybook.yml
 Committer: Daniel Oh <doh@danieloh.redhat.com>
Your name and email address were configured automatically based
on your username and hostname. Please check that they are accurate.
You can suppress this message by setting them explicitly. Run the
following command and follow the instructions in your editor to
edit
your configuration file:

    git config --global --edit

After doing this, you may fix the identity used for this commit
with:
```

```
git commit --amend --reset-author

1 file changed, 1 insertion(+), 1 deletion(-)
```

5. Right now, all of these changes live solely in the working copy on your local machine. This is good by itself, but it would be better if the code was available to everyone who needs to view it on the version control system. To push your updated commits back to (for example) GitHub, run the following command:

```
$ git push
Enumerating objects: 5, done.
Counting objects: 100% (5/5), done.
Delta compression using up to 8 threads
Compressing objects: 100% (3/3), done.
Writing objects: 100% (3/3), 297 bytes | 297.00 KiB/s, done.
Total 3 (delta 2), reused 0 (delta 0)
remote: Resolving deltas: 100% (2/2), completed with 2 local
objects.
To https://github.com/<YOUR_GIT_ACCOUNT>/<GIT_REPO>.git
   0d00263..ed14138 master -> master
```

That's all there is to it!

6. Now, other collaborators can clone your code just as we did in *step 1*. Alternatively, if they already have a working copy of your repository, they can update their working copy using the following command (you can also do this if you want to update your working copy to see changes made by someone else):

```
$ git pull
```

There are some incredibly advanced topics and use cases for Git that are beyond the scope of this book. However, you will find that roughly 80% of the time, the preceding commands are all the Git command-line knowledge you need. There are also a number of graphical frontends to Git, as well as code editors and **Integrated Development Environments (IDEs)**, that integrate with Git repositories and can assist you further in taking advantage of them. With that complete, let's take a look at how to ensure you can use the same playbook (or role) across multiple hosts, even though they might have different OSes and versions.

Setting OS and distribution variances

As stated earlier, our goal is to try to use the same automation code as widely as possible. However, as much as we try to standardize our technology environments, variants always creep in. For example, it is impossible to simultaneously perform a major upgrade on all your servers in one go, so when a major new OS version comes out, such as **Red Hat Enterprise Linux (RHEL)** 8 or Ubuntu Server 20.04, it is inevitable that some machines will remain on older versions as others are upgraded. Similarly, an environment might be standardized on Ubuntu, but then an application is introduced that has only been certified to run on CentOS. In short, as important as standardization is, variances will always creep in.

When writing Ansible playbooks, especially roles, your goal should be for them to be as widely applicable as possible throughout your environment. A classic example of this is package management—let's say you are writing a role to install the Apache 2 web server. If you have to support both Ubuntu and CentOS with this role, not only do you have different package managers to deal with (`yum` and `apt`), you also have different package names (`httpd` and `apache2`).

In `Chapter 4`, *Playbooks and Roles*, we looked at how to apply conditions to tasks using the `when` clause, along with facts gathered by Ansible, such as `ansible_distribution`. However, there is another way of running tasks on specific hosts that we haven't yet looked at. In the same chapter, we also looked at the concept of defining multiple plays in one playbook—there is a special module that can create inventory groups for us based on Ansible facts and we can leverage this along with multiple plays to create a playbook that runs the appropriate tasks on each host based on its type. This is best explained by a practical example, so let's get started.

Assume that we are using the following simple inventory file for this example, which has two hosts in a single group called `app`:

```
[app]
app01.dev.example.com
app02.dev.example.com
```

Let's now build a simple playbook that demonstrates how you can group differing plays using an Ansible fact so that the OS distribution determines which play in a playbook gets run. Follow these steps to create this playbook and observe it's operation:

1. Start by creating a new playbook—we'll call it `osvariants.yml`—with the following `Play` definition. It will also contain a single task, as shown:

```
---
- name: Play to demonstrate group_by module
  hosts: all

  tasks:
    - name: Create inventory groups based on host facts
      group_by:
        key: os_{{ ansible_facts['distribution'] }}
```

The playbook structure will be, by now, incredibly familiar to you. However, the use of the `group_by` module is new. It dynamically creates new inventory groups based on the key that we specify—in this example, we are creating groups based on a key comprised of the `os_` fixed string, followed by the OS distribution fact obtained from the `Gathering Facts` stage. The original inventory group structure is preserved and unmodified, but all the hosts are also added to the newly created groups according to their facts.

So, the two servers in our simple inventory remain in the `app` group, but if they are based on Ubuntu, they will be added to a newly created inventory group called `os_Ubuntu`. Similarly, if they are based on CentOS, they will be added to a group called `os_CentOS`.

2. Armed with this information, we can go ahead and create additional plays based on the newly created groups. Let's add the following `Play` definition to the same playbook file to install Apache on CentOS:

```
- name: Play to install Apache on CentOS
  hosts: os_CentOS
  become: true

  tasks:
    - name: Install Apache on CentOS
      yum:
        name: httpd
        state: present
```

This is a perfectly normal `Play` definition that uses the `yum` module to install the `httpd` package (as required on CentOS). The only thing that differentiates it from our earlier work is the `hosts` definition at the top of the play. This uses the newly created inventory group created by the `group_by` module in the first play.

3. We can, similarly, add a third `Play` definition, this time for installing the `apache2` package on Ubuntu using the `apt` module:

```
- name: Play to install Apache on Ubuntu
  hosts: os_Ubuntu
  become: true

  tasks:
    - name: Install Apache on Ubuntu
      apt:
        name: apache2
        state: present
```

4. If our environment is based on CentOS servers and we run this playbook, the results are as follows:

```
$ ansible-playbook -i hosts osvariants.yml

PLAY [Play to demonstrate group_by module]
************************************

TASK [Gathering Facts]
********************************************************
ok: [app02.dev.example.com]
ok: [app01.dev.example.com]

TASK [Create inventory groups based on host facts]
***************************
ok: [app01.dev.example.com]
ok: [app02.dev.example.com]

PLAY [Play to install Apache on CentOS]
****************************************

TASK [Gathering Facts]
********************************************************
ok: [app01.dev.example.com]
ok: [app02.dev.example.com]

TASK [Install Apache on CentOS]
***********************************************
changed: [app02.dev.example.com]
```

```
changed: [app01.dev.example.com]
[WARNING]: Could not match supplied host pattern, ignoring:
os_Ubuntu

PLAY [Play to install Apache on Ubuntu]
*****************************************
skipping: no hosts matched

PLAY RECAP
*********************************************************************
**
app01.dev.example.com : ok=4 changed=2 unreachable=0 failed=0
skipped=0 rescued=0 ignored=0
app02.dev.example.com : ok=4 changed=2 unreachable=0 failed=0
skipped=0 rescued=0 ignored=0
```

Notice how the task to install Apache on CentOS was run. It was run this way because the `group_by` module created a group called `os_CentOS` and our second play only runs on hosts in the group called `os_CentOS`. As there were no servers running on Ubuntu in the inventory, the `os_Ubuntu` group was never created and so the third play does not run. We receive a warning about the fact that there is no host pattern that matches `os_Ubuntu`, but the playbook does not fail—it simply skips this play.

We provided this example to show you another way of managing the inevitable variance in OS types that you will come across in your automation coding. At the end of the day, it is up to you to choose the coding style most appropriate to you. You can make use of the `group_by` module, as detailed here, or write your tasks in blocks and add a when clause to the blocks so that they only run when a certain fact-based condition is met (for example, the OS distribution is CentOS)—or perhaps even a combination of the two. The choice is ultimately yours and these different examples are provided to empower you with multiple options that you can choose between to create the best possible solution for your scenario.

Finally, let's round off this chapter with a look at porting your automation code between Ansible versions.

Porting between Ansible versions

Ansible is a fast-moving project, and with releases and new features added, new modules (and module enhancements) are released and the inevitable bugs that come with the software are fixed. There is no doubt that you will end up writing your code against one version of Ansible only to need to run it on a newer version again at some point. By way of example, when we started writing this book, the current release of Ansible was 2.7. As we are editing this book ready for publication, version 2.9.6 is the current stable version.

Often, you will find that your code from an earlier version "just about works" when you upgrade it, but this isn't always a given. Modules are sometimes deprecated (although usually not without warning) and features do change. Several major changes are expected when Ansible 2.10 is released. So, the question remains—how can you ensure that your playbooks, roles, modules, and plugins still work when you update your Ansible installation?

The first part of the answer is to establish which version of Ansible you are starting from. For example, let's say you are preparing for the release of Ansible 2.10. If you query the version of Ansible you already have installed and see something like the following, then you know you are starting from Ansible release 2.9:

```
$ ansible --version
ansible 2.9.6
  config file = /etc/ansible/ansible.cfg
  configured module search path = [u'/home/james/.ansible/plugins/modules',
u'/usr/share/ansible/plugins/modules']
  ansible python module location = /usr/lib/python2.7/site-packages/ansible
  executable location = /usr/bin/ansible
  python version = 2.7.5 (default, Aug 7 2019, 00:51:29) [GCC 4.8.5
20150623 (Red Hat 4.8.5-39)]
```

So, your first port of call should be to review the porting guide for the Ansible 2.10 release; a porting guide is normally written for every major release (such as 2.8, 2.9, and so on). The guide for 2.10 can be found at https://docs.ansible.com/ansible/devel/porting_guides/porting_guide_2.10.html.

If we review this document, we can see that there are a number of changes coming—whether they are significant to you really depends on the code you are running. For example, if we review the *Modules Removed* section of the guide, we can see that the letsencrypt module has been removed and it is suggested that you use the acme_certificate module instead. If you are generating free SSL certificates using the letsencrypt module in Ansible, then you would certainly need to update your playbooks and roles to accommodate this change.

As you can see in the preceding link, there are a great number of changes between the 2.9 and 2.10 releases of Ansible. To that end, it's also important to note that the porting guides are written from the perspective of an upgrade from the previous major release. That is to say, if you query your Ansible version and it returns the following, you are porting from Ansible 2.8:

```
$ ansible --version
ansible 2.8.4
  config file = /etc/ansible/ansible.cfg
  configured module search path = [u'/home/james/.ansible/plugins/modules',
u'/usr/share/ansible/plugins/modules']
  ansible python module location = /usr/lib/python2.7/site-packages/ansible
  executable location = /usr/bin/ansible
  python version = 2.7.5 (default, Aug 7 2019, 00:51:29) [GCC 4.8.5
20150623 (Red Hat 4.8.5-39)]
```

If you move straight to Ansible 2.10 when it comes out, then you need to review the porting guides for both 2.9 (which covers the changes required to your code between releases 2.8 and 2.9) and 2.10 (which covers the changes required to upgrade from 2.9 to 2.10). An index of all the porting guides can be found on the official Ansible website at `https://docs.ansible.com/ansible/devel/porting_guides/porting_guides.html`.

Another great source of information, especially more fine-grained information, on the changes between releases are the changelogs. These are released and updated for every minor release and can currently be found at the official Ansible GitHub repository on the `stable` branch for the release you wish to query. For example, if you wish to review all the changelogs for Ansible 2.9, you would need to go to `https://github.com/ansible/ansible/blob/stable-2.9/changelogs/CHANGELOG-v2.9.rst`.

The trick to porting code between Ansible releases (if, indeed, you can call it a trick) is simply to read the excellent documentation released by the Ansible project team. A lot of effort goes into creating this documentation, so you are advised to make good use of it. That concludes our look at the best practices for working with Ansible. We hope you have found this chapter valuable.

Summary

Ansible automation projects often start out small, but as people come to realize the power and simplicity of Ansible, both the code and the inventories tend to grow at an exponential pace (at least in my experience). It is important that in the push for greater automation, the Ansible automation code and infrastructure itself doesn't become another headache. By embedding a few good practices early on and applying them consistently throughout your automation journey with Ansible, you will find that managing your Ansible automation is simple and easy and is a true benefit to your technology infrastructure.

In this chapter, you learned about the best practices for directory layout that you should adopt for your playbooks and the steps you should adopt when working with cloud inventories. You then learned new ways of differentiating environments by OS type, as well as more about variable precedence and how to leverage it when working with host and group variables. You then explored the importance of the top-level playbook, before looking at how to make use of version control tools to manage your automation code. Finally, you explored the new techniques for creating single playbooks that will manage servers of different OS versions and distributions, before finally looking at the important topic of porting your code to new Ansible versions.

In the next chapter, we will look at some of the more advanced ways that you can use Ansible to take care of some special cases that may arise on your automation journey.

Questions

1. What is a safe and easy way to manage (that is, modify, fix, and create) code changes continuously and share them with others?

   A) Playbook revision

   B) Task history

   C) Ad hoc creation

   D) With a Git repository

   E) Log management

2. True or false – Ansible Galaxy supports sharing roles with other users from a central, community-supported repository.

   A) True

   B) False

3. True or false – Ansible modules are guaranteed to be available in all future releases of Ansible.

   A) True

   B) False

Further reading

Manage multiple repositories, versions, or tasks by creating branches and tags to control multiple versions effectively. Refer to the following links for more details:

- How to use Git tagging: `https://git-scm.com/book/en/v2/Git-Basics-Tagging`
- How to use Git branches: `https://git-scm.com/docs/git-branch`

8
Advanced Ansible Topics

Up to this point, we have worked hard to give you a solid foundation of Ansible, so that whatever your desired automation task, you can implement it with ease and confidence. However, when you really start to ramp up your automation, how do you ensure that you can handle any condition that arises in a graceful manner? For example, how can you ensure that when you have to initiate long-running actions, you can run them asynchronously and come back to them to check on the results reliably later? Or, if you are updating a large group of servers, how can you ensure that the play fails early if a handful of servers suffer failures? The last thing you want to do is to roll out a broken update (let's face it, problems do occur with everyone's code from time to time) across a hundred servers—far better to detect that a small percentage have failed and abort the entire play on this basis than attempt to continue and break an entire load-balanced cluster.

In this chapter, we will look at how to solve these particular issues, as well as many more, using some of the more advanced features of Ansible to control playbook flow and error handling. We will explore, through practical examples, how to perform rolling updates with Ansible, how to work with proxies and jump hosts (which is vital for secure environments and often for core network configuration), and how to secure sensitive Ansible data at rest using the native Ansible Vault technology. By the end of this chapter, you will have a full picture of how to run Ansible not only in a small environment but also in a large, secure, mission-critical environment.

In this chapter, we will cover the following topics:

- Asynchronous versus synchronous actions
- Controlling play execution for rolling updates
- Configuring the maximum failure percentage
- Setting task execution delegation
- Using the `run_once` option
- Running playbooks locally
- Working with proxies and jump hosts
- Configuring playbook prompts
- Placing tags in the plays and tasks
- Securing data with Ansible Vault

Technical requirements

This chapter assumes that you have set up your control host with Ansible, as detailed in `Chapter 1`, *Getting Started with Ansible*, and are using the most recent version available. The examples in this chapter are tested with Ansible 2.9. This chapter also assumes that you have at least one additional host to test against and ideally, this should be Linux-based. Although we will give specific examples of hostnames in this chapter, you are free to substitute them with your own hostname and/or IP addresses; details of how to do this are provided at the appropriate places.

The code bundle for this chapter is available at `https://github.com/PacktPublishing/Ansible-2-Cookbook/tree/master/Chapter%20 8`.

Asynchronous versus synchronous actions

As we have seen in this book so far, Ansible plays are executed in sequence, with each task running to completion before the next task is started. Although this is often advantageous for flow control and logical sequencing, there are times when you may not want this. In particular, it might be the case that a particular task runs for longer than the configured SSH connection timeout and as Ansible uses SSH to perform its automation tasks on most platforms, this would be an issue.

Fortunately, Ansible tasks can be run asynchronously—that is to say, tasks can be run in the background on the target host and polled on a regular basis. This is in contrast to synchronous tasks, where the connection to the target host is kept open until the task completes (which runs the risk of a timeout occurring).

As ever, let's explore this through a practical example. Suppose we have two servers in a simple INI-formatted inventory:

```
[frontends]
frt01.example.com
frt02.example.com
```

Now, in order to simulate a long-running task, we'll run the `sleep` command using the `shell` module. However, rather than have it run with the SSH connection blocked for the duration of the `sleep` command, we'll add two special parameters to the task, as shown:

```
---
- name: Play to demonstrate asynchronous tasks
  hosts: frontends
  become: true

  tasks:
    - name: A simulated long running task
      shell: "sleep 20"
      async: 30
      poll: 5
```

The two new parameters are `async` and `poll`. The `async` parameter tells Ansible that this task should be run asynchronously (so that the SSH connection will not be blocked) for a maximum of 30 seconds. If the task runs for longer than this configured time, Ansible considers the task to have failed and the play is failed, accordingly. When `poll` is set to a positive integer, Ansible checks the status of the asynchronous task at the specified interval—in this example, every 5 seconds. If `poll` is set to 0, then the task is run in the background and never checked—it is up to you to write a task to manually check its status later on.

If you don't specify the `poll` value, it will be set to the default value defined by the `DEFAULT_POLL_INTERVAL` configuration parameter of Ansible (which is `10` seconds).

When you run this playbook, you will find that it runs just like any other playbook; from the terminal output, you won't be able to see any difference. But behind the scenes, Ansible checks the task every `5` seconds until it succeeds or reaches the `async` timeout value of `30` seconds:

```
$ ansible-playbook -i hosts async.yml

PLAY [Play to demonstrate asynchronous tasks]
********************************

TASK [Gathering Facts]
*******************************************************
ok: [frt02.example.com]
ok: [frt01.example.com]

TASK [A simulated long running task]
********************************************
changed: [frt02.example.com]
changed: [frt01.example.com]

PLAY RECAP
**************************************************************************
frt01.example.com : ok=2 changed=1 unreachable=0 failed=0 skipped=0
rescued=0 ignored=0
frt02.example.com : ok=2 changed=1 unreachable=0 failed=0 skipped=0
rescued=0 ignored=0
```

If you want to check on the task later (that is, if `poll` is set to `0`), you could add a second task to your playbook so that it looks as follows:

```
---
- name: Play to demonstrate asynchronous tasks
  hosts: frontends
  become: true

  tasks:
    - name: A simulated long running task
      shell: "sleep 20"
      async: 30
      poll: 0
      register: long_task
```

```
  - name: Check on the asynchronous task
    async_status:
      jid: "{{ long_task.ansible_job_id }}"
    register: async_result
    until: async_result.finished
    retries: 30
```

In this playbook, the initial asynchronous task is defined as before, except we have now set poll to 0. We have also chosen to register the result of this task to a variable called long_task—this is so that we can query the job ID for the task when we check it later on. The next (new) task in the play uses the async_status module to check on the job ID we registered from the first task and loops until the job either finishes or reaches 30 retries—whichever comes first. When using these in a playbook, you almost certainly wouldn't add the two tasks back to back like this—usually, you would perform additional tasks in between them—but to keep this example simple, we will run the two tasks sequentially. Running this playbook should yield an output similar to the following:

```
$ ansible-playbook -i hosts async2.yml

PLAY [Play to demonstrate asynchronous tasks]
*********************************

TASK [Gathering Facts]
***********************************************************
ok: [frt01.example.com]
ok: [frt02.example.com]

TASK [A simulated long running task]
*******************************************
changed: [frt02.example.com]
changed: [frt01.example.com]

TASK [Check on the asynchronous task]
********************************************
FAILED - RETRYING: Check on the asynchronous task (30 retries left).
FAILED - RETRYING: Check on the asynchronous task (30 retries left).
FAILED - RETRYING: Check on the asynchronous task (29 retries left).
FAILED - RETRYING: Check on the asynchronous task (29 retries left).
FAILED - RETRYING: Check on the asynchronous task (28 retries left).
FAILED - RETRYING: Check on the asynchronous task (28 retries left).
FAILED - RETRYING: Check on the asynchronous task (27 retries left).
FAILED - RETRYING: Check on the asynchronous task (27 retries left).
changed: [frt01.example.com]
changed: [frt02.example.com]

PLAY RECAP
```

```
*************************************************************************
frt01.example.com : ok=3 changed=2 unreachable=0 failed=0 skipped=0
rescued=0 ignored=0
frt02.example.com : ok=3 changed=2 unreachable=0 failed=0 skipped=0
rescued=0 ignored=0
```

In the preceding code block, we can see that the long-running task is left running and the next task polls its status until the conditions we set are met. In this case, we can see that the task finished successfully and the overall play result was successful. Asynchronous actions are especially useful for large downloads, package updates, and other tasks that might take a long time to run. You may find them useful in your playbook development, especially in more complex infrastructures.

With this under our belt, let's take a look at another advanced technique that might be useful in large infrastructures—performing rolling updates with Ansible.

Control play execution for rolling updates

By default, Ansible parallelizes tasks on multiple hosts at the same time to speed up automation tasks in large inventories. The setting for this is defined by the `forks` parameter in the Ansible configuration file, which defaults to 5 (so, by default, Ansible attempts to run its automation job on five hosts at the same time).

In a load-balanced environment, this is not ideal, especially if you want to avoid downtime. Suppose we have five frontend servers in an inventory (or perhaps even fewer). If we allow Ansible to update all of these at the same time, the end users may experience a loss of service. So, it is important to consider updating all of the servers at different times. Let's reuse our inventory from the previous section with just two servers in it. Obviously, if these were in a load-balanced environment, it would be vital that we only update one of these at a time; if both were taken out of service simultaneously, then end users would definitely lose access to the service until the Ansible play completes successfully.

The answer to this is to use the `serial` keyword in the play definition to determine how many hosts are operated on at once. Let's demonstrate this through a practical example:

1. Create the following simple playbook to run two commands on the two hosts in our inventory. The content of the command is not important at this stage, but if you run the `date` command using the `command` module, you will be able to see the time that each task is run, as well as if you specify `-v` to increase the verbosity when you run the play:

```
---
- name: Simple serial demonstration play
  hosts: frontends
  gather_facts: false

  tasks:
    - name: First task
      command: date
    - name: Second task
      command: date
```

2. Now, if you run this play, you will see that it performs all the operations on each host simultaneously, as we have fewer hosts than the default number of forks—5. This behavior is normal for Ansible, but not really what we want as our users will experience service outage:

```
$ ansible-playbook -i hosts serial.yml

PLAY [Simple serial demonstration play]
**************************************

TASK [First task]
*************************************************************
changed: [frt02.example.com]
changed: [frt01.example.com]

TASK [Second task]
*************************************************************
changed: [frt01.example.com]
changed: [frt02.example.com]


PLAY RECAP
*******************************************************************
**
frt01.example.com : ok=2 changed=2 unreachable=0 failed=0 skipped=0
rescued=0 ignored=0
```

```
frt02.example.com : ok=2 changed=2 unreachable=0 failed=0 skipped=0
rescued=0 ignored=0
```

3. Now, let's modify the play definition, as shown. We'll leave the `tasks` sections exactly as they were in *step 1*:

```
---
- name: Simple serial demonstration play
  hosts: frontends
  serial: 1
  gather_facts: false
```

4. Notice the presence of the `serial: 1` line. This tells Ansible to complete the play on `1` host at a time before moving on to the next. If we run the play again, we can see this in action:

```
$ ansible-playbook -i hosts serial.yml

PLAY [Simple serial demonstration play]
****************************************

TASK [First task]
*************************************************************
changed: [frt01.example.com]

TASK [Second task]
*************************************************************
changed: [frt01.example.com]

PLAY [Simple serial demonstration play]
****************************************

TASK [First task]
*************************************************************
changed: [frt02.example.com]

TASK [Second task]
*************************************************************
changed: [frt02.example.com]

PLAY RECAP
*******************************************************************
**
frt01.example.com : ok=2 changed=2 unreachable=0 failed=0 skipped=0
rescued=0 ignored=0
frt02.example.com : ok=2 changed=2 unreachable=0 failed=0 skipped=0
rescued=0 ignored=0
```

Much better! If you imagine that this playbook actually disables these hosts on a load balancer, performs an upgrade, and then re-enables the hosts on the load balancer, this is exactly how you would want the operation to proceed. Doing so without the `serial: 1` directive would result in all the hosts being removed from the load balancer at once, causing a loss of service.

It is useful to note that the `serial` directive can also take a percentage instead of an integer. When you specify a percentage, you are telling Ansible to run the play on that percentage of hosts at one time. So, if you have 4 hosts in your inventory and specify `serial: 25%`, Ansible will only run the play on one host at a time. If you have 8 hosts in your inventory, it will run the play on two hosts at a time. I'm sure you get the idea!

You can even build on this by passing a list to the `serial` directive. Consider the following code:

```
serial:
  - 1
  - 3
  - 5
```

This tells Ansible to run the play on 1 host, initially, then on the next 3, and then on batches of 5 at a time until the inventory is completed. You can also specify a list of percentages in place of the integer numbers of hosts. In doing this, you will build up a robust playbook that can perform rolling updates without causing a loss of service to end users. With this complete, let's further build on this knowledge by looking at controlling the maximum failure percentage that Ansible can tolerate before it aborts a play, which will again be useful in highly available or load-balanced environments such as this.

Configuring the maximum failure percentage

In its default mode of operation, Ansible continues to execute a play on a batch of servers (the batch size is determined by the `serial` directive we discussed in the preceding section) as long as there are hosts in the inventory and a failure isn't recorded. Obviously, in a highly available or load-balanced environment (such as the one we discussed previously), this is not ideal. If there is a bug in your play, or perhaps a problem with the code being rolled out, the last thing that you want is for Ansible to faithfully roll it out to all servers in the cluster, causing a service outage because all the nodes suffered a failed upgrade. It would be far better, in this kind of environment, to fail early on and leave at least some hosts in the cluster untouched until someone can intervene and resolve the issue.

For our practical example, let's consider an expanded inventory with 10 hosts in it. We'll define this as follows:

```
[frontends]
frt[01:10].example.com
```

Now, let's create a simple playbook to run on these hosts. We will set our batch size to 5 and `max_fail_percentage` to 50% in the play definition:

1. Create the following play definition to demonstrate the use of the `max_fail_percentage` directive:

   ```
   ---
   - name: A simple play to demonstrate use of max_fail_percentage
     hosts: frontends
     gather_facts: no
     serial: 5
     max_fail_percentage: 50
   ```

   We have defined 10 hosts in our inventory, so it will process them in batches of 5 (as specified by `serial: 5`). We will fail the entire play and stop performing processing if more than 50% of the hosts in one batch fails.

    The number of failed hosts must exceed the value of `max_fail_percentage`; if it is equal, the play continues. So, in our example, if exactly 50% of our hosts failed, the play would still continue.

2. Next, we will define two simple tasks. The first task has a special clause under it that we use to deliberately simulate a failure—this line starts with `failed_when` and we use it to tell the task that if it runs this task on the first three hosts in the batch, then it should deliberately fail this task regardless of the result; otherwise, it should allow the task to run as normal:

   ```
   tasks:
     - name: A task that will sometimes fail
       debug:
         msg: This might fail
       failed_when: inventory_hostname in ansible_play_batch[0:3]
   ```

3. Finally, we'll add a second task that will always succeed. This is run if the play is allowed to continue, but not if it is aborted:

   ```
     - name: A task that will succeed
       debug:
         msg: Success!
   ```

So, we have deliberately constructed a playbook that will run on a 10-host inventory in batches of 5 hosts at a time, but the play is aborted if more than 50% of the hosts in any given batch experiences a failure. We have also deliberately set up a failure condition that causes three of the hosts in the first batch of 5 (60%) to fail.

4. Run the playbook and let's observe what happens:

```
$ ansible-playbook -i morehosts maxfail.yml

PLAY [A simple play to demonstrate use of max_fail_percentage]
*****************

TASK [A task that will sometimes fail]
******************************************
fatal: [frt01.example.com]: FAILED! => {
    "msg": "This might fail"
}
fatal: [frt02.example.com]: FAILED! => {
    "msg": "This might fail"
}
fatal: [frt03.example.com]: FAILED! => {
    "msg": "This might fail"
}
ok: [frt04.example.com] => {
    "msg": "This might fail"
}
ok: [frt05.example.com] => {
    "msg": "This might fail"
}

NO MORE HOSTS LEFT
*************************************************************

NO MORE HOSTS LEFT
*************************************************************

PLAY RECAP
*****************************************************************
**
frt01.example.com : ok=0 changed=0 unreachable=0 failed=1 skipped=0
rescued=0 ignored=0
frt02.example.com : ok=0 changed=0 unreachable=0 failed=1 skipped=0
rescued=0 ignored=0
frt03.example.com : ok=0 changed=0 unreachable=0 failed=1 skipped=0
rescued=0 ignored=0
frt04.example.com : ok=1 changed=0 unreachable=0 failed=0 skipped=0
```

```
             rescued=0 ignored=0
             frt05.example.com : ok=1 changed=0 unreachable=0 failed=0 skipped=0
             rescued=0 ignored=0
```

Notice the results of this playbook. We deliberately failed three of the first batch of 5, exceeding the threshold for max_fail_percentage that we set. This immediately causes the play to abort and the second task is not performed on the first batch of 5. You will also notice that the second batch of 5, out of the 10 hosts, is never processed, so our play was truly aborted. This is exactly the behavior you would want to see to prevent a failed update from rolling out across a cluster. Through the careful use of batches and max_fail_percentage, you can safely run automated tasks across an entire cluster without the fear of breaking the entire cluster in the event of an issue. In the next section, we will take a look at another feature of Ansible that can be incredibly useful when it comes to working with clusters—task delegation.

Setting task execution delegation

In every play we have run so far, we have assumed that all the tasks are executed on each host in the inventory in turn. However, what if you need to run one or two tasks on a different host? For example, we have talked about the concept of automating upgrades on clusters. Logically, however, we would want to automate the entire process, including the removal of each host in turn from the load balancer and its return after the task is completed.

Although we still want to run our play across our entire inventory, we certainly don't want to run the load balancer commands from those hosts. Let's once again explain this in more detail with a practical example. We'll reuse the two simple host inventories that we used earlier in this chapter:

```
[frontends]
frt01.example.com
frt02.example.com
```

Now, to work on this, let's create two simple shell scripts in the same directory as our playbook. These are only examples as setting up a load balancer is beyond the scope of this book. However, imagine that you have a shell script (or other executables) that you can call that can add and remove hosts to and from a load balancer:

1. For our example, let's create a script called `remove_from_loadbalancer.sh`, which will contain the following:

   ```
   #!/bin/sh
   echo Removing $1 from load balancer...
   ```

2. We will also create a script called `add_to_loadbalancer.sh`, which will contain the following:

   ```
   #!/bin/sh
   echo Adding $1 to load balancer...
   ```

   Obviously, in a real-world example, there would be much more code in these scripts!

3. Now, let's create a playbook that will perform the logic we outlined here. We'll first create a very simple play definition (you are free to experiment with the `serial` and `max_fail_percentage` directives as you wish) and an initial task:

   ```
   ---
   - name: Play to demonstrate task delegation
     hosts: frontends

     tasks:
       - name: Remove host from the load balancer
         command: ./remove_from_loadbalancer.sh {{ inventory_hostname }}
         args:
           chdir: "{{ playbook_dir }}"
         delegate_to: localhost
   ```

Notice the task structure—most of it will be familiar to you. We are using the `command` module to call the script we created earlier, passing the hostname from the inventory being removed from the load balancer to the script. We use the `chdir` argument with the `playbook_dir` magic variable to tell Ansible that the script is to be run from the same directory as the playbook.

The special part of this task is the `delegate_to` directive, which tells Ansible that even though we're iterating through an inventory that doesn't contain `localhost`, we should run this action on `localhost` (we aren't copying the script to our remote hosts, so it won't run if we attempt to run it from there).

4. After this, we add a task where the upgrade work is carried out. This task has no `delegate_to` directive, and so it is actually run on the remote host from the inventory (as desired):

```
- name: Deploy code to host
  debug:
    msg: Deployment code would go here....
```

5. Finally, we add the host back to the load balancer using the second script we created earlier. This task is almost identical to the first:

```
- name: Add host back to the load balancer
  command: ./add_to_loadbalancer.sh {{ inventory_hostname }}
  args:
    chdir: "{{ playbook_dir }}"
  delegate_to: localhost
```

6. Let's see this playbook in action:

```
$ ansible-playbook -i hosts delegate.yml

PLAY [Play to demonstrate task delegation]
*************************************

TASK [Gathering Facts]
*********************************************************
ok: [frt01.example.com]
ok: [frt02.example.com]

TASK [Remove host from the load balancer]
*************************************
changed: [frt02.example.com -> localhost]
changed: [frt01.example.com -> localhost]

TASK [Deploy code to host]
****************************************************
ok: [frt01.example.com] => {
    "msg": "Deployment code would go here...."
}
ok: [frt02.example.com] => {
    "msg": "Deployment code would go here...."
}
```

```
TASK [Add host back to the load balancer]
****************************************
changed: [frt01.example.com -> localhost]
changed: [frt02.example.com -> localhost]

PLAY RECAP
***********************************************************************
**
frt01.example.com : ok=4 changed=2 unreachable=0 failed=0 skipped=0
rescued=0 ignored=0
frt02.example.com : ok=4 changed=2 unreachable=0 failed=0 skipped=0
rescued=0 ignored=0
```

Notice how even though Ansible is working through the inventory (which doesn't feature `localhost`), the load balancer-related scripts are actually run from `localhost`, while the upgrade task is performed directly on the remote host. This, of course, isn't the only thing you can do with task delegation, but it's a common example of a way that it can help you.

In truth, you can delegate any task to `localhost`, or even another non-inventory host. You could, for example, run an `rsync` command delegated to `localhost` to copy files to remote hosts using a similar task definition to the previous one. This is useful because although Ansible has a `copy` module, it can't perform the advanced recursive `copy` and `update` functions that `rsync` is capable of.

Also, note that you can choose to use a form of shorthand notation in your playbooks (and roles) for `delegate_to`, called `local_action`. This allows you to specify a task on a single line that would ordinarily be run with `delegate_to: localhost` added below it. Wrapping this all up into a second example, our playbook will look as follows:

```
---
- name: Second task delegation example
  hosts: frontends

  tasks:
  - name: Perform an rsync from localhost to inventory hosts
    local_action: command rsync -a /tmp/ {{ inventory_hostname
}}:/tmp/target/
```

The preceding shorthand notation is equivalent to the following:

```
tasks:
  - name: Perform an rsync from localhost to inventory hosts
    command: rsync -a /tmp/ {{ inventory_hostname }}:/tmp/target/
    delegate_to: localhost
```

If we run this playbook, we can see that `local_action` does indeed run `rsync` from `localhost`, enabling us to efficiently copy whole directory trees across to remote servers in the inventory:

```
$ ansible-playbook -i hosts delegate2.yml

PLAY [Second task delegation example]
*****************************************

TASK [Gathering Facts]
***********************************************************
ok: [frt02.example.com]
ok: [frt01.example.com]

TASK [Perform an rsync from localhost to inventory hosts]
***********************
changed: [frt02.example.com -> localhost]
changed: [frt01.example.com -> localhost]

PLAY RECAP
******************************************************************
frt01.example.com : ok=2 changed=1 unreachable=0 failed=0 skipped=0
rescued=0 ignored=0
frt02.example.com : ok=2 changed=1 unreachable=0 failed=0 skipped=0
rescued=0 ignored=0
```

This concludes our look at task delegation, although as stated, these are just two common examples. I'm sure you can think up some more advanced use cases for this capability. Let's continue looking at controlling the flow of Ansible code by proceeding, in the next section, to look at the special `run_once` option.

Using the run_once option

When working with clusters, you will sometimes encounter a task that should only be executed once for the entire cluster. For example, you might want to upgrade the schema of a clustered database or issue a command to reconfigure a Pacemaker cluster that would normally be issued on one node and replicated to all other nodes by Pacemaker. You could, of course, address this with a special inventory with only one host in it, or even by writing a special play that references one host from the inventory, but this is inefficient and starts to make your code fragmented.

Instead, you can write your code as you normally would, but make use of the special
`run_once` directive for any tasks you want to run only once on your inventory. For
example, let's reuse the 10-host inventory that we defined earlier in this chapter. Now, let's
proceed to demonstrate this option, as follows:

1. Create the simple playbook as in the following code block. We're using a debug
   statement to display some output, but in real life, you would insert your script or
   command that performs your one-off cluster function here (for example,
   upgrading a database schema):

```
---
- name: Play to demonstrate the run_once directive
  hosts: frontends

  tasks:
    - name: Upgrade database schema
      debug:
        msg: Upgrading database schema...
      run_once: true
```

2. Now, let's run this playbook and see what happens:

```
$ ansible-playbook -i morehosts runonce.yml

PLAY [Play to demonstrate the run_once directive]
*****************************

TASK [Gathering Facts]
*******************************************************
ok: [frt02.example.com]
ok: [frt05.example.com]
ok: [frt03.example.com]
ok: [frt01.example.com]
ok: [frt04.example.com]
ok: [frt06.example.com]
ok: [frt08.example.com]
ok: [frt09.example.com]
ok: [frt07.example.com]
ok: [frt10.example.com]

TASK [Upgrade database schema]
*************************************************
ok: [frt01.example.com] => {
    "msg": "Upgrading database schema..."
}
---
```

```
PLAY RECAP
*********************************************************************
**
frt01.example.com : ok=2 changed=0 unreachable=0 failed=0 skipped=0
rescued=0 ignored=0
frt02.example.com : ok=1 changed=0 unreachable=0 failed=0 skipped=0
rescued=0 ignored=0
frt03.example.com : ok=1 changed=0 unreachable=0 failed=0 skipped=0
rescued=0 ignored=0
frt04.example.com : ok=1 changed=0 unreachable=0 failed=0 skipped=0
rescued=0 ignored=0
frt05.example.com : ok=1 changed=0 unreachable=0 failed=0 skipped=0
rescued=0 ignored=0
frt06.example.com : ok=1 changed=0 unreachable=0 failed=0 skipped=0
rescued=0 ignored=0
frt07.example.com : ok=1 changed=0 unreachable=0 failed=0 skipped=0
rescued=0 ignored=0
frt08.example.com : ok=1 changed=0 unreachable=0 failed=0 skipped=0
rescued=0 ignored=0
frt09.example.com : ok=1 changed=0 unreachable=0 failed=0 skipped=0
rescued=0 ignored=0
frt10.example.com : ok=1 changed=0 unreachable=0 failed=0 skipped=0
rescued=0 ignored=0
```

Notice that, just as desired, although the playbook was run on all 10 hosts (and, indeed, gathered facts from all 10 hosts), we only ran the upgrade task on one host.

3. It's important to note that the `run_once` option applies per batch of servers, so if we add `serial: 5` to our play definition (running our play in two batches of 5 on our inventory of 10 servers), the schema upgrade task actually runs twice! It runs once as requested, but once per batch of servers, not once for the entire inventory. Be careful of this nuance when working with this directive in a clustered environment.

Add `serial: 5` to your play definition and rerun the playbook. The output should appear as follows:

```
$ ansible-playbook -i morehosts runonce.yml

PLAY [Play to demonstrate the run_once directive]
*****************************

TASK [Gathering Facts]
*******************************************************
ok: [frt04.example.com]
ok: [frt01.example.com]
```

```
ok: [frt02.example.com]
ok: [frt03.example.com]
ok: [frt05.example.com]

TASK [Upgrade database schema]
************************************************
ok: [frt01.example.com] => {
    "msg": "Upgrading database schema..."
}

PLAY [Play to demonstrate the run_once directive]
*****************************

TASK [Gathering Facts]
*******************************************************
ok: [frt08.example.com]
ok: [frt06.example.com]
ok: [frt07.example.com]
ok: [frt10.example.com]
ok: [frt09.example.com]

TASK [Upgrade database schema]
************************************************
ok: [frt06.example.com] => {
    "msg": "Upgrading database schema..."
}

PLAY RECAP
****************************************************************
**
frt01.example.com : ok=2 changed=0 unreachable=0 failed=0 skipped=0
rescued=0 ignored=0
frt02.example.com : ok=1 changed=0 unreachable=0 failed=0 skipped=0
rescued=0 ignored=0
frt03.example.com : ok=1 changed=0 unreachable=0 failed=0 skipped=0
rescued=0 ignored=0
frt04.example.com : ok=1 changed=0 unreachable=0 failed=0 skipped=0
rescued=0 ignored=0
frt05.example.com : ok=1 changed=0 unreachable=0 failed=0 skipped=0
rescued=0 ignored=0
frt06.example.com : ok=2 changed=0 unreachable=0 failed=0 skipped=0
rescued=0 ignored=0
frt07.example.com : ok=1 changed=0 unreachable=0 failed=0 skipped=0
rescued=0 ignored=0
frt08.example.com : ok=1 changed=0 unreachable=0 failed=0 skipped=0
rescued=0 ignored=0
frt09.example.com : ok=1 changed=0 unreachable=0 failed=0 skipped=0
rescued=0 ignored=0
```

```
frt10.example.com : ok=1 changed=0 unreachable=0 failed=0 skipped=0
rescued=0 ignored=0
```

This is how the `run_once` option is designed to work—you can observe, in the preceding output, that our schema upgrade ran twice, which is probably not something we wanted! However, with this awareness, you should be able to take advantage of this option to control your playbook flow across clusters and still achieve the results you want. Let's now move away from cluster-related Ansible tasks and look at the subtle but important difference between running playbooks locally and running them on `localhost`.

Running playbooks locally

It is important to note that when we talk about running a playbook locally with Ansible, it is not the same as talking about running it on `localhost`. If we run a playbook on `localhost`, Ansible actually sets up an SSH connection to `localhost` (it doesn't differentiate its behavior or attempt to detect whether a host in the inventory is local or remote—it simply tries faithfully to connect).

Indeed, we can try creating a `local` inventory file with the following contents:

```
[local]
localhost
```

Now, if we attempt to run the `ping` module in an ad hoc command against this inventory, we see the following:

```
$ ansible -i localhosts -m ping all --ask-pass
The authenticity of host 'localhost (::1)' can't be established.
ECDSA key fingerprint is
SHA256:DUwVxH+45432pSr9qsN8Av4l0KJJ+r5jTo123n3XGvZs.
ECDSA key fingerprint is
MD5:78:d1:dc:23:cc:28:51:42:eb:fb:58:49:ab:92:b6:96.
Are you sure you want to continue connecting (yes/no)? yes
SSH password:
localhost | SUCCESS => {
    "ansible_facts": {
        "discovered_interpreter_python": "/usr/bin/python"
    },
    "changed": false,
    "ping": "pong"
}
```

As you can see, Ansible set up an SSH connection that needed the host key to validate, as well as our SSH password. Now, although you could add the host key (as we did in the preceding code block), add key-based SSH authentication to your `localhost`, and so on, there is a more direct way of doing this.

We can now modify our inventory so that it looks as follows:

```
[local]
localhost ansible_connection=local
```

We've added a special variable to our `localhost` entry—the `ansible_connection` variable—which defines which protocol is used to connect to this inventory host. So, we have told it to use a direct local connection instead of an SSH-based connectivity (which is the default).

It should be noted that this special value for the `ansible_connection` variable actually overrides the hostname you have put in your inventory. So, if we change our inventory to look as follows, Ansible will not even attempt to connect to the remote host called `frt01.example.com`—it will connect locally to the machine running the playbook (without SSH):

```
[local]
frt01.example.com ansible_connection=local
```

We can demonstrate this very simply. Let's first check for the absence of a test file in our local `/tmp` directory:

```
ls -l /tmp/foo
ls: cannot access /tmp/foo: No such file or directory
```

Now, let's run an ad hoc command to touch this file on all hosts in the new inventory we just defined:

```
$ ansible -i localhosts2 -m file -a "path=/tmp/foo state=touch" all
frt01.example.com | CHANGED => {
    "ansible_facts": {
        "discovered_interpreter_python": "/usr/bin/python"
    },
    "changed": true,
    "dest": "/tmp/foo",
    "gid": 0,
    "group": "root",
    "mode": "0644",
    "owner": "root",
    "size": 0,
    "state": "file",
    "uid": 0
}
```

The command ran successfully, so let's see whether the test file is present on the local machine:

```
$ ls -l /tmp/foo
-rw-r--r-- 1 root root 0 Apr 24 16:28 /tmp/foo
```

It is! So, the ad hoc command did not attempt to connect to `frt01.example.com`, even though this host name was in the inventory. The presence of `ansible_connection=local` meant that this command was run on the local machine without using SSH.

This ability to run commands locally without the need to set up SSH connectivity, SSH keys, and so on can be incredibly valuable, especially if you need to get things up and running quickly on your local machine. With this complete, let's take a look at how you can work with proxies and jump hosts using Ansible.

Working with proxies and jump hosts

Often, when it comes to configuring core network devices, these are isolated from the main network via a proxy or jump host. Ansible lends itself well to automating network device configuration as most of it is performed over SSH: however, this is only helpful in a scenario where Ansible can either be installed and operated from the jump host—or, better yet, can operate via a host such as this.

Fortunately, Ansible can do exactly that. Let's assume that you have two Cumulus Networks switches in your network (these are based on a special distribution of Linux for switching hardware, which is very similar to Debian). These two switches have the `cmls01.example.com` and `cmls02.example.com` hostnames, but both can only be accessed from a host called `bastion.example.com`.

The configuration to support our `bastion` host is performed in the inventory, rather than in the playbook. We begin by defining an inventory group with the switches in, in the normal manner:

```
[switches]
cmls01.example.com
cmls02.example.com
```

However, we can now start to get clever by adding some special SSH arguments into the inventory variables for this group. Add the following code to your inventory file:

```
[switches:vars]
ansible_ssh_common_args='-o ProxyCommand="ssh -W %h:%p -q
bastion.example.com"'
```

This special variable content tells Ansible to add extra options when it sets up an SSH connection, including to proxy via the `bastion.example.com` host. The `-W %h:%p` options tell SSH to proxy the connection and to connect to the host specified by `%h` (this is either `cmls01.example.com` or `cmls02.example.com`) on the port specified by `%p` (usually port 22).

Now, if we attempt to run the Ansible `ping` module against this inventory, we can see whether it works:

```
$ ansible -i switches -m ping all
cmls02.example.com | SUCCESS => {
    "ansible_facts": {
        "discovered_interpreter_python": "/usr/bin/python"
    },
    "changed": false,
127.0.0.1 app02.example.com
    "ping": "pong"
}
cmls01.example.com | SUCCESS => {
    "ansible_facts": {
        "discovered_interpreter_python": "/usr/bin/python"
    },
    "changed": false,
    "ping": "pong"
}
```

You will notice that we can't actually see any differences in Ansible's behavior from the command-line output. On the surface, Ansible works just as it normally does and connects successfully to the two hosts. However, behind the scenes it proxies via `bastion.example.com`.

Note that this simple example assumes that you are connecting to both the `bastion` host and `switches` using the same username and SSH credentials (or in this case, keys). There are ways to provide separate credentials for both variables, but this involves more advanced usage of OpenSSH, which is beyond the scope of this book. However, this section intends to give you a starting point and demonstrate the possibility of this, and you are free to explore OpenSSH proxying by yourself.

Let's now change track and explore how it is possible to set up Ansible to prompt you for data during a playbook run.

Configuring playbook prompts

So far, all of our playbooks have had their data specified for them at run time in variables we defined within the playbook. However, what if you actually want to obtain information from someone during a playbook run? Perhaps you want a user to select a version of a package to install? Or, perhaps you want to obtain a password from a user for an authentication task without storing it anywhere. (Although Ansible Value can encrypt the data at rest, some companies may forbid the storing of passwords and other such credentials in tools that they have not evaluated.) Fortunately for these instances (and many more), Ansible can prompt you for user input and store the input in a variable for future processing.

Let's reuse the two host frontend inventories we defined at the beginning of this chapter. Now, let's demonstrate how to capture data from users during a playbook run with a practical example:

1. Create a simple play definition in the usual manner, as follows:

```
---
- name: A simple play to demonstrate prompting in a playbook
  hosts: frontends
```

2. Now, we'll add a special section to the play definition. We previously defined a
   `vars` section, but this time we will define one called `vars_prompt` (which
   enables you to do just that—define variables through user prompts). In this
   section, we will prompt for two variables—one for a user ID and one for a
   password. One will be echoed to the screen, while the other won't be, by setting
   `private: yes`:

```
vars_prompt:
  - name: loginid
    prompt: "Enter your username"
    private: no
  - name: password
    prompt: "Enter your password"
    private: yes
```

3. We'll now add a single task to our playbook to demonstrate this prompting
   process of setting the variables:

```
tasks:
  - name: Proceed with login
    debug:
      msg: "Logging in as {{ loginid }}..."
```

4. Now, let's run the playbook and see how it behaves:

```
$ ansible-playbook -i hosts prompt.yml
Enter your username: james
Enter your password:

PLAY [A simple play to demonstrate prompting in a playbook]
********************

TASK [Gathering Facts]
*******************************************************
ok: [frt01.example.com]
ok: [frt02.example.com]

TASK [Proceed with login]
****************************************************
ok: [frt01.example.com] => {
    "msg": "Logging in as james..."
}
ok: [frt02.example.com] => {
    "msg": "Logging in as james..."
}

PLAY RECAP
```

```
******************************************************************
**
frt01.example.com : ok=2 changed=0 unreachable=0 failed=0 skipped=0
rescued=0 ignored=0
frt02.example.com : ok=2 changed=0 unreachable=0 failed=0 skipped=0
rescued=0 ignored=0
```

As you can see, we are prompted for both variables, yet the password is not echoed to the terminal, which is important for security reasons. We can then make use of the variables later in the playbook. Here, we just used a simple `debug` command to demonstrate that the variables have been set; however, you would instead implement an actual authentication function in place of this.

With this complete, let's proceed to the next section and look at how you can selectively run your tasks from within your plays with the use of tags.

Placing tags in the plays and tasks

We have discussed, at many points in this book, that as your confidence and experience with Ansible grows, it is likely that your playbooks will grow in size, scale, and complexity. While this is undoubtedly a good thing, there may be times when you only want to run a subset of a playbook, rather than running it from beginning to end. We have discussed how to conditionally run tasks based on the value of a variable or fact, but is there a way we can run them on the basis of a selection made at the time that the playbook is run?

Tags in Ansible plays are the solution to this, and in this section we will build a simple playbook with two tasks—each bearing a different tag—to show you how tags work. We will work with the two simple host inventories that we worked with previously:

1. Create the following simple playbook to perform two tasks—one to install the `nginx` package and the other to deploy a configuration file from a template:

```
---
- name: Simple play to demonstrate use of tags
  hosts: frontends

  tasks:
    - name: Install nginx
      yum:
        name: nginx
        state: present
      tags:
        - install
```

```
- name: Install nginx configuration from template
  template:
    src: templates/nginx.conf.j2
    dest: /etc/nginx.conf
  tags:
    - customize
```

2. Now, let's run the playbook in the usual manner, but with one difference—this
   time, we'll add the `--tags` switch to the command line. This switch tells Ansible
   to only run the tasks that have tags matching the ones that are specified. So, for
   example, run the following command:

   ```
   $ ansible-playbook -i hosts tags.yml --tags install

   PLAY [Simple play to demonstrate use of tags]
   ********************************

   TASK [Gathering Facts]
   ***********************************************************
   ok: [frt02.example.com]
   ok: [frt01.example.com]

   TASK [Install nginx]
   ***********************************************************
   changed: [frt02.example.com]
   changed: [frt01.example.com]

   PLAY RECAP
   ***************************************************************************
   **
   frt01.example.com : ok=2 changed=1 unreachable=0 failed=0 skipped=0
   rescued=0 ignored=0
   frt02.example.com : ok=2 changed=1 unreachable=0 failed=0 skipped=0
   rescued=0 ignored=0
   ```

   Notice that the task to deploy the configuration file doesn't run. This is because it
   is tagged with `customize` and we did not specify this tag when running the
   playbook.

3. There is also a `--skip-tags` switch that does the reverse of the previous
   switch—it tells Ansible to skip the tags listed. So, if we run the playbook again
   but skip the `customize` tag, we should see an output similar to the following:

   ```
   $ ansible-playbook -i hosts tags.yml --skip-tags customize

   PLAY [Simple play to demonstrate use of tags]
   ********************************
   ```

```
TASK [Gathering Facts]
*********************************************************
ok: [frt02.example.com]
ok: [frt01.example.com]

TASK [Install nginx]
***********************************************************
ok: [frt02.example.com]
ok: [frt01.example.com]

PLAY RECAP
****************************************************************
**
frt01.example.com : ok=2 changed=0 unreachable=0 failed=0 skipped=0
rescued=0 ignored=0
frt02.example.com : ok=2 changed=0 unreachable=0 failed=0 skipped=0
rescued=0 ignored=0
```

This play run is identical because, rather than including only the install-tagged tasks, we skipped the tasks tagged with customize.

 Note that if you don't specify either --tags or --skip-tags, then all the tasks are run, regardless of their tag.

A few notes about tags—first of all, each task can have more than one tag, so we see them specified in a YAML list format. If you use the --tags switch, a task will run if any of it's tags match the tag that was specified on the command line. Secondly, tags can be reused, so we could have five tasks that are all tagged install, and all five tasks would be performed or skipped if you requested them to do so via --tags or --skip-tags, respectively.

You can also specify more than one tag on the command line, running all the tasks that match any of the specified tags. Although the logic behind tags is relatively simple, it can take a little while to get used to it and the last thing you want to do is run your playbook on real hosts to check whether you understand tagging! A great way to figure this out is to add --list-tasks to your command, which—rather than running the playbook—lists the tasks from the playbook that would perform if you run it. Some examples are provided for you in the following code block, based on the example playbook we just created:

```
$ ansible-playbook -i hosts tags.yml --skip-tags customize --list-tasks

playbook: tags.yml

  play #1 (frontends): Simple play to demonstrate use of tags TAGS: []
```

```
    tasks:
       Install nginx TAGS: [install]

$ ansible-playbook -i hosts tags.yml --tags install,customize --list-tasks

playbook: tags.yml

   play #1 (frontends): Simple play to demonstrate use of tags TAGS: []
      tasks:
         Install nginx TAGS: [install]
         Install nginx configuration from template TAGS: [customize]

$ ansible-playbook -i hosts tags.yml --list-tasks

playbook: tags.yml

   play #1 (frontends): Simple play to demonstrate use of tags TAGS: []
      tasks:
         Install nginx TAGS: [install]
         Install nginx configuration from template TAGS: [customize]
```

As you can see, not only does `--list-tasks` show you which tasks would run, it also shows you which tags are associated with them, which helps you further understand how tagging works and ensure that you achieve the playbook flow that you wanted. Tags are an incredibly simple yet powerful way to control which parts of your playbook run and often when it comes to creating and maintaining large playbooks, it is better to be able to run only selected parts of the playbook at once. From here, we will move on to the final section of this chapter, where we will look at securing your variable data at rest by encrypting it with Ansible Vault.

Securing data with Ansible Vault

Ansible Vault is a tool included with Ansible that allows you to encrypt your sensitive data at rest, while also using it in a playbook. Often, it is necessary to store login credentials or other sensitive data in a variable to allow a playbook to run unattended. However, this risks exposing your data to people who might use it with malicious intent. Fortunately, Ansible Vault secures your data at rest using AES-256 encryption, meaning your sensitive data is safe from prying eyes.

Let's proceed with a simple example that shows you how you can use Ansible Vault:

1. Start by creating a new vault to store sensitive data in; we'll call this file `secret.yml`. You can create this using the following command:

```
$ ansible-vault create secret.yml
New Vault password:
Confirm New Vault password:
```

Enter the password you have chosen for the vault when prompted and confirm it by entering it a second time (the vault that accompanies this book on GitHub is encrypted with the `secure` password).

2. When you have entered the password, you will be set to your normal editor (defined by the `EDITOR` shell variable). On my test system, this is `vi`. Within this editor, you should create a `vars` file, in the normal manner, containing your sensitive data:

```
---

secretdata: "Ansible is cool!"
```

3. Save and exit the editor (press *Esc*, then `:wq` in `vi`). You will exit to the shell. Now, if you look at the contents of your file, you will see that they are encrypted and are safe from anyone who shouldn't be able to read the file:

```
$ cat secret.yml
$ANSIBLE_VAULT;1.1;AES256
63333734623764633865633237333166333636343533343738623463346463313031 6
3653931306138
63343564653964636439363231633231323738363336461370a34323638626631333
1653964326334
62363737663165333653396332623666363833364343663396335643635623463 62633
6643732613830
6139363035373736370a64666613964643863646539356363666336636232616353 53
8626230616630
35346465346430636463323838613037386663333334356265623964633763333 53
2366561323266
36646136626432633834646437346336323831383636636323730
```

4. However, the great thing about Ansible Vault is that you can use this encrypted file in a playbook as if it were a normal `variables` file (although, obviously, you have to tell Ansible your vault password). Let's create a simple playbook as follows:

```
---
- name: A play that makes use of an Ansible Vault
  hosts: frontends

  vars_files:
    - secret.yml

  tasks:
    - name: Tell me a secret
      debug:
        msg: "Your secret data is: {{ secretdata }}"
```

The `vars_files` directive is used in exactly the same way as it would be if you were using an unencrypted `variables` file. Ansible reads the headers of the `variables` files at run time and determines whether they are encrypted or not.

5. Try running the playbook without telling Ansible what the vault password is—in this instance, you should receive an error such as this:

```
$ ansible-playbook -i hosts vaultplaybook.yml
ERROR! Attempting to decrypt but no vault secrets found
```

6. Ansible correctly understands that we are trying to load a `variables` file that is encrypted with `ansible-vault`, but we must manually tell it the password for it to proceed. There are a number of ways of specifying passwords for vaults (more on this in a minute), but for simplicity, try running the following command and enter your vault password when prompted:

```
$ ansible-playbook -i hosts vaultplaybook.yml --ask-vault-pass
Vault password:

PLAY [A play that makes use of an Ansible Vault]
******************************

TASK [Gathering Facts]
*******************************************************
ok: [frt01.example.com]
ok: [frt02.example.com]

TASK [Tell me a secret]
*******************************************************
```

```
        ok: [frt01.example.com] => {
            "msg": "Your secret data is: Ansible is cool!"
        }
        ok: [frt02.example.com] => {
            "msg": "Your secret data is: Ansible is cool!"
        }

        PLAY RECAP
        *********************************************************************
        **
        frt01.example.com : ok=2 changed=0 unreachable=0 failed=0 skipped=0
        rescued=0 ignored=0
        frt02.example.com : ok=2 changed=0 unreachable=0 failed=0 skipped=0
        rescued=0 ignored=0
```

Success! Ansible decrypted our vault file and loaded the variables into the playbook, which we can see from the debug statement we created. Naturally, this defeats the purpose of using a vault, but it makes for a nice example.

This is a very simple example of what you can do with vaults. There are multiple ways that you can specify passwords; you don't have to be prompted for them on the command line—they can be provided either by a plain text file that contains the vault password or via a script that could obtain the password from a secure location at run time (think of a dynamic inventory script, only for returning a password rather than a hostname). The ansible-vault tool itself can also be used to edit, view, and change the passwords in a vault file, or even decrypt it and turn it back into plain text. The user guide for Ansible Vault is a great place to start for more information (https://docs.ansible.com/ansible/latest/user_guide/vault.html).

One thing to note is that you don't actually have to have a separate vault file for your sensitive data; you can actually include it inline in your playbook. For example, let's try re-encrypting our sensitive data for inclusion in an otherwise unencrypted playbook (again, use the secure password for the vault if you are testing the examples from the GitHub repository accompanying this book). Run the following command in your shell (it should produce an output similar to what is shown):

```
$ ansible-vault encrypt_string 'Ansible is cool!' --name secretdata
New Vault password:
Confirm New Vault password:
secretdata: !vault |
          $ANSIBLE_VAULT;1.1;AES256
34393431303339353735656236656130336664663373637323762623438376637383934656
23930
33666230613063646439666666565316235313136633264310a623736643362663035373861
343435
```

```
62346264313638656363323835323833363326463656136633932633235643038373465303
06637
37363365336562303 80a31636431383166646364353463353039333734616435663461306 53
96434
333163383362 6663666635333346438653638303465666663313037636435643230 65
Encryption successful
```

You can copy and paste the output of this command into a playbook. So, if we modify our earlier example, it would appear as follows:

```
---
- name: A play that makes use of an Ansible Vault
  hosts: frontends

  vars:
    secretdata: !vault |
          $ANSIBLE_VAULT;1.1;AES256
343934313033393537356562366561303366646663373637323762623438376637383934656
23930
336662306130636464396666656531623531313663326431 0a62373664336266303 5373 8613
43435
62346264313638656363323835323833363326463656136633932633235643038373465303
06637
37363365336562303 80a31636431383166646364353463353039333734616435663461306 53
96434
333163383362 6663666635333346438653638303465666663313037636435643230 65

  tasks:
    - name: Tell me a secret
      debug:
        msg: "Your secret data is: {{ secretdata }}"
```

Now, when you run this playbook in exactly the same manner as we did before (specifying the vault password using a user prompt), you should see that it runs just as when we used an external encrypted `variables` file:

```
$ ansible-playbook -i hosts inlinevaultplaybook.yml --ask-vault-pass
Vault password:

PLAY [A play that makes use of an Ansible Vault]
*******************************

TASK [Gathering Facts]
*********************************************************
ok: [frt02.example.com]
ok: [frt01.example.com]

TASK [Tell me a secret]
```

```
*********************************************************
ok: [frt01.example.com] => {
    "msg": "Your secret data is: Ansible is cool!"
}
ok: [frt02.example.com] => {
    "msg": "Your secret data is: Ansible is cool!"
}

PLAY RECAP
**************************************************************************
frt01.example.com : ok=2 changed=0 unreachable=0 failed=0 skipped=0
rescued=0 ignored=0
frt02.example.com : ok=2 changed=0 unreachable=0 failed=0 skipped=0
rescued=0 ignored=0
```

Ansible Vault is a powerful and versatile tool for encrypting your sensitive playbook data at rest and should enable you (with a little care) to run most of your playbooks unattended without ever leaving passwords or other sensitive data in the clear. That concludes this section and this chapter; I hope that it has been useful for you.

Summary

Ansible has many advanced features that allow you to run your playbooks in a variety of scenarios, whether that is upgrading a cluster of servers in a controlled manner; working with devices on a secure, isolated network; or controlling your playbook flow with prompts and tags. Ansible has been adopted by a large and ever-growing user base and, as such, is designed and evolved around solving real-world problems. Most of the advanced features of Ansible we discussed are centered around exactly this—solving real-world problems.

In this chapter, you learned about running tasks asynchronously in Ansible, before looking at the various features available for running playbooks to upgrade a cluster, such as running tasks on small batches of inventory hosts, failing a play early if a certain percentage of hosts fail, delegating tasks to a specific host, and even running tasks once, regardless of your inventory (or batch) size. You also learned about the difference between running playbooks locally as opposed to on `localhost` and how to use SSH-proxying to automate tasks on an isolated network via a `bastion` host. Finally, you learned about handling sensitive data without storing it unencrypted at rest, either through prompting the user at run time or through the use of Ansible Vault. You even learned about running a subset of your playbook tasks with tagging.

In the next chapter, we will explore a topic we touched on briefly in this chapter in more detail—automating network device management with Ansible.

Questions

1. Which parameter allows you to configure the maximum number of hosts in a batch that will fail before a play is aborted?

   A) `percentage`

   B) `max_fail`

   C) `max_fail_percentage`

   D) `max_percentage`

   E) `fail_percentage`

2. True or false – you can use the `--connect=local` parameter to run any playbooks locally without using SSH:

   A) True

   B) False

3. True or false – in order to run a playbook asynchronously, you need to use the `async` keyword:

   A) True

   B) False

Further reading

If you install Passlib, which is a password-hashing library for Python 2 and 3, `vars_prompt` is encrypted with any crypt scheme (such as `descrypt`, `md5crypt`, `sha56_crypt`, and more):

- `https://passlib.readthedocs.io/en/stable/`

Section 3: Using Ansible in an Enterprise

3

In this section, we will take a practically based look at how to get the most out of Ansible in an enterprise environment. We will start by looking at how to automate your network devices with Ansible, before moving onto the use of Ansible to manage both cloud and container environments. We will then look at some of the more advanced testing and troubleshooting strategies that will assist you in your use of Ansible in an enterprise, before finally looking at the Ansible Tower/AWX product, which provides rich **Role-Based Access Control (RBAC)** and auditing capabilities in enterprise settings.

This section contains the following chapters:

- Chapter 9, *Network Automation with Ansible*
- Chapter 10, *Container and Cloud Management*
- Chapter 11, *Troubleshooting and Testing Strategies*
- Chapter 12, *Getting Started with Ansible Tower*

9
Network Automation with Ansible

Years ago, the standard practice was to configure every single network device by hand. This was possible mainly because the routers and switches were routing the traffic of physical servers, so not much configuration was needed on each networking device, and changes were slow-paced. In addition, humans were the only ones to have enough information on machines to set up networking. Everything was very manual in terms of both planning and execution.

Virtualization changed this paradigm, as it has resulted in thousands of machines being connected to the same switch or router, each with potentially different networking requirements. Changes are fast-paced and expected frequently, and with virtual infrastructures defined in code, it becomes a full-time job for a human administrator to just keep up with the changes to the infrastructure. Virtualization orchestration platforms have far better knowledge of the machine's location, and can even generate an inventory for us, as we saw in earlier chapters. Practically speaking, there is no way a human being can memorize or manage a modern, large-scale, virtualized infrastructure. As a result, it becomes clear that automation is a requirement when it comes to configuring the network infrastructure.

We will learn more about this, and what we can do to automate our network, in this chapter by covering the following topics:

- Why automate network management?
- How Ansible manages networking devices
- How to enable network automation
- The available Ansible networking modules
- Connecting to network devices
- Environment variables for network devices
- Custom conditional statements for networking devices

Let's get started!

Technical requirements

This chapter assumes that you have set up your control host with Ansible, as detailed in Chapter 1, *Getting Started with Ansible*, and are using the most recent version available – the examples in this chapter were tested with Ansible 2.9. This chapter also assumes that you have at least one additional host to test against, and ideally, this should be Linux-based. Since this chapter is network device-centric, we understand that not everyone will have access to specific networking equipment to test on (for example, Cisco switches). Where examples are given and you have access to such devices, please feel free to explore the examples. However, if you do not have access to any network hardware, we will give an example using the freely available Cumulus VX, which offers a fully-featured demo of Cumulus Networks' switching environment. Although we will give specific examples of hostnames in this chapter, you are free to substitute them with your own hostname and/or IP addresses. Details of how to do this will be provided in the appropriate places.

The code bundle for this chapter is available here: https://github.com/PacktPublishing/ Practical-Ansible-2/tree/master/Chapter%209.

Why automate network management?

The way that we design data centers has radically changed in the last 30 years. In the 90s, a typical data center was full of physical machines, each with a very specific purpose. In many companies, the servers were bought by different vendors based on the purpose of the machine. This meant that there was a need for machines, network devices, and storage devices and that those devices were bought, provisioned, configured, and delivered.

The big drawback here was the significant lag between identifying the need for the machine and its delivery. In that period, this was acceptable, since the majority of companies had very few systems and they tended to change very rarely. Also, this approach was very expensive as a lot of devices were under-utilized.

With the progress of society and companies in the world of technology, we know that today, it has become important for companies to cut their infrastructure deployment time and costs. This opened the road for a new idea: virtualization. By creating a virtualization cluster, you do not need to have physical hosts that are of the correct size, so you can provision a number of them up front, add them to a resource pool, and then create the right-sized machines in your virtualization platform. This means that when a new machine is needed, you can create it with a few clicks and it will be ready in seconds.

This shift also allowed enterprises to move from a per-project infrastructure, with each project being deployed with its own unique data center requirements, to one large central infrastructure that can have its behavior defined by software and configuration. This means that one single network infrastructure can support all projects, regardless of their scale. We call this a virtual data center infrastructure, and in this infrastructure, we try to make use of generic design patters as much as possible. This allows enterprises to deploy, switch, and serve infrastructure at a large scale to enable a multitude of projects so that they can be successfully implemented by simply subdividing them (for example, by creating virtual servers).

Another big advantage that virtualization brought is the decoupling of workloads and physical hosts. Historically, since a workload was tied to a physical host, if the host died, the workload itself died, if not properly replicated on different hardware. Virtualization solved this problem since the workload is now tied to one or more virtual hosts, but those can be moved freely from a physical host to another one.

This ability to provision machines quickly and the ability of such machines to move from one host to another created an issue with networking configuration management. Before, it was acceptable for a human to tweak the configuration details while installing the new machine, but now, machines move from one host to another (and therefore from one physical switch port to another) without any human intervention. This means that the system needed to update network configurations as well.

In the same time period, VLANs affirmed their presence in networking, which allowed the utilization of network devices to be dramatically improved, and therefore optimize their costs.

Today, we work at an even larger scale, where virtual objects (machines, containers, functions, and so on) move in our data centers, fully managed by software systems, and where humans are less and less involved in the process.

In this kind of environment, automating networking is a key part of their success.

Today, there are some companies (the famous "cloud providers") that work at a scale where manual network management is not only impracticable but impossible, even when employing huge teams of network engineers. On the other hand, there are many environments where it would be technically possible to manage network configurations (at least partially) manually, but it's still impractical.

Aside from the time required to configure a network device, the biggest advantage – from my perspective – of network automation is the opportunity to drastically reduce human errors. If a human has to configure a VLAN on 100 devices, chances are, they are going to make a few errors in the process. This is absolutely normal, but still problematic since those configurations will need to be fully tested and amended. Often, the problem doesn't stop here, because when a device breaks and therefore needs to be replaced, a human has to configure the new device in the same way the old one was configured. Often – over time – the configurations change and – very often – there is no clear way to trace this, so while replacing a faulty network device, there might be problems for some rules that were present in the previous device but are not present in the new one.

Now that we have discussed the need to automate network management, let's look at how to manage networking devices with Ansible.

Learning how Ansible manages networking devices

Ansible allows you to manage many different networking devices, including Arista EOS, Cisco ASA, Cisco IOS, Cisco IOS XR, Cisco NX-OS, Dell OS 6, Dell OS 9, Dell OS 10, Extreme EXOS, Extreme IronWare, Extreme NOS, Extreme SLX-OS, Extreme VOSS, F5 BIG-IP, F5 BIG-IQ, Junos OS, Lenovo CNOS, Lenovo ENOS, MikroTik RouterOS, Nokia SR OS, Pluribus Netvisor, VyOS, and OS, which supports NETCONF. As you can imagine, there are various ways we can make Ansible communicate with them.

Also, we have to remember that Ansible networking modules run on the controller host (the one where you issued the `ansible` command), while usually, the Ansible modules run on the target host. This difference is important because it allows Ansible to use different connection mechanisms based on the target device type. Remember that even when you have a host that has SSH management capabilities (which many switches have), Ansible, by very virtue of running its modules on the target host, needs the target host to have Python installed. Most switches (and embedded hardware) lack Python environments, and so we must make use of other connection protocols. The key ones supported by Ansible for network device management are given here.

There are five main connection types that Ansible uses for connecting to those network devices, as follows:

- `network_cli`
- `netconf`
- `httpapi`
- `local`
- `ssh`

When you create a connection with your networking device, you need to choose the connection mechanism based on the ones supported by your devices and your needs:

- `network_cli` is supported by the majority of modules and it is the most similar to the way Ansible usually works with the non-networking modules. This mode uses a CLI via SSH. This protocol creates a persistent connection at the beginning of the configuration and keeps it alive for the whole duration of the task so that you don't have to provide credentials for every subsequent task.
- `netconf` is supported by very few modules (at the time of writing, these modules are just OSes that support NETCONF and Junos OS). This mode uses XML via SSH, so basically, it applies XML-based configurations to the device. This protocol creates a persistent connection at the beginning of the configuration and keeps it alive for the whole duration of the task so that you don't have to provide credentials for every subsequent task.
- `httpapi` is supported by a few modules (at the time of writing, these are Arista EOS, Cisco NX-OS, and Extreme EXOS). This mode uses the HTTP API that the device publishes. This protocol creates a persistent connection at the beginning of the configuration and keeps it alive for the whole duration of the task so that you don't have to provide credentials for every subsequent task.

- `Local` is supported by the majority of devices but is a deprecated mode. This is basically a vendor-dependent connection mode that may require some vendor packages to be used. This mode does not create a persistent connection, so at the start of every task, you will need to pass the credentials. When possible, avoid this mode.
- `ssh` must not be forgotten in this section. Although a large number of devices depend upon the connection modes listed here, a new breed of devices is being created that run Linux natively on white box switch hardware. One such example is Cumulus Networks, and as the software is Linux-based, all configuration can be performed over SSH, as if the switch was actually just another Linux server.

Knowing how Ansible connects to and communicates with your networking hardware is important as it gives you the understanding you need to build your Ansible playbooks and debug issues when things go wrong. In this section, we covered the communication protocols you will come across when working with networking hardware. We will build on this in the next section by looking at the fundamentals of starting out on our network automation journey with Ansible.

Enabling network automation

Before you can use Ansible for network automation, you need to make sure you have everything you need.

Based on the kind of connection method we are going to use, we need different dependencies. As an example, we are going to use a Cisco IOS device with `network_cli` connectivity.

The only requirements for Ansible network automation to work are as follows:

- Ansible 2.5+
- Proper connectivity with the network device

First, we need to check the Ansible version:

1. To ensure that you have a recent Ansible version, you can run the following command:

    ```
    $ ansible --version
    ```

    This will tell you the version of your Ansible installation.

2. If it's 2.5 or better, you can issue the following command (with the appropriate options) to check the connectivity of your network device:

```
$ ansible all -i n1.example.com, -c network_cli -u my_user -k -m
ios_facts -e ansible_network_os=ios all
```

This should return your device's facts, which proves that we are able to connect. As for any other target, Ansible is able to retrieve facts, and this is usually the first thing Ansible does when interacting with a target.

This is a key step since this allows Ansible to know the current state of the device and therefore act appropriately.

By running the `ios_facts` module on our target device, we are just executing this first standard step (so no changes will be performed on the device itself or its configurations), but this will confirm that Ansible is able to connect all the way to the device and perform commands on it.

Now, obviously, you could only actually run the preceding command and explore its behavior if you have access to a network device running Cisco IOS. We understand that not everyone will have the same networking equipment available to them for testing purposes (or indeed any!). Fortunately for us, a new breed of switches is becoming available – "white box" switches. These switches are made by a variety of manufacturers and are based on standardized hardware where you can install your own network operating system. One such operating system is Cumulus Linux, and a freely available test version of this, called Cumulus VX, is available for you to download.

 At the time of writing, the download link for Cumulus VX is `https://cumulusnetworks.com/products/cumulus-vx/`. You will need to register to download it, but doing so gives you free access to the world of open networking.

Simply download the image appropriate to your hypervisor (for example, VirtualBox) and then run it just as you would run any other Linux virtual machine. Once you've done this, you can connect to the Cumulus VX switch, just like you would any other SSH device. For example, to run an ad hoc command to gather facts about all the switch port interfaces (which are enumerated as `swp1`, `swp2`, and `swpX` on Cumulus VX), you would run the following command:

```
$ ansible -i vx01.example.com, -u cumulus -m setup -a 'filter=ansible_swp*'
all --ask-pass
```

If successful, this should result in pages of information about the switch port interface for your Cumulus VX-powered virtual switch. On my test system, the first part of this output looks like this:

```
vx01.example.com | SUCCESS => {
    "ansible_facts": {
        "ansible_swp1": {
            "active": false,
            "device": "swp1",
            "features": {
                "esp_hw_offload": "off [fixed]",
                "esp_tx_csum_hw_offload": "off [fixed]",
                "fcoe_mtu": "off [fixed]",
                "generic_receive_offload": "on",
                "generic_segmentation_offload": "on",
                "highdma": "off [fixed]",
    ...
```

As you can see, working with white box switches using an operating system such as Cumulus Linux has the advantage that you can connect using the standard SSH protocol, and you can even use the built-in `setup` module to gather facts about it. Working with other proprietary hardware is not much more difficult, but simply requires more parameters to be specified, as we showed earlier in this chapter.

Now that you know the fundamentals of enabling network automation, let's learn how to discover the appropriate networking modules for our desired automation task in Ansible.

Reviewing the available Ansible networking modules

At the moment, there are thousands of modules on a total of more than 20 different networking platforms. Let's learn how to find the ones more relevant to you:

1. First of all, you need to know which device type you have and how Ansible calls it. On the `https://docs.ansible.com/ansible/latest/network/user_guide/platform_index.html` page, you can find the different device types that Ansible supports and how they are designated. In our example, we will use Cisco IOS as an example.

2. On the `https://docs.ansible.com/ansible/latest/modules/list_of_network_modules.html` page, you can search for the category dedicated to the family of switches you need, and you'll be able to see all the modules you can use.

The list of modules is way too big and family-specific for us to talk about them in depth. This list is getting larger every release, with often hundreds of new additions in every release.

If you are familiar with how to configure the device in a manual fashion, you will quickly find the name of the modules fairly natural, so it will be easy for you to understand what they do. However, let's go through a handful of examples from the collection of Cisco IOS modules – specifically, with reference to `https://docs.ansible.com/ansible/latest/modules/list_of_network_modules.html#ios`:

- `ios_banner`: As the name suggests, this module will allow you to tweak and modify the login banner (what in many systems is called `motd`).
- `ios_bgp`: This module allows you to configure BGP routes.
- `ios_command`: This is the IOS equivalent of the Ansible `command` module, and it allows you to perform many different commands. As for the `command` module, this is a very powerful module, but it's better to use specific modules for the operation we are going to perform, if they are available.
- `ios_config`: This module allows us to make pretty much any changes to the configuration file of the device. As for the `ios_command` module, this is a very powerful module, but it's better to use specific modules for the operation we are going to perform, if they are available. The idempotency for this module is only guaranteed if no abbreviated commands are used.
- `ios_vlan`: This module allows the configuration of VLANs.

These are just a few examples, but there are many more modules for Cisco IOS (27, at the time of writing), and if you cannot find a specific module to perform the operation you want, you can always fall back to `ios_command` and `ios_config`, which, thanks to their flexibility, will allow you to perform any operation you can think of.

In contrast, if you are working with a Cumulus Linux switch, you'll find there is just one module – `nclu` (see `https://docs.ansible.com/ansible/latest/modules/list_of_network_modules.html#cumulus`). This reflects the fact that all configuration work in Cumulus Linux is handled with this command. If you need to customize the message of the day or other aspects of the Linux operating system, you can do this in the normal manner (for example, using the `template` or `copy` modules, which we have demonstrated previously in this book).

As ever, the Ansible documentation is your friend, and it should be your first port of call when you are learning how to automate commands on a new class of device. In this section, we have demonstrated a simple process for finding out which Ansible modules are available for your class of network device, using Cisco as a specific example (though you could apply these principles to any other device). Now, let's look at how Ansible connects to network devices.

Connecting to network devices

As we have seen, there are some peculiarities in Ansible networking, so specific configurations are required.

In order to manage network devices with Ansible, you need to have at least one to test on. Let's assume we have a Cisco IOS system available to us. It is accepted that not everyone will have such a device to test on, so the following is offered as a hypothetical example only.

Going by the `https://docs.ansible.com/ansible/latest/network/user_guide/platform_index.html` page, we can see that the correct `ansible_network_os` for this device is `ios` and that we can connect to it using both `network_cli` and `local`. Since `local` is deprecated, we are going to use `network_cli`. Follow these steps to configure Ansible so that you can manage IOS devices:

1. First, let's create the inventory file with our devices in the `routers` group:

   ```
   [routers]
   n1.example.com
   n2.example.com

   [cumulusvx]
   vx01.example.com
   ```

2. To know which connection parameters to use, we will set Ansible's special connection variables so that they define the connection parameters. We'll do this in a group variables subdirectory of our playbook, so we will need to create the `group_vars/routers.yml` file with the following content:

   ```
   ---
   ansible_connection: network_cli
   ansible_network_os: ios
   ansible_become: True
   ansible_become_method: enable
   ```

By virtue of these special Ansible variables, it will know how to connect to your devices. We covered some of these examples earlier in this book, but as a recap, Ansible uses the values of those variables to determine its behavior in the following ways:

- `ansible_connection`: This variable is used by Ansible to decide how to connect to the device. By choosing `network_cli`, we are instructing Ansible to connect to the CLI over SSH mode, as we discussed in the previous paragraph.
- `ansible_network_os`: This variable is used by Ansible to understand the device family of the device we are going to use. By choosing `ios`, we are instructing Ansible to expect a Cisco IOS device.
- `ansible_become`: This variable is used by Ansible so that we decide whether to perform privilege escalation on the device or not. By specifying `True`, we are telling Ansible to perform privilege escalation.
- `ansible_become_method`: There are many different ways to perform privilege escalation on the various devices (normally `sudo` on a Linux server – this is the default setting), and for Cisco IOS , we must set this to `enable`.

With that, you have learned the necessary steps to connect to network devices.

To validate that the connection is working as expected (assuming you have access to a router running Cisco IOS), you can run this simple playbook, called `ios_facts.yaml`:

```
---
- name: Play to return facts from a Cisco IOS device
  hosts: routers
  gather_facts: False
  tasks:
    - name: Gather IOS facts
      ios_facts:
        gather_subset: all
```

You can run this using a command such as the following:

```
$ ansible-playbook -i hosts ios_facts.yml --ask-pass
```

If it returns successfully, this means that your configuration is correct and you've been able to give Ansible the necessary authorization to manage your IOS device.

Similarly, if you wanted to connect to a Cumulus VX device, you could add another group variables file called `group_vars/cumulusvx.yml` containing the following code:

```
---
ansible_user: cumulus
become: false
```

An analogous playbook that returns all the facts about our Cumulus VX switches could look like this:

```
---
- name: Simply play to gather Cumulus VX switch facts
  hosts: cumulusvx
  gather_facts: no

  tasks:
    - name: Gather facts
      setup:
        gather_subset: all
```

You can run this in a normal manner by using a command such as the following:

```
$ ansible-playbook -i hosts cumulusvx_facts.yml --ask-pass
```

If successful, you should see the following output from your playbook run:

```
SSH password:

PLAY [Simply play to gather Cumulus VX switch facts]
************************************************************************
********************

TASK [Gather facts]
************************************************************************
********************
ok: [vx01.example.com]

PLAY RECAP
************************************************************************
********************
vx01.example.com : ok=1 changed=0 unreachable=0 failed=0 skipped=0
rescued=0 ignored=0
```

This demonstrates the techniques for connecting to two different types of network devices in Ansible, including one you can test by yourself without access to any special hardware. Now, let's build on this by looking at how to set environment variables for network devices in Ansible.

Environment variables for network devices

Very often, the complexity of networks is high and the network systems are very varied. For those reasons, Ansible has a huge amount of variables that can help you tweak it so that you can make Ansible fit your environment.

Let's suppose you have two different networks (that is, one for computing and one for network devices) that can't communicate directly, but have to pass through a bastion host to reach one from the other. Since we have Ansible in the computing network, we will need to jump networks using the bastion host to configure an IOS router in the management network. Also, our target switch needs a proxy to reach the internet.

To connect to the IOS router in the database network, we will need to create a new group for our network devices, which are on a separate network. For this example, this might be specified as follows:

```
[bastion_routers]
n1.example.com
n2.example.com

[bastion_cumulusvx]
vx01.example.com
```

Following the creation of our updated inventory, we can create a new group variables file, such as group_vars/bastion_routers.yaml, with the following content:

```
---
ansible_connection: network_cli
ansible_network_os: ios
ansible_become: True
ansible_become_method: enable
ansible_ssh_common_args: '-o ProxyCommand="ssh -W %h:%p -q
bastion.example.com"'
proxy_env:
    http_proxy: http://proxy.example.com:8080
```

We can also do the same for our Cumulus VX switches if they are behind a bastion server by creating a group_vars/bastion_cumulusvx.yml file:

```
---
ansible_user: cumulus
ansible_become: false
ansible_ssh_common_args: '-o ProxyCommand="ssh -W %h:%p -q
bastion.example.com"'
proxy_env:
    http_proxy: http://proxy.example.com:8080
```

In addition to the options we discussed in the previous section, we now have two additional options:

- `ansible_ssh_common_args`: This is a very powerful option that allows us to add additional options to the SSH connections so that we can tweak their behavior. These options should be fairly straightforward to identify since you are already using them in your SSH configurations to simply SSH to the target machine. In this specific case, we are adding a `ProxyCommand`, which is the SSH directive to perform a jump to a host (usually a bastion host) so that we can enter the target host securely.
- `http_proxy`: This option, which is below the `proxy_env` option, is key in environments where network isolation is strong, and therefore your machines can't interact with the internet unless they use a proxy.

Assuming you have set up passwordless (for example, SSH key-based) access to your bastion host, you should be able to run an ad hoc Ansible `ping` command against your Cumulus VX host, as follows:

```
$ ansible -i hosts -m ping -u cumulus --ask-pass bastion_cumulusvx
SSH password:

vx01.example.com | SUCCESS => {
    "ansible_facts": {
        "discovered_interpreter_python": "/usr/bin/python"
    },
    "changed": false,
    "ping": "pong"
}
```

Note that the use of the bastion server becomes transparent – you can carry on automating with Ansible as if you were on the same flat network. If you have access to a Cisco IOS-based device, you should be able to run a similar command against the `bastion_routers` group as well and achieve similarly positive results. Now that you have learned the necessary steps to set environment variables for network devices, and indeed access them with Ansible, even when they are on isolated networks, let's learn how to set conditional statements for networking devices.

Conditional statements for networking devices

Although there are no networking-specific Ansible conditionals, conditionals are fairly common in networking-related Ansible usage.

In networking, it's common to enable and disable ports. To have data pass through the cable, both ports at the ends of the cable should be enabled and result in a "connected" state (some vendors will use different names for this, but the idea is the same).

Let's suppose we have two Arista Networks EOS devices and we issued the ON status on the ports and need to wait for the connection to be up before proceeding.

To wait for the `Ethernet4` interface to be enabled, we will need to add the following task in our playbook:

```
- name: Wait for interface to be enabled
  eos_command:
    commands:
      - show interface Ethernet4 | json
    wait_for:
      - "result[0].interfaces.Ethernet4.interfaceStatus eq connected"
```

`eos_command` is the module that allows us to issue free-formed commands to an Arista Networks EOS device. The command itself needs to be specified in an array in the `commands` option. With the `wait_for` option, we can specify a condition, and Ansible will reiterate on the specified task until the condition is satisfied. Since the command's output is redirected to the `json` utility, the output will be a JSON, so we can traverse its structure using Ansible's ability to manipulate JSON data.

We can achieve similar results on Cumulus VX – for example, we can query the facts gathered from the switch to see if port `swp2` is enabled. If it is not, then we will enable it; however, if it is enabled, we will skip the command. We can do this with a simple playbook, follows:

```
---
- name: Simple play to demonstrate conditional on Cumulus Linux
  hosts: cumulusvx

  tasks:
    - name: Enable swp2 if it is disabled
      nclu:
        commands:
          - add int swp2
```

```
      commit: yes
    when: ansible_swp2.active == false
```

Notice the use of the `when` clause in our task, meaning we should only issue the configuration directive if `swp2` is not active. If we were to run this playbook for the first time on an unconfigured Cumulus Linux switch, we should see an output similar to the following:

```
PLAY [Simple play to demonstrate conditional on Cumulus Linux]
****************************************************************

TASK [Gathering Facts]
****************************************************************
ok: [vx01.example.com]

TASK [Enable swp2 if it is disabled]
****************************************************************
changed: [vx01.example.com]

PLAY RECAP
****************************************************************
vx01.example.com : ok=2 changed=1 unreachable=0 failed=0 skipped=0
rescued=0 ignored=0
```

As we can see, the `nclu` module committed our change to the switch configuration. However, if we were to run the playbook a second time, the output should be more like this:

```
PLAY [Simple play to demonstrate conditional on Cumulus Linux]
****************************************************************

TASK [Gathering Facts]
****************************************************************
ok: [vx01.example.com]

TASK [Enable swp2 if it is disabled]
****************************************************************
skipping: [vx01.example.com]

PLAY RECAP
****************************************************************
vx01.example.com : ok=1 changed=0 unreachable=0 failed=0 skipped=1
rescued=0 ignored=0
```

This time, the task was skipped as the Ansible facts show that port `swp2` is already enabled. This is obviously an incredibly simple example, but it shows how you can work with conditionals on a network device very much in the same way that you have already seen conditionals being used on Linux servers, earlier in this book.

That concludes our brief look at network device automation with Ansible – more in-depth work would require a look at network configurations and necessitate more hardware, so this is beyond the scope of this book. However, I hope that this information demonstrates to you that Ansible can be used effectively to automate and configure a wide array of network devices.

Summary

Modern large-scale infrastructures that change rapidly necessitate automation of network tasks. Fortunately, Ansible supports a wide array of network devices, from proprietary hardware such as Cisco IOS-based devices, through to open standards such as white box switches that run operating systems such as Cumulus Linux. Ansible is a powerful and supportive tool when it comes to managing your network configuration and allows you to implement changes quickly and safely. You can even replace entire devices in your network and be confident in your ability to put the correct configuration on the new device in place by virtue of your Ansible playbooks.

In this chapter, you learned about the reasons for automating network management. You then looked at how Ansible manages network devices, how to enable network automation in Ansible, and how to locate the Ansible modules necessary to perform the automation tasks you wish to complete. Then, through practical examples, you learned how to connect to network devices, how to set environment variables (and connect to isolated networks via bastion hosts), and how to apply conditional statements to Ansible tasks for network device configuration.

In the next chapter, we will learn how to manage Linux containers and cloud infrastructures using Ansible.

Questions

1. Which of these is NOT one of the four major connection types that Ansible uses for connecting to those network devices?

   A) `netconf`

   B) `network_cli`

   C) `local`

   D) `netstat`

   E) `httpapi`

2. True or False: The `ansible_network_os` variable is used by Ansible to understand the device family of the device we are going to use.

   A) True

   B) False

3. True or False: In order to connect to an IOS router in a separate network, you need to specify the special connection variables for the host, possibly as inventory group variables.

   A) True

   B) False

Further reading

- The official documentation about Ansible networking: `https://docs.ansible.com/ansible/latest/network/index.html`

10
Container and Cloud Management

Ansible is a very flexible automation tool and can be easily used to automate any aspect of your infrastructure. In the last few years, container-based workloads and cloud workloads have become more and more popular, and for this reason, we are going to look at how you can automate tasks related to those kinds of workloads with Ansible. In this chapter, we will start by designing and building containers with Ansible. We will then look at how to run those containers, and finally, we will look at ways to manage various cloud platforms with Ansible.

Specifically, we will be covering the following topics in this chapter:

- Designing and building containers with playbooks
- Managing multiple container platforms
- Automating Docker with Ansible
- Exploring container-focused modules
- Automating against Amazon Web Services
- Complementing Google Cloud Platform with automation
- Seamless automation integration to Azure
- Expanding your environment with Rackspace Cloud
- Using Ansible to orchestrate OpenStack

Let's get started!

Technical requirements

This chapter assumes that you have set up your control host with Ansible, as detailed in `Chapter 1`, *Getting Started with Ansible,* and are using the most recent version available – the examples in this chapter were tested with Ansible 2.9. Although we will give specific examples of hostnames in this chapter, you are free to substitute them with your own hostname and/or IP addresses. Details of how to do this will be provided in the appropriate places. This chapter also assumes you have access to a Docker host, and although it's possible to install Docker on the majority – if not all – operating systems, all the commands provided in this chapter are for GNU/Linux and have been tested solely on this platform.

All the examples in this chapter can be found in this book's GitHub repository at `https://github.com/PacktPublishing/Practical-Ansible-2/tree/master/Chapter%2010`.

Designing and building containers with playbooks

Building containers with Dockerfiles is probably the most common way of doing this, but this does not mean that this is the best way.

First of all, even if you are in a very good place in your automation path and you have a lot of Ansible roles written for your infrastructure, you can't leverage them in Dockerfiles, so you would end up replicating your work to create containers. Aside from the time required to do this and the fact that you need to learn a new language to do so, it is very rare that a company is able to drop all their infrastructure and switch to containers overnight. This means that you need to keep two copies of the same automation section active and up-to-date, thus putting yourself in the position to make mistakes and have inconsistent behaviors between environments.

If this is not enough of a problem, this situation quickly deteriorates when you start considering cloud environments. All cloud environments have their own control planes and native automation languages, so in a very short time, you would find yourself rewriting the automation for the same operation over and over, thus wasting time and deteriorating the consistency of your environments.

Ansible provides `ansible-container` so that you can create containers using the same components you would use for creating machines. The first thing you should do is ensure that you have `ansible-container` installed. There are a few ways to install it, but the most straightforward is using `pip`. To do so, you can run the following command:

```
$ sudo pip install ansible-container[docker,k8s]
```

The `ansible-container` tool comes with three supported engines at the time of writing:

- `docker`: This is needed if you want to use it with Docker Engine (that is, on your local machine).
- `k8s`: This is needed if you want to use it with a Kubernetes cluster, both local (that is, MiniKube) or remote (that is, a production cluster).
- `openshift`: This is needed if you want to use it with an OpenShift cluster, both local (that is, MiniShift) or remote (that is, a production cluster).

Follow these steps to build the container using playbooks:

1. Issuing the `ansible-container init` command will give us the following output:

```
$ ansible-container init
Ansible Container initialized.
```

Running this command will also create the following files:

- `ansible.cfg`: An empty file to be (eventually) used to override Ansible system configurations
- `ansible-requirements.txt`: An empty file to (eventually) list the Python requirements for the building process of your containers
- `container.yml`: A file that contains the Ansible code for the build
- `meta.yml`: A file that contains the metadata for Ansible Galaxy
- `requirements.yml`: An empty file to (eventually) list the Ansible roles that are required for your build

2. Let's try building our own container using this tool – replace the contents of `container.yml` with the following:

```
version: "2"
settings:
  conductor:
    base: centos:7
  project_name: http-server
services:
  web:
    from: "centos:7"
    roles:
      - geerlingguy.apache
    ports:
      - "80:80"
    command:
      - "/usr/bin/dumb-init"
      - "/usr/sbin/apache2ctl"
      - "-D"
      - "FOREGROUND"
    dev_overrides:
      environment:
        - "DEBUG=1"
```

We can now run `ansible-container build` to initiate the build.

At the end of the building process, we will have a container built with the `geerlingguy.apache` role applied to it. The `ansible-container` tool performs a multi-stage build capability, spinning up an Ansible container that is then used to build the real container.

If we specified more than one role to be applied, the output would be an image with more layers, since Ansible will create a layer for every specified role. In this way, containers can easily be built using your existing Ansible roles rather than Dockerfiles.

Now that you have learned how to design and building containers with playbooks, you'll learn how to manage multiple container platforms.

Managing multiple container platforms

In today's world, simply being able to run an image is not considered a production-ready setup.

To be able to call a deployment "production-ready," you need to be able to demonstrate that the service your application is delivering will run reasonably, even in the case of a single application crash, as well as hardware failure. Often, you'll have even more reliability constraints from your customer.

Luckily, your software is not the only data that has those requirements, so orchestration solutions have been developed for this purpose.

Today, the most successful one is Kubernetes due to its various distributions/versions, so we are going to focus on it primarily.

The idea of Kubernetes is that you inform the Kubernetes Control Plane that you want X number of instances of your Y application, and Kubernetes will count how many instances of the Y application are running on the Kubernetes Nodes to ensure that the number of instances are X. If there are too few instances, Kubernetes will take care to start more instances, while if there are too many instances, the exceeding instances will be stopped.

Since Kubernetes constantly checks that the requested amount of instances are running, in the case of an application failure or a node failure, Kubernetes will restart the lost instances.

Due to the complexity of installing and managing Kubernetes, multiple companies have started to sell distributions of Kubernetes that simplify their operations and that they are willing to support.

The most widely used distribution by far, at the moment, is OpenShift: the Red Hat Kubernetes distribution.

To simplify the life of the developers and operation teams, Ansible provides `ansible-container`, which, as we saw in the previous section, is a tool that's used to create containers, as well as to support the whole life cycle of the container itself.

Deploying to Kubernetes with ansible-container

Let's learn how to run the image we just built with `ansible-container`.

First of all, we need the image itself, and you should have it since this is the output of the previous section!

We will assume that you have access to either a Kubernetes or OpenShift cluster for testing. Setting these up is out the scope of this book, so you might want to look at a distribution such as Minikube or Minishift, both of which are designed to be quick and easy to set up so that you can start learning these technologies rapidly. We also need to have the `kubectl` client or the `oc` client, based on the fact that we have deployed Kubernetes or OpenShift, properly configured. Let's get started:

1. To deploy your application to your cluster, you need to change the `container.yml` file so that you can add some additional information. More specifically, we will need to add a section called `settings` and a section called `k8s_namespace` to declare our deployment settings. This section will look something like this:

   ```
   k8s_namespace:
     name: http-server
     description: An HTTP server
     display_name: HTTP server
   ```

2. Now that we have added the necessary information about the Kubernetes deployment, we can proceed with the deployment:

   ```
   $ ansible-container --engine kubernetes deploy
   ```

As soon as Ansible has completed its execution, you will be able to find the `http-server` deployment on your Kubernetes cluster.

What happens behind the scenes is that Ansible has a set of modules (whose name usually starts with `k8s`) that are used to drive a Kubernetes cluster, and it uses them to deploy the application automatically.

Based on the image that we built in the previous section and the additional information we added at the beginning of this section, Ansible is able to populate a deployment template and then deploy it using the `k8s` module.

Now that you have learned how to deploy your container on a Kubernetes cluster, you'll learn how to interact with the Kubernetes cluster with Ansible.

Managing Kubernetes objects with Ansible

Now that you have deployed your first application with `ansible-container`, it would be useful to interact with this application. It can come in handy to obtain information around the state of your Kubernetes objects or to deploy an application to it, and more generally, to interact with the Kubernetes APIs without `ansible-containers`.

Installing Ansible Kubernetes dependencies

First of all, you need to install the Python `openshift` package (you can install it either via pip or via your OS packaging system).

We are now ready for our first Kubernetes playbook!

Listing Kubernetes namespaces with Ansible

A Kubernetes cluster has multiple namespaces internally, and you can usually find the ones a cluster has with `kubectl get namespaces`. You can do the same with Ansible by creating a file called `k8s-ns-show.yaml` with the following content:

```
---
- hosts: localhost
  tasks:
    - name: Get information from K8s
      k8s_info:
        api_version: v1
        kind: Namespace
      register: ns
    - name: Print info
      debug:
        var: ns
```

We can now execute this, as follows:

```
$ ansible-playbook k8s-ns-show.yaml
```

You will now see information regarding the namespaces in the output.

Notice that in the seventh line of the code (`kind: Namespace`), we are specifying the type of resources we are interested in. You can specify other Kubernetes object types to see them (for example, you can try this with Deployments, Services, and Pods).

Creating a Kubernetes namespace with Ansible

So far, we have learned how to show existing namespaces, but usually, Ansible is used in a declarative way to achieve a desired state. So, let's create a new playbook called `k8s-ns.yaml` with the following content:

```yaml
---
- hosts: localhost
  tasks:
    - name: Ensure the myns namespace exists
      k8s:
        api_version: v1
        kind: Namespace
        name: myns
        state: present
```

Before running it, we can execute `kubectl get ns` so that we can ensure `myns` is not present. In my case, the output is as follows:

```
$ kubectl get ns
NAME STATUS AGE
default Active 69m
kube-node-lease Active 69m
kube-public Active 69m
kube-system Active 69m
```

We can now run the playbook with the following command:

```
$ ansible-playbook k8s-ns.yaml
```

The output should resemble the following one:

```
PLAY [localhost]
******************************************************************
TASK [Gathering Facts]
*****************************************************************
ok: [localhost]

TASK [Ensure the myns namespace exists]
*****************************************
changed: [localhost]

PLAY RECAP
***********************************************************************
localhost : ok=2 changed=1 unreachable=0 failed=0 skipped=0 rescued=0
ignored=0
```

As you can see, Ansible reports that it changed the namespace state. If I execute `kubectl get ns` again, is clear that Ansible created the namespace we were expecting:

```
$ kubectl get ns
NAME STATUS AGE
default Active 74m
kube-node-lease Active 74m
kube-public Active 74m
kube-system Active 74m
myns Active 22s
```

Now, let's create a Service.

Creating a Kubernetes Service with Ansible

So far, we have seen how to create namespaces from Ansible, so now, let's put a Service in the namespace we just created. Let's create a new playbook called `k8s-svc.yaml` with the following content:

```
---
- hosts: localhost
  tasks:
    - name: Ensure the Service mysvc is present
      k8s:
        state: present
        definition:
          apiVersion: v1
          kind: Service
          metadata:
            name: mysvc
            namespace: myns
          spec:
            selector:
              app: myapp
              service: mysvc
            ports:
              - protocol: TCP
                targetPort: 800
                name: port-80-tcp
                port: 80
```

Before running it, we can execute `kubectl get svc` to ensure that the namespace has no Services. Make sure you're in the right namespace before running it! In my case, the output is as follows:

```
$ kubectl get svc
No resources found in myns namespace.
```

We can now run it with the following command:

```
$ ansible-playbook k8s-svc.yaml
```

The output should resemble the following one:

```
PLAY [localhost]
********************************************************************

TASK [Gathering Facts]
*************************************************************
ok: [localhost]

TASK [Ensure the myns namespace exists]
*****************************************
changed: [localhost]

PLAY RECAP
***********************************************************************
localhost : ok=2 changed=1 unreachable=0 failed=0 skipped=0 rescued=0
ignored=0
```

As you can see, Ansible reports that it changed the Service state. If I execute `kubectl get svc` again, is clear that Ansible created the Service we were expecting:

```
$ kubectl get svc
NAME TYPE CLUSTER-IP EXTERNAL-IP PORT(S) AGE
mysvc ClusterIP 10.0.0.84 <none> 80/TCP 10s
```

As you can see, we followed the same procedure that we used in the namespace case, but we specified a different Kubernetes object type and specified the various parameters that are needed for the Service type. You can do the same for all other Kubernetes object types.

Now that you have learned how to deal with Kubernetes clusters, you'll learn how to automate Docker with Ansible.

Automating Docker with Ansible

Docker is now a very common and ubiquitous tool. In production, it is often managed by an orchestrator (or at least it should be, in the majority of cases), but in development, environments are often used directly.

With Ansible, you can easily manage your Docker instance.

Since we are going to manage a Docker instance, we need to make sure we have one at hand and that the `docker` command on our machine is configured properly. We need to do this to ensure this is enough to run `docker images` on the Terminal. Let's say you get a result similar to the following:

```
REPOSITORY TAG IMAGE ID CREATED SIZE
```

This means that everything is working properly. More lines may be provided as output if you have already-cloned images.

On the other hand, let's say it returns something like this:

```
Cannot connect to the Docker daemon at unix:///var/run/docker.sock. Is the
docker daemon running?
```

This means that we don't have a Docker daemon running or that our Docker console has been configured incorrectly.

Also, it's important to ensure that you have the `docker` Python module since Ansible will try to use it to communicate with the Docker daemon. Let's take a look:

1. First of all, we need to create a playbook called `start-docker-container.yaml` that will contain the following code:

```
---
- hosts: localhost
  tasks:
    - name: Start a container with a command
      docker_container:
        name: test-container
        image: alpine
        command:
          - echo
          - "Hello, World!"
```

2. Now that we have the Ansible playbook, we just need to execute it:

```
$ ansible-playbook start-docker-container.yaml
```

As you may expect, it will give you an output similar to the following:

```
PLAY [localhost]
*********************************************************************
**

TASK [Gathering Facts]
*********************************************************************
ok: [localhost]

TASK [Start a container with a command]
*********************************************
changed: [localhost]

PLAY RECAP
*********************************************************************
********
localhost : ok=2 changed=1 unreachable=0 failed=0 skipped=0
rescued=0 ignored=0
```

3. We can now check that our command executed properly, as follows:

```
$ docker container list -a
```

This will show the container that was run:

```
CONTAINER ID IMAGE   COMMAND                CREATED        STATUS
PORTS NAMES
c706ec55fc0d alpine "echo Hello, World!" 3 minutes ago Exited (0) About a
minute ago          test-container
```

This proves that a container was executed.

To check that the `echo` command was executed, we can run the following code:

```
$ docker logs c706ec55fc0d
```

This will return the following output:

```
Hello, World!
```

In this section, we executed the `docker_container` module. This is not the only module Ansible has to control the Docker daemon, but it is probably one of the most widely used since it's used to control containers running on Docker.

Other modules include the following:

- `docker_config`: Used to change the configurations of the Docker daemon
- `docker_container_info`: Used to gather information from (inspect) a container
- `docker_network`: Used to manage Docker networking configuration

There are also many modules that start with `docker_` but are actually used to manage Docker Swarm clusters, and not Docker instances. Some examples are as follows:

- `docker_node`: Used to manage a node in a Docker Swarm cluster
- `docker_node_info`: Used to retrieve information about a specific node in a Docker Swarm cluster
- `docker_swarm_info`: Used to retrieve information about a Docker Swarm cluster

As we will see in the next section, there many more modules that can be used to manage containers that are orchestrated in various ways.

Now that you have learned how to automate Docker with Ansible, you will explore container-focused modules.

Exploring container-focused modules

Often, when organizations grow, they start to use multiple technologies in different parts of the organization. Another thing that usually happens is that after a department has found that a vendor worked well for them, they will be more inclined to try new technologies offered by this vendor. A mix of those two factors and time (usually, fewer technologies cycles) will end up creating multiple solutions for the same problem within the same organization.

If your organization is in this situation with containers, Ansible can come to rescue, thanks to its ability to interoperate with the majority of, if not all, container platforms.

Many times, the biggest problem to do something with Ansible is finding the name of the modules you need to use to achieve what you want to achieve. In this section, we will try to help in this effort, mainly in terms of the containerization space, but this might help you in the quest to find different kinds of modules.

The starting point for all Ansible module research should be the Module index (`https://docs.ansible.com/ansible/latest/modules/modules_by_category.html`). Very often, you can find a category that is clearly a match for what you are looking for, but this is not always the case.

Containers are one of those exceptions (at least at the time of writing), and therefore there is no "containers" category. The solution is to go to **All modules**. From here, you can search by using your browser's built-in feature (usually, this can be reached by using *Ctrl+F*) to find the strings that might match the package name or short description.

Every module in Ansible is classified in one category, but very often, modules fit more than one category, so it's not always easy to find them.

For instance, many Ansible modules relative to container Services are in the **Cloud modules** category (ECS, Docker, LXC, LXD, and Podman), while others are in the **Clustering modules** category (Kubernetes, OpenShift, and so on).

To help you further, let's take a look at some of the main container platforms and the main modules Ansible provides.

Amazon Web Services, back in 2014, launched **Elastic Container Service (ECS)**, which is a way to deploy and orchestrate Docker containers within their infrastructure. In the following year, **Amazon Web Services (AWS)** also launched **Elastic Container Registry (ECR)**, a managed Docker Registry service. The service did not become as ubiquitous as AWS hoped, so in 2018, AWS launched **Elastic Kubernetes Service (EKS)** to allow people that wanted to run Kubernetes on AWS to have a managed service. If you are using or plan to use EKS, this is just a standard managed Kubernetes cluster, so you can use the Kubernetes-specific modules that we are going to cover shortly. If you decide to use ECS, there are several modules that can help you. The most important ones are `ecs_cluster`, which allows you to create or terminate ECS clusters; `ecs_ecr`, which allows you to manage ECR; `ecs_service`, which allows you to create, terminate, start, or stop a service in ECS; and `ecs_task`, which allows you to run, start, or stop a task in ECS. In addition to those, there are `ecs_service_facts` that allow Ansible to list or describe services in ECS.

Microsoft Azure, in 2018, announced **Azure Container Service (ACS)**, and then announced **Azure Kubernetes Service (AKS)**. These services are managed by Kubernetes solutions, so they can both be managed with the Kubernetes modules. In addition to those, Ansible provided two specific modules: the `azure_rm_acs` module allows us to create, update, and delete Azure Container Service instances, while the `azure_rm_aks` module allows us to create, update, and delete Azure Kubernetes Service instances.

Google Cloud launched **Google Kubernetes Engine (GKE)** in 2015. GKE is the Google Cloud Platform version of managed Kubernetes, and therefore compatible with Ansible Kubernetes modules. In addition to those, there are various GKE-specific modules, some of which are as follows:

- `gcp_container_cluster`: Allows you to create a GCP Cluster
- `gcp_container_cluster_facts`: Allows you to gather facts for a GCP Cluster
- `gcp_container_node_pool`: Allows you to create a GCP NodePool
- `gcp_container_node_pool_facts`: Allows you to gather facts for a GCP NodePool

Red Hat started OpenShift in 2011, and at the time, it was based on its own container runtime. In version 3, which was released in 2015, it was completely rebased on Kubernetes, so all Ansible Kubernetes modules work. In addition to those, there is the `oc` module, which is currently still present but in a deprecated state, giving preference to the Kubernetes modules.

In 2015, Google released Kubernetes and quickly, a huge community started to build around it. Ansible allows you to manage your Kubernetes clusters with some modules:

- `k8s`: Allows you to manage any kind of Kubernetes object
- `k8s_auth`: Allows you to authenticate to Kubernetes clusters that require an explicit login step
- `k8s_facts`: Allows you to inspect Kubernetes objects
- `k8s_scale`: Allows you to set a new size for a Deployment, ReplicaSet, Replication Controller, or Job
- `k8s_service`: Allows you to manage Services on Kubernetes

LXC and LXD are also systems that can be used to run containers in Linux. These systems are also supported by Ansible, thanks to the following modules:

- `lxc_container`: Allows you to manage LXC containers
- `lxd_container`: Allows you to manage LXD containers
- `lxd_profile`: Allows you to manage LXD profiles

Now that you have learned how to explore container-focused modules, you'll learn how to automate against Amazon Web Services.

Automating against Amazon Web Services

In many organizations, cloud providers are being used widely, while in others, they are just being introduced. However, in one way or the other, you will probably have to deal with some cloud provider doing your job. AWS is the biggest and the oldest, and is perhaps something you will have to work with.

Installation

To be able to use Ansible to automate your Amazon Web Service estate, you'll need to install the `boto` library. To do so, run the following command:

```
$ pip install boto
```

Now that you have all the necessary software installed, you can set up authentication.

Authentication

The `boto` library looks up the necessary credentials in the `~/.aws/credentials` file. There are two different ways to ensure that the credentials file is configured properly.

It is possible to use the AWS CLI tool. Alternatively, this can be done with a text editor of your choice by creating a file with the following structure:

```
[default]
aws_access_key_id = [YOUR_KEY_HERE]
aws_secret_access_key = [YOUR_SECRET_ACCESS_KEY_HERE]
```

Now that you've created the file with the necessary credentials, `boto` will be able to work against your AWS environment. Since Ansible uses `boto` for every single communication with AWS systems, this means that Ansible will be appropriately configured, even without you have to change any Ansible-specific configuration.

Creating your first machine

Now that Ansible is able to connect to your AWS environment, you can proceed with the actual playbook by following these steps:

1. Create the `aws.yaml` Playbook with the following content:

```yaml
---
- hosts: localhost
  tasks:
    - name: Ensure key pair is present
      ec2_key:
        name: fale
        key_material: "{{ lookup('file', '~/.ssh/fale.pub') }}"
    - name: Gather information of the EC2 VPC net in eu-west-1
      ec2_vpc_net_facts:
        region: eu-west-1
      register: aws_simple_net
    - name: Gather information of the EC2 VPC subnet in eu-west-1
      ec2_vpc_subnet_facts:
        region: eu-west-1
        filters:
          vpc-id: '{{ aws_simple_net.vpcs.0.id }}'
      register: aws_simple_subnet
    - name: Ensure wssg Security Group is present
      ec2_group:
        name: wssg
        description: Web Security Group
        region: eu-west-1
        vpc_id: '{{ aws_simple_net.vpcs.0.id }}'
        rules:
          - proto: tcp
            from_port: 22
            to_port: 22
            cidr_ip: 0.0.0.0/0
          - proto: tcp
            from_port: 80
            to_port: 80
            cidr_ip: 0.0.0.0/0
          - proto: tcp
            from_port: 443
            to_port: 443
            cidr_ip: 0.0.0.0/0
        rules_egress:
          - proto: all
            cidr_ip: 0.0.0.0/0
      register: aws_simple_wssg
```

```
- name: Setup instance
  ec2:
    assign_public_ip: true
    image: ami-3548444c
    region: eu-west-1
    exact_count: 1
    key_name: fale
    count_tag:
      Name: ws01.ansible2cookbook.com
    instance_tags:
      Name: ws01.ansible2cookbook.coms
    instance_type: t2.micro
    group_id: '{{ aws_simple_wssg.group_id }}'
    vpc_subnet_id: '{{ aws_simple_subnet.subnets.0.id }}'
    volumes:
      - device_name: /dev/sda1
        volume_type: gp2
        volume_size: 10
        delete_on_termination: True
```

2. Run it using the following command:

```
$ ansible-playbook aws.yaml
```

This command will return something like the following:

```
PLAY [localhost]
***********************************************************************
***************

TASK [Gathering Facts]
***********************************************************************
*********
ok: [localhost]

TASK [Ensure key pair is present]
***********************************************************************
ok: [localhost]

TASK [Gather information of the EC2 VPC net in eu-west-1]
****************************************
ok: [localhost]

TASK [Gather information of the EC2 VPC subnet in eu-west-1]
****************************************
ok: [localhost]

TASK [Ensure wssg Security Group is present]
```

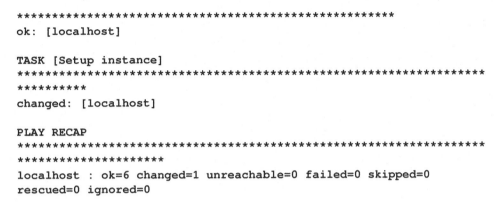

```
*********************************************************
ok: [localhost]

TASK [Setup instance]
***********************************************************************
**********
changed: [localhost]

PLAY RECAP
***********************************************************************
********************
localhost : ok=6 changed=1 unreachable=0 failed=0 skipped=0
rescued=0 ignored=0
```

If you check AWS Console, you will see that you now have one machine up and running!

To launch a virtual machine in AWS, we need a few things to be in place, as follows:

- An SSH key pair
- A network
- A subnetwork
- A security group

By default, a network and a subnetwork are already available in your accounts, but you need to retrieve their IDs.

That's why we started by uploading the public part of an SSH keypair to AWS, then queried for information about the network and the subnetwork, then ensured that the Security Group we wanted to use was present, and lastly triggered the machine build.

Now you have learned how to automate against Amazon Web Services, you'll learn how to complement Google Cloud Platform with automation.

Complementing Google Cloud Platform with automation

Another global cloud provider is Google, with its Google Cloud Platform. Google's approach to the cloud is relatively different from other providers' since Google does not try to simulate the data center in a virtual environment. This is because Google wishes to rethink the concept of cloud provision in order to simplify it.

Installation

You need to ensure that you have the proper components installed before you can start using Google Cloud Platform with Ansible. More specifically, you will require the Python `requests` and `google-auth` modules. To install these modules, run the following command:

```
$ pip install requests google-auth
```

Now that you have all the dependencies present, you can start the authentication process.

Authentication

There are two different approaches to obtain a working set of credentials in Google Cloud Platform:

- The Service Account
- The Machine Account

The first approach is the suggested one in the majority of cases since the second applies only to circumstances where Ansible is run directly within the Google Cloud Platform environment.

Once you have created the Service Account, you should set the following environmental variables:

- GCP_AUTH_KIND
- GCP_SERVICE_ACCOUNT_EMAIL
- GCP_SERVICE_ACCOUNT_FILE
- GCP_SCOPES

Now, Ansible can use the proper Service Account.

The second approach is by far the easiest since Ansible will be able to auto-detect the Machine Account if you are running it in a Google Cloud instance.

Creating your first machine

Now that Ansible is able to connect to your GCP environment, you can proceed with the actual Playbook:

1. Create the `gce.yaml` Playbook with the following content:

```
---
- hosts: localhost
  tasks:
    - name: create a instance
      gcp_compute_instance:
        name: TestMachine
        machine_type: n1-standard-1
        disks:
        - auto_delete: 'true'
          boot: 'true'
          initialize_params:
            source_image: family/centos-7
            disk_size_gb: 10
        zone: eu-west1-c
        auth_kind: serviceaccount
        service_account_file: "~/sa.json"
        state: present
```

Execute it with the following command:

```
$ ansible-playbook gce.yaml
```

This will create an output like the following one:

```
PLAY [localhost]
****************************************************************
***************

TASK [Gathering Facts]
****************************************************************
*********
ok: [localhost]

TASK [create a instance]
****************************************************************
*******
changed: [localhost]

PLAY RECAP
****************************************************************
********************
```

```
localhost : ok=2 changed=1 unreachable=0 failed=0 skipped=0
rescued=0 ignored=0
```

As for the AWS example, running a machine in the cloud is very easy with Ansible.

In the case of GCE, you don't need to set up the networks beforehand since the GCE defaults will kick in and provide a functional machine either way.

As for AWS, the list of modules you can use is huge. You can find the full list at `https://docs.ansible.com/ansible/latest/modules/list_of_cloud_modules.html#google`.

Now that you have learned how to complement Google Cloud Platform with automation, you will learn how to seamlessly perform automation integration to Azure.

Seamless automation integration to Azure

Another global cloud that Ansible can manage is Microsoft Azure.

Azure integration, like the AWS one, requires quite a few steps to be performed in Playbooks.

The first thing you will need to do is set up the authentication so that Ansible is allowed to control your Azure account.

Installation

To let Ansible manage the Azure cloud, you need to install the Azure SDK for Python. Do this by executing the following command:

```
$ pip install 'ansible[azure]'
```

Now that you have all the dependencies present, you can start the authentication process.

Authentication

There are different ways to ensure that Ansible is able to manage Azure for you, based on the way your Azure account is set up, but they can all be configured in the `~/.azure/credentials` file.

If you want Ansible to use the principal credentials for the Azure account, you will need to create a file that resembles the following:

```
[default]
subscription_id = [YOUR_SUBSCIRPTION_ID_HERE]
client_id = [YOUR_CLIENT_ID_HERE]
secret = [YOUR_SECRET_HERE]
tenant = [YOUR_TENANT_HERE]
```

If you prefer to use Active Directories with a username and password, you can do something like this:

```
[default]
ad_user = [YOUR_AD_USER_HERE]
password = [YOUR_AD_PASSWORD_HERE]
```

Lastly, you can opt for an Active Directory login with ADFS. In this case, you'll need to set some additional parameters. You'll end up with something like this:

```
[default]
ad_user = [YOUR_AD_USER_HERE]
password = [YOUR_AD_PASSWORD_HERE]
client_id = [YOUR_CLIENT_ID_HERE]
tenant = [YOUR_TENANT_HERE]
adfs_authority_url = [YOUR_ADFS_AUTHORITY_URL_HERE]
```

The same parameters can be passed as parameters or as environmental variables if it makes more sense.

Creating your first machine

Now that Ansible is able to connect to your Azure environment, you can proceed with the actual Playbook:

1. Create the `azure.yaml` Playbook with the following content:

```yaml
---
- hosts: localhost
  tasks:
    - name: Ensure the Storage Account is present
      azure_rm_storageaccount:
        resource_group: Testing
        name: mysa
        account_type: Standard_LRS
    - name: Ensure the Virtual Network is present
      azure_rm_virtualnetwork:
        resource_group: Testing
        name: myvn
        address_prefixes: "10.10.0.0/16"
    - name: Ensure the Subnet is present
      azure_rm_subnet:
        resource_group: Testing
        name: mysn
        address_prefix: "10.10.0.0/24"
        virtual_network: myvn
    - name: Ensure that the Public IP is set
      azure_rm_publicipaddress:
        resource_group: Testing
        allocation_method: Static
        name: myip
    - name: Ensure a Security Group allowing SSH is present
      azure_rm_securitygroup:
        resource_group: Testing
        name: mysg
        rules:
          - name: SSH
            protocol: Tcp
            destination_port_range: 22
            access: Allow
            priority: 101
            direction: Inbound
    - name: Ensure the NIC is present
      azure_rm_networkinterface:
        resource_group: Testing
        name: testnic001
        virtual_network: myvn
```

```
      subnet: mysn
      public_ip_name: myip
      security_group: mysg
    - name: Ensure the Virtual Machine is present
      azure_rm_virtualmachine:
        resource_group: Testing
        name: myvm01
        vm_size: Standard_D1
        storage_account: mysa
        storage_container: myvm01
        storage_blob: myvm01.vhd
        admin_username: admin
        admin_password: Password!
        network_interfaces: testnic001
        image:
          offer: CentOS
          publisher: OpenLogic
          sku: '8.0'
          version: latest
```

2. We can run it with the following command:

   $ ansible-playbook azure.yaml

   This will return something like the following:

   PLAY [localhost]
   ****
   ****

   TASK [Gathering Facts]
   ****
   ****
   ok: [localhost]

   TASK [Ensure the Storage Account is present]
   ****
   changed: [localhost]

   TASK [Ensure the Virtual Network is present]
   ****
   changed: [localhost]

   TASK [Ensure the Subnet is present]
   ****
   changed: [localhost]

   TASK [Ensure that the Public IP is set]
```
```

```
**************************************************************
changed: [localhost]

TASK [Ensure a Security Group allowing SSH is present]
*******************************************
changed: [localhost]

TASK [Ensure the NIC is present]
*********************************************************************
changed: [localhost]

TASK [Ensure the Virtual Machine is present]
*****************************************************
changed: [localhost]

PLAY RECAP
*********************************************************************
*********************
localhost : ok=8 changed=7 unreachable=0 failed=0 skipped=0
rescued=0 ignored=0
```

You now have your machine running in the Azure cloud!

As you can see, in Azure, you will need all the resources to be ready before you can issue the machine creation command. This is the reason you create the Storage Account, the Virtual Network, the Subnet, the Public IP, the security Group, and the NIC first, and only at that point, the machine itself.

Outside the three major players in the market, there are many additional cloud options. One very interesting option is RackSpace, due to its history: Rackspace Cloud.

Expanding your environment with Rackspace Cloud

Rackspace was one of the first companies in the public cloud business. Also, in a joint effort with NASA, Rackspace created OpenStack in 2010. In the last 10 years, Rackspace has been a very influential provider for the world of cloud infrastructure, OpenStack, and, more generally, the hosting scene.

Installation

To be able to manage Rackspace from Ansible, you will need to install pyrax.

The easiest way to install it is by running the following command:

```
$ pip install pyrax
```

You can also install it via your system package manager if it's available.

Authentication

Since pyrax does not have a default location for the credentials file, you will need to create a file and then set an environmental variable by instructing pyrax to do this at the file's location.

Let's start by creating a file in ~/.rackspace_credentials with the following content:

```
[rackspace_cloud]
username = [YOUR_USERNAME_HERE]
api_key = [YOUR_API_KEY_HERE]
```

We can now proceed by setting the RAX_CREDS_FILE variable to the right location:

```
$ export RAX_CREDS_FILE=~/.rackspace_credentials
```

Let's go ahead and create a machine using Rackspace Cloud.

Creating your first machine

Creating a machine in Rackspace Cloud is very simple since it's a single-step operation:

1. Create the `rax.yaml` Playbook with the following content:

```
---
- hosts: localhost
  tasks:
    - name: Ensure the my_machine exists
      rax:
        name: my_machine
        flavor: 4
        image: centos-8
        count: 1
        group: my_group
        wait: True
```

2. Now, you can execute it with the following command:

```
$ ansible-playbook rax.yaml
```

3. This should result in something like the following:

```
PLAY [localhost]
**************************************************************************
***************

TASK [Gathering Facts]
**************************************************************************
*********
ok: [localhost]

TASK [Ensure the my_machine exists]
*********************************************************************
changed: [localhost]

PLAY RECAP
*********************************************************************
*********************
localhost : ok=2 changed=1 unreachable=0 failed=0 skipped=0
rescued=0 ignored=0
```

As you can see, creating machines in Rackspace Cloud is very straightforward, and the default Ansible module has some interesting concepts already integrated into it, such as group and count. Those options allow you to create and manage groups of instances in the same way you would do with a single instance.

Using Ansible to orchestrate OpenStack

As opposed to the various cloud services we just discussed, all of which are public clouds, OpenStack allows you to create your own (private) cloud.

Private clouds have the disadvantage that they expose more complexity to the administrator and to the user, but this is the reason why they can be customized to suit an organization perfectly.

Installation

The first step to being able to control an OpenStack cluster with Ansible is to ensure that openstacksdk is installed.

To install openstacksdk, you need to execute the following command:

```
$ pip install openstacksdk
```

Now that you have installed openstacksdk, you can start the authentication process.

Authentication

Since Ansible will use openstacksdk as its backend, you will need to ensure that openstacksdk is able to connect to the OpenStack cluster.

To do this, you can change the ~/.config/openstack/clouds.yaml file, ensuring that there is a configuration for the cloud you want to use it for.

An example of what a correct OpenStack credentials set could look like is as follows:

```
clouds:
  test_cloud:
    region_name: MyRegion
    auth:
      auth_url: http://[YOUR_AUTH_URL_HERE]:5000/v2.0/
      username: [YOUR_USERNAME_HERE]
      password: [YOUR_PASSWORD_HERE]
      project_name: myProject
```

It's also possible to set a different config file location if you are willing to export the `OS_CLIENT_CONFIG_FILE` variable as an environment variable.

Now that you have set up the required security so that Ansible can manage your cluster, you can create your first Playbook.

Creating your first machine

Since OpenStack is very flexible, many of its components can have many different implementations, which means they may differ slightly in terms of their behavior. To be able to accommodate all the various cases, the Ansible modules that manage OpenStack tend to have a lower level of abstraction compared to the ones for many public clouds.

So, to create a machine, you will need to ensure that the public SSH key is known to OpenStack and ensure that the OS image is present as well. After doing this, you can set up networks, subnetworks, and routers to ensure that the machine we are going to create can communicate via the network. Then, you can create the security group and its rules so that the machine can receive connections (pings and SSH traffic, in this case). Finally, you can create a machine instance.

To complete all the steps we've just described, you need to create a file called `openstack.yaml` with the following content:

```
---
- hosts: localhost
  tasks:
    - name: Ensure the SSH key is present on OpenStack
      os_keypair:
        state: present
        name: ansible_key
        public_key_file: "{{ '~' | expanduser }}/.ssh/id_rsa.pub"
    - name: Ensure we have a CentOS image
      get_url:
        url:
http://cloud.centos.org/centos/8/x86_64/images/CentOS-8-GenericCloud-8.1.19
11-20200113.3.x86_64.qcow2
        dest: /tmp/CentOS-8-GenericCloud-8.1.1911-20200113.3.x86_64.qcow2
    - name: Ensure the CentOS image is in OpenStack
      os_image:
        name: centos
        container_format: bare
        disk_format: qcow2
        state: present
        filename: /tmp/CentOS-8-
```

```
GenericCloud-8.1.1911-20200113.3.x86_64.qcow2
    - name: Ensure the Network is present
      os_network:
        state: present
        name: mynet
        external: False
        shared: False
      register: net_out
    - name: Ensure the Subnetwork is present
      os_subnet:
        state: present
        network_name: "{{ net_out.id }}"
        name: mysubnet
        ip_version: 4
        cidr: 192.168.0.0/24
        gateway_ip: 192.168.0.1
        enable_dhcp: yes
        dns_nameservers:
          - 8.8.8.8
    - name: Ensure the Router is present
      os_router:
        state: present
        name: myrouter
        network: nova
        external_fixed_ips:
          - subnet: nova
        interfaces:
          - mysubnet
    - name: Ensure the Security Group is present
      os_security_group:
        state: present
        name: mysg
    - name: Ensure the Security Group allows ICMP traffic
      os_security_group_rule:
        security_group: mysg
        protocol: icmp
        remote_ip_prefix: 0.0.0.0/0
    - name: Ensure the Security Group allows SSH traffic
      os_security_group_rule:
        security_group: mysg
        protocol: tcp
        port_range_min: 22
        port_range_max: 22
        remote_ip_prefix: 0.0.0.0/0
    - name: Ensure the Instance exists
      os_server:
        state: present
        name: myInstance
```

```
          image: centos
          flavor: m1.small
          security_groups: mysg
          key_name: ansible_key
          nics:
            - net-id: "{{ net_out.id }}"
```

Now, you can run it, as follows:

```
$ ansible-playbook openstack.yaml
```

The output should be as follows:

```
PLAY [localhost]
***************************************************************************
******

TASK [Gathering Facts]
***************************************************************************
*
ok: [localhost]

TASK [Ensure the SSH key is present on OpenStack]
************************************************
changed: [localhost]

TASK [Ensure we have a CentOS image]
*****************************************************
changed: [localhost]

TASK [Ensure the CentOS image is in OpenStack]
****************************************************
changed: [localhost]

TASK [Ensure the Network is present]
**********************************************************
changed: [localhost]

TASK [Ensure the Subnetwork is present]
*********************************************************
changed: [localhost]

TASK [Ensure the Router is present]
***********************************************************
changed: [localhost]

TASK [Ensure the Security Group is present]
**********************************************************
```

```
changed: [localhost]

TASK [Ensure the Security Group allows ICMP traffic]
************************************************
changed: [localhost]

TASK [Ensure the Security Group allows SSH traffic]
*************************************************
changed: [localhost]

TASK [Ensure the Instance exists]
****************************************************************
changed: [localhost]

PLAY RECAP
*****************************************************************************
*************
localhost : ok=11 changed=10 unreachable=0 failed=0 skipped=0 rescued=0
ignored=0
```

As you can see, this process was longer than the public cloud ones we covered. However, you did get to upload the image that you wanted to run, which is something many clouds do not allow (or allow with very complex processes).

Summary

In this chapter, you learned how to automate tasks, from designing and building containers with playbooks to managing the deployment on Kubernetes, as well as managing Kubernetes objects and automating Docker with Ansible. You also explored the modules that can help you automate cloud environments, such as AWS, Google Cloud Platform, Azure, Rackspace, and OpenShift. You also learned about the different approaches various cloud providers use, including their defaults and the parameters that you will always need to add.

Now that you have an understanding of how Ansible interacts with the clouds, you can immediately start to automate your cloud workflows. Also, remember to check the documentation in the *Further reading* section to take a look at all the cloud modules that Ansible supports and their options.

In the next chapter, you will learn how to troubleshoot and create testing strategies.

Questions

1. Which of the following is NOT a GKE Ansible module?

    A) `gcp_container_cluster`
    B) `gcp_container_node_pool`
    C) `gcp_container_node_pool_facts`
    D) `gcp_container_node_pool_count`
    E) `gcp_container_cluster_facts`

2. True or False: In order to manage containers in Kubernetes, you need to add `k8s_namespace` in the settings section.

    A) True
    B) False

3. True or False: When working with Azure, you don't need to create a **Network Interface Controller (NIC)** before creating an instance.

    A) True
    B) False

4. True or False: `Ansible-Container` is the only way to interact with Kubernetes and Doc.

    A) True
    B) False

5. True or False: When working with AWS, it's necessary to create a Security Group before creating an EC2 instance.

    A) True
    B) False

Further reading

- **More AWS modules:** `https://docs.ansible.com/ansible/latest/modules/list_of_cloud_modules.html#amazon`
- **More Azure modules:** `https://docs.ansible.com/ansible/latest/modules/list_of_cloud_modules.html#azure`
- **More Docker modules:** `https://docs.ansible.com/ansible/latest/modules/list_of_cloud_modules.html#docker`
- **More GCP modules:** `https://docs.ansible.com/ansible/latest/modules/list_of_cloud_modules.html#google`
- **More OpenStack modules:** `https://docs.ansible.com/ansible/latest/modules/list_of_cloud_modules.html#openstack`
- **More Rackspace modules:** `https://docs.ansible.com/ansible/latest/modules/list_of_cloud_modules.html#rackspace`

11
Troubleshooting and Testing Strategies

In a similar way to any other kind of code, Ansible code can contain issues and bugs. Ansible tries to make it as safe as possible by checking the task syntax before the task is executed. This check, however, only saves you from a small number of possible types of errors, such as incorrect task parameters, but it will not protect you from others.

It's also important to remember that, due to its nature, in Ansible code, we describe the desired state rather than stating a sequence of steps to obtain the desired state. This difference means that the system is less prone to logical errors.
Nevertheless, a bug in a Playbook could mean a potential misconfiguration on all of your machines. This should be taken very seriously. It is even more critical when critical parts of the system are changed, such as SSH daemon or sudo configuration, since the risk is you locking yourself out of the system.

There are a bunch of different ways to prevent or mitigate a bug in Ansible playbooks. In this chapter, we will cover the following topics:

- Digging into playbook execution problems
- Using host facts to diagnose failures
- Testing with a playbook
- Using check mode
- Solving host connection issues
- Passing working variables via the CLI
- Limiting the host's execution
- Flushing the code cache
- Checking for bad syntax

Technical requirements

This chapter assumes that you have set up your control host with Ansible, as detailed in Chapter 1, *Getting Started with Ansible,* and are using the most recent version available – the examples in this chapter were tested with Ansible 2.9. Although we will give specific examples of hostnames in this chapter, you are free to substitute them with your own hostname and/or IP addresses. Details of how to do this will be provided at the appropriate places.

The examples in this chapter can be found in this book's GitHub repository at `https://github.com/PacktPublishing/Practical-Ansible-2/tree/master/Chapter%2011`.

Digging into playbook execution problems

There are cases where an Ansible execution will interrupt. Many things can cause these situations.

The single most frequent cause of problems I've found while executing Ansible playbooks is the network. Since the machine that is issuing the commands and the one that is performing them are usually linked through the network, a problem in the network will immediately show itself as an Ansible execution problem.

Sometimes, and this is particularly true for some modules, such as `shell` or `command`, the return code is non-zero, even though the execution was successful. In those cases, you can ignore the error by using the following line in your module:

```
ignore_errors: yes
```

For instance, if you run the `/bin/false` command, it will always return 1. To execute this in a playbook so that you can avoid it blocking there, you can write something like the following:

```
- name: Run a command that will return 1
  command: /bin/false
  ignore_errors: yes
```

As we have seen, `/bin/false` will always return 1 as return code, but we still managed to go forward in the execution. Be aware that this is a particular case, and often, the best approach is to fix your application so that you're following UNIX standards and return 0 if the application runs appropriately, instead of putting a workaround in your Playbooks.

Next, we will talk more about the methods we can use to diagnose Ansible execution problems.

Using host facts to diagnose failures

Some execution failures derive from the state of the target machine. The most common problem of this kind is the case where Ansible expects a file or variable to be present, but it's not.

Sometimes, it can be enough to print the machine facts to find the problem.

To do so, we need to create a simple playbook, called `print_facts.yaml`, which contains the following content:

```
---
- hosts: target_host
  tasks:
    - name: Display all variables/facts known for a host
      debug:
        var: hostvars[inventory_hostname]
```

This technique will give you a lot of information about the state of the target machine during Ansible execution.

Testing with a playbook

One of the most complex things in the IT field is not creating software and systems, but debugging them when they have problems. Ansible is not an exception. No matter how good you are at creating Ansible playbooks, sooner or later, you'll find yourself debugging a playbook that is not behaving as you thought it would.

The simplest way of performing basic tests is to print out the values of variables during execution. Let's learn how to do this with Ansible, as follows:

1. First of all, we need a playbook called `debug.yaml` with the following content:

```
---
- hosts: localhost
  tasks:
    - shell: /usr/bin/uptime
      register: result
    - debug:
        var: result
```

2. Run it with the following command:

   $ ansible-playbook debug.yaml

You will receive an output similar to the following:

```
PLAY [localhost]
********************************************************************
**********

TASK [Gathering Facts]
********************************************************************
*****
ok: [localhost]

TASK [shell]
********************************************************************
***************
changed: [localhost]

TASK [debug]
********************************************************************
***************
ok: [localhost] => {
    "result": {
        "changed": true,
        "cmd": "/usr/bin/uptime",
        "delta": "0:00:00.003461",
        "end": "2019-06-16 11:30:51.087322",
        "failed": false,
        "rc": 0,
        "start": "2019-06-16 11:30:51.083861",
        "stderr": "",
        "stderr_lines": [],
        "stdout": " 11:30:51 up 40 min, 1 user, load average: 1.11,
```

```
        0.73, 0.53",
            "stdout_lines": [
                " 11:30:51 up 40 min, 1 user, load average: 1.11, 0.73,
        0.53"
            ]
        }
    }

    PLAY RECAP
    *************************************************************************
    *****************
    localhost : ok=3 changed=1 unreachable=0 failed=0 skipped=0 rescued=0
    ignored=0
```

In the first task, we used the command module to execute the uptime command and saved its output in the result variable. Then, in the second task, we used the debug module to print the content of the result variable.

The debug module is the module that allows you to print the value of a variable (by using the var option) or a fixed string (by using the msg option) during Ansible's execution.

The debug module also provides the verbosity option. Let's say you change the playbook in the following way:

```
---
- hosts: localhost
  tasks:
    - shell: /usr/bin/uptime
      register: result
    - debug:
        var: result
        verbosity: 2
```

Now, if you try to execute it in the same way you did previously, you will notice that the debug step won't be executed and that the following line will appear in the output instead:

```
TASK [debug]
*************************************************************************
***********
skipping: [localhost]
```

This is because we set the minimum required verbosity to 2, and by default, Ansible runs with a verbosity of 0.

To see the result of using the debug module with this new playbook, we will need to run a slightly different command:

```
$ ansible-playbook debug2.yaml -vv
```

By putting two -v options in the command line, we will be running Ansible with verbosity of 2. This will not only affect this specific module but all the modules (or Ansible itself) that are set to behave differently at different debug levels.

Now that you have learned how to test with a playbook, let's learn how to use check mode.

Using check mode

Although you might be confident in the code you have written, it still pays to test it before running it for real in a production environment. In such cases, it is a good idea to be able to run your code, but with a safety net in place. This is what check mode is for. Follow these steps:

1. First of all, we need to create an easy playbook to test this feature. Let's create a playbook called check-mode.yaml that contains the following content:

```
---
- hosts: localhost
  tasks:
    - name: Touch a file
      file:
        path: /tmp/myfile
        state: touch
```

2. Now, we can run the playbook in the check mode by specifying the --check option in the invocation:

```
$ ansible-playbook check-mode.yaml --check
```

This will output everything as if it was really performing the operation, as follows:

```
PLAY [localhost]
****************************************************************************
*******

TASK [Gathering Facts]
****************************************************************************
*
ok: [localhost]
```

```
TASK [Touch a file]
*********************************************************************
****
ok: [localhost]

PLAY RECAP
*********************************************************************
*************
localhost : ok=2 changed=0 unreachable=0 failed=0 skipped=0 rescued=0
ignored=0
```

However, if you look in /tmp, you won't find myfile.

Ansible check mode is usually called a dry run. The idea is that the run won't change the state of the machine and will only highlight the differences between the current status and the status declared in the playbook.

> Not all modules support check mode, but all major modules do, and more and more modules are being added at every release. In particular, note that the command and shell modules do not support it because it is impossible for the module to tell what commands will result in a change, and what won't. Therefore, these modules will always return changed when they're run outside of check mode because they assume a change has been made.

A similar feature to check mode is the --diff flag. What this flag allows us to do is track what exactly changed during an Ansible execution. So, let's say we run the same playbook with the following command:

```
$ ansible-playbook check-mode.yaml --diff
```

This will return something like the following:

```
PLAY [localhost]
*********************************************************************
*******

TASK [Gathering Facts]
*********************************************************************
*
ok: [localhost]

TASK [Touch a file]
*********************************************************************
****
--- before
+++ after
```

```
@@ -1,6 +1,6 @@
 {
- "atime": 1560693571.3594637,
- "mtime": 1560693571.3594637,
+ "atime": 1560693571.3620908,
+ "mtime": 1560693571.3620908,
     "path": "/tmp/myfile",
- "state": "absent"
+ "state": "touch"
 }

changed: [localhost]

PLAY RECAP
*************************************************************************
*************
localhost : ok=2 changed=1 unreachable=0 failed=0 skipped=0 rescued=0
ignored=0
```

As you can see, the output says changed, which means that something was changed (more specifically, the file was created), and in the output, we can see a diff-like output that tells us that the state moved from absent to touch, which means the file was created. mtime and atime also changed, but this is probably due to how files are created and checked.

Now that you have learned how to use check mode, let's learn how to solve host connection issues.

Solving host connection issues

Ansible is often used to manage remote hosts or systems. To do this, Ansible will need to be able to connect to the remote host, and only after that will it be able to issue commands. Sometimes, the problem is that Ansible is unable to connect to the remote host. A typical example of this is when you try to manage a machine that hasn't booted yet. Being able to quickly recognize these kinds of problems and fix them promptly will help you save a lot of time.

Follow these steps to get started:

1. Let's create a playbook called `remote.yaml` with the following content:

```
---
- hosts: all
  tasks:
    - name: Touch a file
      file:
        path: /tmp/myfile
        state: touch
```

2. We can try to run the `remote.yaml` playbook against a non-existent FQDN, as follows:

```
$ ansible-playbook -i host.example.com, remote.yaml
```

In this case, the output will clearly inform us that the SSH service did not reply in time:

```
PLAY [all]
***********************************************************************
************

TASK [Gathering Facts]
***********************************************************************
*
fatal: [host.example.com]: UNREACHABLE! => {"changed": false, "msg":
"Failed to connect to the host via ssh: ssh: Could not resolve hostname
host.example.com: Name or service not known", "unreachable": true}

PLAY RECAP
***********************************************************************
************
host.example.com : ok=0 changed=0 unreachable=1 failed=0 skipped=0
rescued=0 ignored=0
```

There is also the possibility that we'll receive a different error:

```
PLAY [all]
***********************************************************************
************

TASK [Gathering Facts]
***********************************************************************
*
fatal: [host.example.com]: UNREACHABLE! => {"changed": false, "msg":
"Failed to connect to the host via ssh: fale@host.example.com: Permission
denied (publickey,gssapi-keyex,gssapi-with-mic).", "unreachable": true}
```

```
PLAY RECAP
*********************************************************************
*************
host.example.com : ok=0 changed=0 unreachable=1 failed=0 skipped=0
rescued=0 ignored=0
```

In this case, the host did reply, but we don't have enough access to be able to SSH into it.

SSH connections usually fail for one of two reasons:

- The SSH client is unable to establish a connection with the SSH server
- The SSH server refuses the credentials provided by the SSH client

Due to OpenSSH's very high stability and backward compatibility, when the first issue occurs, it's very probable that the IP address or the port is wrong, so the TCP connection isn't feasible. Very rarely, this kind of error occurs in SSH-specific problems. Usually, double-checking the IP and the hostname (if it's a DNS, check that it resolves to the right IP) solves the problem. To investigate this further, you can try performing an SSH connection from the same machine to check if there are problems. For instance, I would do this like so:

```
$ ssh host.example.com -vvv
```

I've taken the hostname from the error itself to ensure that I'm simulating exactly what Ansible is doing. I'm doing this to ensure that I can see all possible logging messages that SSH is able to give me to troubleshoot the problem.

The second problem might be a little bit more complex to debug since it can happen for multiple reasons. One of those is that you are trying to connect to the wrong host and you don't have the credentials for that machine. Another common case is that the username is wrong. To debug it, you can take the user@host address that is shown in the error (in my case, fale@host.example.com) and use the same command you used previously:

```
$ ssh fale@host.example.com -vvv
```

This should raise the same error that Ansible reported to you, but with much more details.

Now that you have learned how to solve host connection issues, let's learn how to pass working variables via the CLI.

Passing working variables via the CLI

One thing that can help during debugging, and definitely helps for code reusability, is passing variables to playbooks via the command line. Every time your application – either an Ansible playbook or any kind of application – receives an input from a third party (a human, in this case), it should ensure that the value is reasonable. An example of this would be to check that the variable has been set and therefore is not an empty string. This is a security golden rule, but should also be applied when the user is trusted since the user might mistype the variable name. The application should identify this and protect the whole system by protecting itself. Follow these steps:

1. The first thing we want to have is a simple playbook that prints the content of a variable. Let's create a playbook called `printvar.yaml` that contains the following content:

   ```
   ---
   - hosts: localhost
     tasks:
       - debug:
           var: variable
   ```

2. Now that we have an Ansible playbook that allows us to see if a variable has been set to what we were expecting, let's run it with `variable` declared in the execution statement:

   ```
   $ ansible-playbook printvar.yaml --extra-vars='{"variable": "Hello, World!"}'
   ```

By running this, we will receive an output similar to the following:

```
PLAY [localhost]
**************************************************************************
*******

TASK [Gathering Facts]
**************************************************************************
*
ok: [localhost]

TASK [debug]
**************************************************************************
***********
ok: [localhost] => {
  "variable": "Hello, World!"
}
```

```
PLAY RECAP
***********************************************************************
*************
localhost : ok=2 changed=0 unreachable=0 failed=0 skipped=0 rescued=0
ignored=0
```

Ansible allows variables to be set in various modes and with different priorities. More specifically, you can set them with the following:

- Command-line values (lowest priority)
- Role defaults
- Inventory files or script group `vars`
- Inventory `group_vars/all`
- Playbook `group_vars/all`
- Inventory `group_vars/*`
- Playbook `group_vars/*`
- Inventory files or script host vars
- Inventory `host_vars/*`
- Playbook `host_vars/*`
- Host facts/cached `set_facts`
- Play `vars`
- Play `vars_prompt`
- Play `vars_files`
- Role `vars` (defined in `role/vars/main.yml`)
- Block `vars` (only for tasks in block)
- Task `vars` (only for the task)
- `include_vars`
- `set_facts`/registered vars
- Role (and `include_role`) params
- `include` params
- Extra vars (highest priority)

As you can see, the last option (and the highest priority of them all) is using `--extra-vars` in the execution command.

Now that you have learned how to pass working variables via CLI, let's learn how to limit the host's execution.

Limiting the host's execution

While testing a playbook, it might make sense to test on a restricted number of machines; for instance, just one. Let's get started:

1. To use the limitation of target hosts on Ansible, we will need a playbook. Create a playbook called `helloworld.yaml` that contains the following content:

```
---
- hosts: all
  tasks:
    - debug:
        msg: "Hello, World!"
```

2. We also need to create an inventory with at least two hosts. In my case, I created a file called `inventory` that contains the following content:

```
[hosts]
host1.example.com
host2.example.com
host3.example.com
```

Let's run the playbook in the usual way with the following command:

```
$ ansible-playbook -i inventory helloworld.yaml
```

By doing this, we will receive the following output:

```
PLAY [all]
*************************************************************************
*************

TASK [Gathering Facts]
*************************************************************************
*
ok: [host1.example.com]
ok: [host3.example.com]
ok: [host2.example.com]

TASK [debug]
*************************************************************************
***********
ok: [host1.example.com] => {
    "msg": "Hello, World!"
}
ok: [host2.example.com] => {
    "msg": "Hello, World!"
}
```

```
ok: [host3.example.com] => {
    "msg": "Hello, World!"
}

PLAY RECAP
**********************************************************************
*************
host1.example.com : ok=2 changed=0 unreachable=0 failed=0 skipped=0
rescued=0 ignored=0
host2.example.com : ok=2 changed=0 unreachable=0 failed=0 skipped=0
rescued=0 ignored=0
host3.example.com : ok=2 changed=0 unreachable=0 failed=0 skipped=0
rescued=0 ignored=0
```

This means that the playbook was executed on all the machines in the inventory. If we just want to run it against host3.example.com, we will need to specify this on the command line, as follows:

```
$ ansible-playbook -i inventory helloworld.yaml --limit=host3.example.com
```

To prove that this works as expected, we can run it. By doing this, we will receive the following output:

```
PLAY [all]
**********************************************************************
*************

TASK [Gathering Facts]
**********************************************************************
*
ok: [host3.example.com]

TASK [debug]
**********************************************************************
***********
ok: [host3.example.com] => {
    "msg": "Hello, World!"
}

PLAY RECAP
**********************************************************************
*************
host3.example.com : ok=2 changed=0 unreachable=0 failed=0 skipped=0
rescued=0 ignored=0
```

Before Ansible executes the playbook we mentioned in the command line, it analyzes the inventory to detect which targets are in scope and which are not. By using the `--limit` keyword, we can force Ansible to ignore all the hosts that are outside what is specified in the limit parameter.

It's possible to specify multiple hosts as a list or with patterns, so both of the following commands will execute the playbook against `host2.example.com` and `host3.example.com`:

```
$ ansible-playbook -i inventory helloworld.yaml --
limit=host2.example.com,host3.example.com

$ ansible-playbook -i inventory helloworld.yaml --
limit=host[2-3].example.com
```

The limit will not override the inventory but will add restrictions to it. So, let's say we limit to a host that is not part of the inventory, as follows:

```
$ ansible-playbook -i inventory helloworld.yaml --limit=host4.example.com
```

Here, we will receive the following error, and nothing will be done:

```
[WARNING]: Could not match supplied host pattern, ignoring:
host4.example.com

ERROR! Specified hosts and/or --limit does not match any hosts
```

Now that you have learned how to limit the host's execution, let's learn how to flush the code cache.

Flushing the code cache

Everywhere in IT, caches are used to speed up operations, and Ansible is not an exception.

Usually, caches are good, and for this reason, they are heavily used ubiquitously. However, they might create some problems if they cache a value they should not have cached or if they are not flushed, even if the value has changed.

Flushing caches in Ansible is very straightforward, and it's enough to run `ansible-playbook`, which we are already running, with the addition of the `--flush-cache` option, as follows:

```
ansible-playbook -i inventory helloworld.yaml --flush-cache
```

Ansible uses Redis to save host variables, as well as execution variables. Sometimes, those variables might be left behind and influence the following executions. When Ansible finds a variable that should be set in the step it just started, Ansible might assume that the step has already been completed, and therefore pick up that old variable as if it has just been created. By using the `--flush-cache` option, we can avoid this since it will ensure that Ansible flushes the Redis cache during its execution.

Now that you have learned how to flush the code cache, let's learn how to check for bad syntax.

Checking for bad syntax

Defining whether a file has the right syntax or not is fairly easy for a machine, but might be more complex for humans. This does not mean that machines are able to fix the code for you, but they can quickly identify whether a problem is present or not. To use Ansible's built-in syntax checker, we need a playbook with a syntax error. Let's get started:

1. Let's create a `syntaxcheck.yaml` file with the following content:

   ```
   ---
   - hosts: all
     tasks:
       - debug:
         msg: "Hello, World!"
   ```

2. Now, we can use the `--syntax-check` command:

   ```
   $ ansible-playbook syntaxcheck.yaml --syntax-check
   ```

   By doing this, we will receive the following output:

   ```
   ERROR! 'msg' is not a valid attribute for a Task

   The error appears to be in
   '/home/fale/ansible/Ansible2Cookbook/Ch11/syntaxcheck.yaml': line
   4, column 7, but may
   be elsewhere in the file depending on the exact syntax problem.

   The offending line appears to be:

     tasks:
       - debug:
         ^ here
   ```

> This error can be suppressed as a warning using the
> "invalid_task_attribute_failed" configuration

3. We can now proceed to fix the indentation problem on line 4:

```
---
- hosts: all
  tasks:
    - debug:
        msg: "Hello, World!"
```

When we recheck the syntax, we will see that it now returns no errors:

```
$  ansible-playbook syntaxcheck-fixed.yaml --syntax-check

playbook: syntaxcheck.yaml
```

When the syntax check doesn't find any errors, the output will resemble the previous one, where it listed the files that were analyzed without listing any errors.

Since Ansible knows all the supported options in all the supported modules, it can quickly read your code and validate whether the YAML you provided contains all the required fields and that it does not contain any unsupported fields.

Summary

In this chapter, you learned about the various options that Ansible provides so that you can look for problems in your Ansible code. More specifically, you learned how to use host facts to diagnose failures, how to include testing within a playbook, how to use check mode, how to solve host connection issues, how to pass variables from the CLI, how to limit the execution to a subset of hosts, how to flush the code cache, and how to check for bad syntax.

In the next chapter, you will learn how to get started with Ansible Tower.

Questions

1. True or False: The debug module allows you to print the value of a variable or a fixed string during Ansible's execution.

    A) True

    B) False

2. Which keyword allows Ansible to force limit the host's execution?

    A) `--limit`

    B) `--max`

    C) `--restrict`

    D) `--force`

    E) `--except`

Further reading

Ansible's official documentation about error handling can be found at `https://docs.ansible.com/ansible/latest/user_guide/playbooks_error_handling.html`.

Getting Started with Ansible Tower

12

Ansible is very powerful, but it does require the user to use the CLI. In some situations, this is not the best option, such as in cases where you need to trigger an Ansible job from another job (where APIs would be better) or in cases where the person that should trigger a job should only be able to trigger that specific job. For these cases, AWX or Ansible Tower are better options to use.

The only differences between AWX and Ansible Tower are that AWX is the upstream and open source version, while Ansible Tower is the Red Hat and downstream product that is officially supported but for a price, and also the delivery method. AWX is available as a Docker container that can run everywhere, while Ansible Tower is installed on the system and requires specific versions of Linux—more specifically, RHEL 7.4+, RHEL 8.0+, and CentOS 7.4+, at the time of writing. In this chapter, we will use AWX and talk about AWX, but everything we discuss also applies to Ansible Tower.

The following topics are covered in this chapter:

- Installing AWX
- Running your first playbook from AWX
- Creating an AWX project
- Creating an inventory
- Creating a job template
- Running a job
- Controlling access to AWX
- Creating a user
- Creating a team
- Creating an organization
- Assigning permissions in AWX

Technical requirements

Although there are several ways to install AWX, we are going to use the suggested AWX installation, which is container-based. For this reason, the following software needs to be installed on your machine:

- Ansible 2.4+.
- Docker.
- The `docker` Python module.
- The `docker-compose` Python module.
- If your system uses **Security-Enhanced Linux (SELinux)**, you also need the `libselinux` Python module.

This chapter assumes that you have set up your control host with Ansible, as detailed in `Chapter 1`, *Getting Started with Ansible*, and that you are using the most recent version available—the examples in this chapter were tested with Ansible 2.9. Although we will give specific examples of hostnames in this chapter, you are free to substitute them with your own hostname and/or IP addresses, and details of how to do this will be provided at the appropriate places. The installation of Docker is beyond the scope of this book, but you can either install the version that ships with your Linux operating system or Docker CE. The requisite Python modules can be installed either by using `pip` or through operating system packages if they are available.

Installing AWX

Before we can further discuss AWX, it is best if you have it installed on your machine so that you can follow the explanation and immediately start to use AWX. The most convenient way of installing AWX is to follow these steps:

1. First of all, we need to clone the AWX Git repository, which can be done by running the following command:

   ```
   $ git clone https://github.com/ansible/awx.git
   ```

2. Modify the `installer/inventory` file by setting sensible values for the passwords and secrets (such as `pg_password`, `rabbitmq_password`, `admin_password`, and `secret_key`).

3. Now that we have downloaded the Ansible AWX code and installer, we can move into the installer folder and execute the installation by running the following code:

```
$ cd awx/installer
$ ansible-playbook -i inventory install.yml
```

The `install.yml` playbook performs the whole installation for us. It starts by checking the environment for possible misconfigurations or missing dependencies. If everything seems to be correct, it moves on to downloading several Docker images (including PostgreSQL, memcached, RabbitMQ, AWX Web, and AWX workers) and then runs them all.

As soon as the playbook completes, you can check the installation by issuing the `docker ps` command, which should output something such as the following:

```
CONTAINER ID   IMAGE                         COMMAND                CREATED
STATUS         PORTS        NAMES
7e388622a9a5   ansible/awx_task:5.0.0        "/tini -- /bin/sh ..."  2 minutes
ago  Up 2 minutes  8052/tcp awx_task
03946e9f7a74   ansible/awx_web:5.0.0         "/tini -- /bin/sh ..."  2 minutes
ago  Up 2 minutes  0.0.0.0:80->8052/tcp awx_web
d1134f5dc89a   ansible/awx_rabbitmq:3.7.4 "docker-entrypoint..."  2 minutes
ago  Up 2 minutes  4369/tcp, 5671-5672/tcp, 15671-15672/tcp, 25672/tcp
awx_rabbitmq
2184596d2584   postgres:9.6                  "docker-entrypoint..."  2 minutes
ago  Up 2 minutes  5432/tcp awx_postgres
dd6ebe2f8c8e   memcached:alpine              "docker-entrypoint..."  2 minutes
ago  Up 2 minutes  11211/tcp awx_memcached
```

As you can see from the output above, our system now has a container called `awx_web`, which has bound itself to port `80`.

You can now access AWX by browsing to `http://<ip address of your AWX host>/` and using the credentials you specified in the `inventory` file earlier on in this section—note that the default administrator username is `admin` unless you change it in the inventory.

Now, you have learned the necessary steps to install AWX. Let's take a look at how to create a project in AWX.

Running your first playbook from AWX

As in Ansible, in AWX, the goal is running an Ansible playbook and each playbook that is run is called a **job**. Since AWX gives you more flexibility and automation than Ansible, it requires a little bit more configuration before you can run your first job, so let's dive into it, starting with creating an AWX project.

Creating an AWX project

AWX uses the term **project** to identify a repository of Ansible playbooks. AWX projects support the placement of playbooks in all major **Source Control Management (SCM)** systems, such as Git, Mercurial, and SVN, but also support playbooks on the filesystem or playbooks provided by Red Hat Insights. To create a project, follow these steps:

1. First of all, you need to go to **Projects** on the left-hand side menu bar, then click on the button with a white plus sign on a green background on the top-left section of the screen. This opens up a window such as the following:

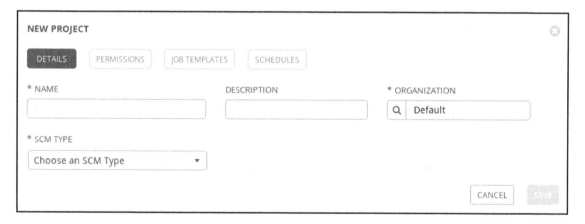

2. By filling in the name (Samples Repo) and selecting **Git** for **SCM TYPE**, the window grows with new parameters:

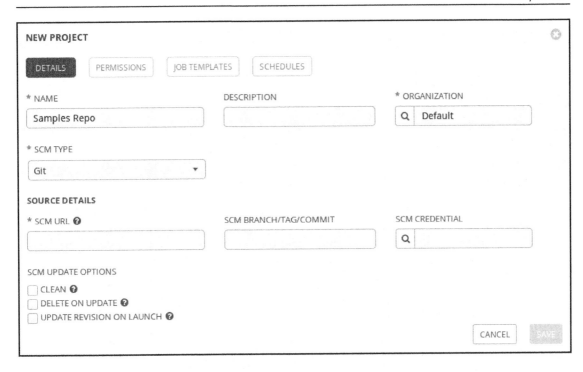

3. You can now add the SCM URL (`https://github.com/ansible/ansible-tower-samples`) and click the **SAVE** button, which should now be clickable.

As we mentioned at the beginning of this section, projects are the system to store and use playbooks in AWX. As you can imagine, there are many interesting additional configurations for AWX projects—and the most interesting one, in my view—is `update revision on launch`.

If flagged, this option instructs Ansible to always update the playbook's repository before running any playbook from that project. This ensures it always executes the latest version of the playbook. This is an important feature to enable as if you don't have it checked, there is the possibility (and sooner or later, this will happen in your environment) that someone notices that there is a problem in a playbook and fixes it, then they run the playbook feeling sure that they are running the latest version. They then forget to run the synchronization task before running the playbook, effectively running the older version of the playbook. This could lead to major problems if the previous version was fairly buggy.

The downside of using this option is that every time you execute a playbook, two playbooks are effectively run, adding time to your task execution. I think this is a very small downside and one that does not offset the benefits of using this option.

Now, you have learned the necessary steps to create a project in Ansible Tower. Let's see how to create an inventory in the next section.

Creating an inventory

As with Ansible Core, to make AWX aware of the machines present in your environment, we use inventories. Inventories, in the AWX world, are not that different from their equivalents in Ansible Core. Let's see how to create your first inventory in AWX by following these steps:

1. Click on the **Inventory** option in the left-hand side menu bar. You will be redirected to the **Inventory** window, where you can create your first inventory by clicking on the button with a white plus sign on a green background on the top-left section of the screen. This is different from when we created a new project as this button does not immediately open the creation form, but will first ask you if you want to create an inventory or a smart inventory.

2. After choosing the **Inventory** option, a box such as the following will appear:

3. In this window, you need to set a name and then save it. After you have clicked **SAVE**, the **Permissions**, **Groups**, **Hosts**, **Sources**, and **Completed Jobs** tabs become clickable, so you can continue with the configuration.

   Since an empty inventory is not useful in any way, we are going to add `localhost` to it.

4. To do this, select the **Hosts** tab, then click on the button with a white plus sign on a green background on the top-left of the screen. This opens a window, as follows:

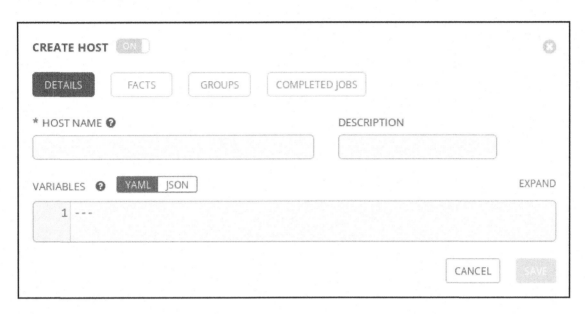

5. We then need to add the hostname (`localhost`) and instruct Ansible to use the local connection by adding the following code to the **VARIABLES** box:

```
---
ansible_connection: local
ansible_python_interpreter: '{{ ansible_playbook_python }}'
```

6. We can now click **SAVE**, saving our inventory.

The first choice we made was between creating an inventory or a smart inventory. What's the difference between these options? In AWX, an inventory is something very similar to an Ansible Core inventory, but with additional features, such as built-in dynamic inventory support, which means you don't need to edit configuration files or install additional Python modules. To enable this, simply go to the **Sources** tab within an inventory to choose to auto-populate the inventory with information from a source of truth, such as a public cloud provider inventory (**Amazon Web Services (AWS)**, Azure, and **Google Cloud Platform (GCP)** are all supported), a private cloud inventory (such as VMWare or OpenStack), or other systems, such as Red Hat Satellite or a custom script.

A special note about the inventory sources is that the **Sourced from a Project** option provides a form such as the following if chosen:

This is a very interesting feature, in my opinion, since it allows the user to check a dynamic inventory script of their own design into a Git repository (either in its own repository or one where you also put in playbooks) and AWX pulls that information from the repository.

As for projects, when you add a source to your inventory, you might choose to select the **Update on launch** option, which behaves in exactly the same way as the **Update on launch** option behaves for projects. For this reason, I strongly suggest you use this option as well.

Smart inventories are inventories that are populated by AWX, starting with the hosts present in other inventories by filtering them using the specific smart host filter that the user selected during creation. This can be incredibly useful for dynamically creating inventories with a specific type of host in them based on a filter and saves the need for manually creating lots of different groups—or worse, having to add the same host multiple times.

Now, you have learned the necessary steps to create an inventory in AWX. Let's see how to create a job template.

Creating a job template

Now that we have the playbooks in our projects and the hosts in our inventories, we can proceed with the creation of a **job template**.

A job template in AWX is a collection of the configurations that are needed to perform a job. This is very similar to the `ansible-playbook` command-line options. The reason why we need to create a job template is so that playbook runs can be launched with little or no user input, meaning they can be delegated to teams who might not know all the details of how a playbook works, or can even be run on a scheduled basis without anyone present:

1. First of all, you need to click on the **Templates** option on the left-hand side menu bar.
2. You can now create a new template by clicking on the button with a white plus sign on a green background on the top-left of the screen. It will ask you whether you want to create a job template or a workflow template—you need to choose **Job template**. The following window will appear:

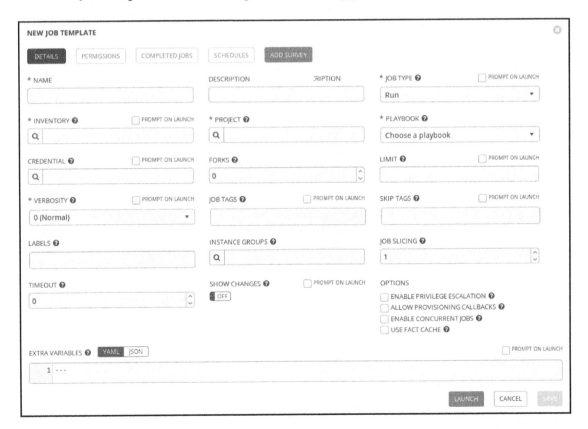

As you can see, there are quite a few fields in this view. The only information needed to proceed is the name (we are going to put in `Hello World`), the inventory (we are going to choose `Test Inventory`, which we created in the previous, *Creating an inventory* section in this chapter), the project (we are going to choose the `Samples Repo` project we created in a previous section in this chapter), and the playbook (we are going to choose `hello_world.yml`, which is the only playbook available). Then, we can click **SAVE**. Note that because we are running it using the local connection to `localhost`, we don't need to create or specify any credentials. However, if you were running a job template against one or more remote hosts, you would need to create a machine credential and associate it with your job template. A machine credential is, for example, an SSH username and password or an SSH username and a private key—these are stored securely in the backend database of AWX, meaning you can again delegate playbook-related tasks to other teams without actually giving them passwords or SSH keys.

The first thing we had to choose was whether we are creating a job template or a workflow template. We chose **Job Template** since we want to be able to create simple jobs out of this template. It's also possible to create more complex jobs, which are the composition of multiple job templates, with flow control features between one job and the next. This allows more complex situations and scenarios where you might want to have multiple jobs (such as the creation of an instance, company customization, the setup of Oracle Database, the setup of a MySQL database, and so on), but you also want to have a one-click deployment that would, for instance, set up the machine, apply all the company customization, and install the MySQL database. Obviously, you might also have another deployment that uses all the same components except the last one and in its place, it uses the Oracle Database piece to create an Oracle Database machine. This allows you to have extreme flexibility and to reuse a lot of components, creating multiple, nearly identical playbooks.

It's interesting to note that many fields in the **Job Template** creation window have an option with the **Prompt on launch** caption. This is to be able to set this value optionally during the creation of the job template, but also allow the user running the job to enter/override it at runtime. This can be incredibly valuable when you have a field that changes on each run (perhaps the `limit` field, which operates in the same way as `--limit` when used with the `ansible-playbook` command) or can also be used as a sanity check, as it prompts the user with the value (and gives them a chance to modify it) before the playbook is actually run. However, it could potentially block scheduled job runs, so exercise caution when enabling this feature.

Now, you have learned the necessary steps to create a job template in AWX. Let's see how to create a job.

Running a job

A job is an instance of a job template, as the name suggests. This means that to perform any action on our machine, we have to create a job template instance—or, more simply, a job—by following these steps:

1. Now that we have set the job template, we can run the job itself. To do so, we need to go the **Templates** item on the left-hand side of the page.
2. Find the job template you want to run (in our case, this is going to be the Hello World one) and then we click on the little rocket on the right-hand side of the page corresponding to the correct job template, as you can see in the following screenshot:

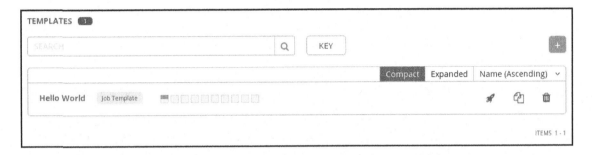

When a job is running, AWX allows us to follow the job execution in the job's dashboard, as in the following screenshot:

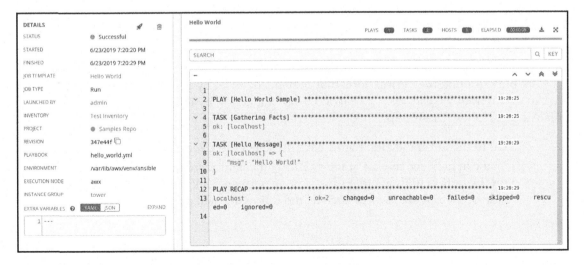

On the right-hand side of the screen, the output of the job loads during the execution, while the left-hand side gives us information about the job. One of the great things about AWX and Ansible Tower is that they archive this job execution output in the backend database, meaning you can, at any point in the future, come back and query a job run to see what changed and what happened. This is incredibly powerful and useful for occasions such as auditing and policy enforcement.

Now, you have learned the necessary steps to create a job in AWX. Let's see how to create a user.

Controlling access to AWX

In my opinion, one of the biggest advantages of AWX compared to Ansible is the fact that AWX allows multiple users to connect and control/perform actions. This allows a company to have a single AWX installation for different teams, a whole organization, or even multiple organizations.

A **Role-Based Access Control (RBAC)** system is in place to manage the users' permissions.

Both AWX and Ansible Tower can link to central directories, such as **Lightweight Directory Access Protocol (LDAP)** and Azure Active Directory—however, we can also create user accounts locally on the AWX server itself. Let's start by creating our first user account locally!

Creating a user

One of the big advantages of AWX is the ability to manage multiple users. This allows us to create a user in AWX for each person that is using the AWX system so that we can ensure they are only granted the permissions that they need. Also, by using individual accounts, we can ensure that we can see who carried out what action by using the audit logs. To create a user, follow these steps:

1. Go to the left-hand side menu bar and select the **Users** option.
2. You can now see the list of users and you can also create a new one by clicking on the button with a white plus sign on a green background at the top-left hand side of the screen. A form such as the following will appear:

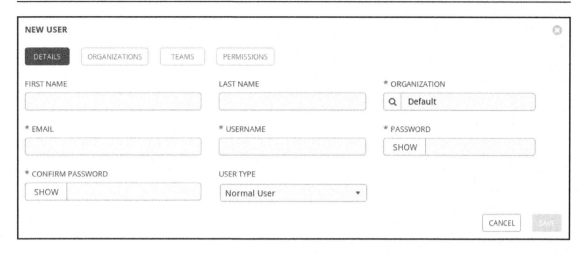

By adding the email address, the username, and the password (with confirmation), you can create the new user.

Users can be of three types:

- **A normal user**: Users of this type do not have any inherited permissions and they need to be awarded specific permissions to be able to do anything.
- **A system auditor**: Users of this type have full read-only privileges on the whole AWX installation.
- **A system administrator**: Users of this type have full privileges on the whole AWX installation.

Now, you have learned the necessary steps to create a user in AWX. Let's have a brief look at teams.

Creating a team

Although having individual user accounts is an incredibly powerful tool, especially for enterprise use cases, it would be incredibly inconvenient and cumbersome to have to set permissions for each object (such as a job template or an inventory) on an individual basis. Every time someone joins a team, their user account has to be manually configured with the correct permissions against every object and, similarly, be removed if they leave.

AWX and Ansible Tower have the same concept of user grouping that you would find in most other RBAC systems. The only slight difference is that in the user interface, they are referred to as **teams**, rather than groups. However, you can create teams simply and easily and then add and remove users as you need to. Doing this through the user interface is very straightforward and you will find the process similar to the way that most RBAC systems handle user groups, so we won't go into any more specific details here.

Once you have your teams set up, I recommend that you assign your permissions to teams, rather than through individual users, as this will make your management of AWX object permissions much easier as your organization grows. Speaking of organizations, let's take a look at the concept of organizations in AWX in the next section.

Creating an organization

Sometimes, you have multiple independent groups of people that you need to manage independent machines. For those kinds of scenarios, the use of organizations can help you. An organization is basically a tenant of AWX, with its own unique user accounts, teams, projects, inventories, and job templates—it's almost like having a separate instance of AWX! To create an organization, you need to perform the follow these steps:

1. To create a new organization, you need to go to the left-hand side of the screen to the **Organizations** option.
2. You can then see the existing organizations and proceed to create a new one by clicking on the button with a white plus sign on a green background at the top-left section of the screen.

A window such as the following will appear:

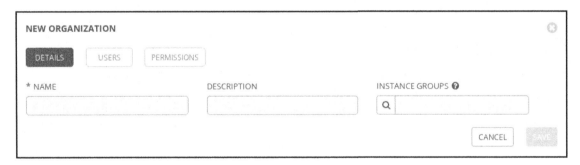

Since the only mandatory field is **NAME**, you can just fill this in and click **SAVE**.

After you create the organization, you can assign any kind of resource to an organization, such as projects, templates, inventories, users, and so on. Organizations are a simple concept to grasp, but also powerful in terms of segregating roles and responsibilities in AWX. Finally, before we complete this section, let's take a look at assigning permissions in AWX.

Assigning permissions in AWX

You will have noticed—on our journey through configuring our first project, inventory, and job template in AWX—that most of the screens we have navigated to have a button on them called **Permissions**. As we navigate the user interface with the administrator account, we get to see all the options—but of course, you would not want to give every single user administrator permissions.

Individual users (or the teams that they belong to) can be granted permissions on a per-object basis. So, for example, you could have a team of database administrators who only have access to see and execute playbooks on an inventory of database servers, using job templates that are specific to their role. Linux system administrators could then have access to the inventories, projects, and job templates that are specific to their role. AWX hides objects that users don't have the privileges to, which means the database administrators never see the Linux system administrator objects and vice versa.

There are a number of different privilege levels that you can award users (or teams) with, which include the following:

- **Admin**: This is the organization-level equivalent of a **system administrator**.
- **Execute**: This kind of user can only execute templates that are part of the organization.
- **Project admin**: This kind of user can alter any project that is part of the organization.
- **Inventory admin**: This kind of user can alter any inventory that is part of the organization.
- **Credential admin**: This kind of user can alter any credential that is part of the organization.
- **Workflow admin**: This kind of user can alter any workflow that is part of the organization.
- **Notification admin**: This kind of user can alter any notification that is part of the organization.

- **Job template admin**: This kind of user can alter any job template that is part of the organization.
- **Auditor**: This is the organization-level equivalent to a **system auditor**.
- **Member**: This is the organization-level equivalent of a **normal user**.
- **Read**: This kind of user is able to view non-sensible objects that are part of the organization.

That concludes our brief look at RBAC in AWX and our look at this powerful tool. AWX is a great addition to the power of Ansible in an enterprise setting and really helps ensure that your users can run Ansible playbooks in a manner that is well managed, secure, and auditable. We have only scratched the surface in this chapter, but hopefully, this chapter has given you a flavor of how AWX can help your team's or enterprise's automation journey.

Summary

AWX and Ansible Tower are powerful, complementary tools that powerfully support the use of Ansible in an enterprise or team-based environment. They can help secure credentials that you would otherwise have to distribute widely, audit the history of playbook runs, and enforce the version control of playbooks. The web-based user interface of these tools creates a low barrier for entry for end users, meaning playbook runs can easily be delegated to teams who otherwise have little knowledge of Ansible (as long as suitable escalation paths are put in place should problems arise). In short, when implementing Ansible in a corporate setting, its usage should not be considered complete without the addition of Ansible Tower or AWX.

In this chapter, you learned how to install AWX on your Linux host, as well as the necessary steps to run your very first playbook from AWX. You also learned about RBAC in AWX and how this can support large, multi-user environments in a corporate setting.

We have now reached the end of this book, since this is the last chapter, and I would like to thank you for reading the entire book, and I hope that it has taught you what you initially hoped to learn about Ansible.

Questions

1. Which objects can you create in Ansible Tower?

   A) Users

   B) Jobs

   C) Job templates

   D) Modules

   E) Projects

2. True or false – AWX is the upstream and open source version of Red Hat Ansible Tower.

   A) True

   B) False

Assessments

Chapter 1

1. A, B
2. C
3. A

Chapter 2

1. C
2. B
3. A

Chapter 3

1. E
2. C
3. A

Chapter 4

1. C
2. A
3. B

Chapter 5

1. D
2. E
3. A

Chapter 6

1. D
2. A
3. A

Chapter 7

1. D
2. A
3. B

Chapter 8

1. C
2. B
3. A

Chapter 9

1. D
2. A
3. A

Chapter 10

1. D
2. A
3. B
4. B
5. A

Chapter 11

1. A
2. A

Chapter 12

1. A,B,C,E
2. A

Other Books You May Enjoy

If you enjoyed this book, you may be interested in these other books by Packt:

Mastering Ansible - Third Edition
James Freeman, Jesse Keating

ISBN: 978-1-78995-154-7

- Gain an in-depth understanding of how Ansible works under the hood
- Fully automate Ansible playbook executions with encrypted data
- Access and manipulate variable data within playbooks
- Use blocks to perform failure recovery or cleanup
- Explore the Playbook debugger and the Ansible Console
- Troubleshoot unexpected behavior effectively
- Work with cloud infrastructure providers and container systems
- Develop custom modules, plugins, and dynamic inventory sources

Learning Ansible 2.7 - Third Edition

Fabio Alessandro Locati

ISBN: 978-1-78995-433-3

- Create a web server using Ansible
- Write a custom module and test it
- Deploy playbooks in the production environment
- Troubleshoot networks using Ansible
- Use Ansible Galaxy and Ansible Tower during deployment
- Deploy an application with Ansible on AWS, Azure and DigitalOcean

Leave a review - let other readers know what you think

Please share your thoughts on this book with others by leaving a review on the site that you bought it from. If you purchased the book from Amazon, please leave us an honest review on this book's Amazon page. This is vital so that other potential readers can see and use your unbiased opinion to make purchasing decisions, we can understand what our customers think about our products, and our authors can see your feedback on the title that they have worked with Packt to create. It will only take a few minutes of your time, but is valuable to other potential customers, our authors, and Packt. Thank you!

Index

Y

Made in the USA
Monee, IL
27 February 2021